A Hard World

A Hard World

An Inside Look at Another Year in Boxing

Thomas Hauser

The University of Arkansas Press
Fayetteville
2016

ISBN: 978-1-68226-013-5
e-ISBN: 978-1-61075-597-9

20   19   18   17   16   5   4   3   2   1

∞The paper used in this publication meets the minimum requirements of the
American National Standard for Permanence of Paper for Printed Library
Materials Z39.48-1984.

Library of Congress Control Number: 2016940660

For Sue Etkin,
An exemplary boxing person

Table of Contents

Issues and Answers

Author's Note

A Hard World contains the articles about professional boxing that I authored in 2015. The articles I wrote about the sweet science prior to that date have been published in *Muhammad Ali & Company*; *A Beautiful Sickness*; *A Year at the Fights*; *The View From Ringside*; *Chaos, Corruption, Courage, and Glory*; *The Lost Legacy of Muhammad Ali*; *I Don't Believe It, But It's True*; *The Greatest Sport of All*, *The Boxing Scene*, *An Unforgiving Sport*, *Boxing Is*, *Winks and Daggers*, *And the New*, *Straight Writes and Jabs*, *Thomas Hauser on Boxing*, and *A Hurting Sport*.

Fighters and Fights

For better or worse, Floyd Mayweather vs. Manny Pacquiao was boxing's 2015 event of the year.

Mayweather–Pacquiao Approaches

The contract weight is 147 pounds. The WBA, WBC, and WBO titles will be on the line. But the sanctioning bodies are irrelevant. On May 2, 2015, at the MGM Grand in Las Vegas, Floyd Mayweather and Manny Pacquiao will be fighting for the championship of each other.

It's an event of staggering economic proportions. But boxing fans won't be tuning in on May 2 to see Mayweather and Pacquiao count money. They want to see them fight each other.

For most of the past decade, either Floyd or Manny has been the consensus choice for top pound-for-pound fighter in the world. For much of that time, whichever of them wasn't ranked #1 was #2.

Mayweather's legs aren't what they used to be. Pacquiao is six years removed from his eleven-month peak (December 6, 2008, through November 14, 2009) when he demolished Oscar De La Hoya, Ricky Hatton, and Miguel Cotto.

But Mayweather and Pacquiao are still two of the best fighters in the world. And the two most marketable.

Mayweather opened as a 5-to-2 betting favorite. The odds have dropped a bit since then but may well rise during fight week when the "smart money" comes in.

The case for a Mayweather victory is simple. He's the naturally bigger man, the physically stronger man, and the more technically proficient fighter. He's also undefeated, while Pacquiao has five losses and two draws on his record. As Floyd noted at the March 11 kick-off press conference, "When you lose, it's in your mind."

Mayweather has three alternative routes to success in Mayweather–Pacquiao:

(1) He can outbox Pacquiao and dictate the distance between them. Either stay too far away for Manny to hit him or smother Pacquiao's punches. (See Mayweather vs. Juan Manuel Marquez as Exhibit A.)

(2) He can throw Pacquiao off his game by roughing him up on the inside. (See Mayweather vs. just about everyone he has fought, and contrast that with Pacquiao vs. Agapito Sanchez, where a rough, sometimes dirty, approach bothered Manny.)

(3) He might land a big punch and whack Manny out. (See Mayweather's check hook vs. Ricky Hatton and Pacquiao-Marquez IV.)

Can Pacquiao give Mayweather trouble by emulating the strategy that Oscar De La Hoya employed en route to a split-decision loss? Probably not. Part of what gave Floyd trouble against Oscar was Oscar's size. De La Hoya used his jab effectively in the first half of that fight to score points and break Mayweather's rhythm. But Manny isn't as tall as Oscar, nor does he have Oscar's reach or timing on the jab.

Add to that the fact that Pacquiao isn't physical enough to force his way inside against Mayweather the way Marcos Maidana did. He'll have to get inside with quickness and angles against an opponent who's a master of angles.

Speaking of Mayweather-Pacquiao, Larry Merchant noted, "One guy [Pacquiao] throws bombs. The other guy [Mayweather] defuses them; that's his priority. One guy's purpose is to hit and not be hit. The other's purpose is to not be hit and hit. In general, defense can shut down offense. Great pitchers shut down great hitters."

The most forceful advocate for a Pacquiao victory on May 2 is Freddie Roach. As Manny's trainer, Roach has a vested interest in the proceedings. But over the years, he has been constant in his observations:

★ "I don't see Mayweather as a great fighter at 147 or 154. Oscar almost beat Mayweather, and Manny didn't lose ten seconds of any round against Oscar."

★ "I've thought about Mayweather for a long time now. His style does pose some problems because he's very good at what he does. I know he's hard to get to, but we will get to him. Manny can match Mayweather's speed, and he has better footwork and more balls. Mayweather is a fragile guy. He'll break down. He can't stand up to Manny's pressure."

★ "Mayweather fights in spurts these days. He likes to lay up on the ropes. He takes a lot of rests in the ring. One of the keys to victory for Manny is to recognize when Floyd is taking a break and to stay on the offensive and keep scoring points. But the big thing is that Manny himself has to recognize when Mayweather is catching a breather. It doesn't help for me to see it from the corner."

★ "Mayweather can't move quite as well as he used to. I think Manny's power will overwhelm him. He has never been against someone with the speed of Pacquiao. Seeing it is one thing. Dealing with it is another."

But there are times when Roach admits that Mayweather is a tall mountain to climb: "Without a doubt, it's the toughest fight in the world for us, I know that. I want to start working on some changes, some new moves, some traps we need to set. This is a whole new ballgame. Everything that worked against De La Hoya, everything that worked against Cotto, everything that worked against Hatton, will not work against Mayweather. We have to come up with a whole new game plan."

But what's the plan?

Prior to Pacquiao's fourth and final fight against Juan Manuel Marquez, Roach told this writer, "I've had three chances to get Manny ready for Marquez, and I haven't gotten it right yet. It works perfectly in camp. Maybe this time I'll say, 'Okay, Manny. Just go out and fucking kill this guy.'"

Pacquiao-Marquez IV ended with Manny face down, unconscious on the ring canvas.

That said; Pacquiao's style is dangerous for any opponent, including Mayweather. And Floyd isn't as good a counterpuncher as Marquez. Juan Manuel lived for the counter and committed to it. Floyd is more likely to pull away from punches without throwing back. If Pacquiao puts his punches together when Mayweather pulls away, he could nail him.

Mike Tyson knows a thing or two about boxing. People tend to lose sight of the fact that he's a serious student of the game. Analyzing Mayweather-Pacquiao, Tyson recently declared, "Manny is going to feint Floyd out of position a lot and make him throw more punches than he's used to, and that will open Floyd up. Floyd has never been tested. Whatever happens in the fight, I think he's going to get hit and hurt more than he has ever before. We're going to see how tough he is."

Pacquiao is more willing than Mayweather to gamble in the ring. In the end, that could be his edge. But Manny will need to gamble successfully to win. And most gamblers who come to Las Vegas go home losers.

So . . . What should boxing fans expect from Mayweather-Pacquiao?

Let's start by cutting through some of the hyperbole. This is not "the most-anticipated fight ever" or "the most important fight ever." Yes; it will gross an enormous amount of money. But Lady Gaga does bigger numbers than Frank Sinatra ever did. That doesn't speak to the quality or relative importance of their work.

There have been many fights that were more important than Mayweather-Pacquiao from a social and political point of view.

Arthur Ashe once said, "Nothing that Frederick Douglass did, nothing that Booker T. Washington did, nothing that any African-American had done up until that time had the same impact as Jack Johnson's fight against Jim Jeffries on July 4, 1910. It completely destroyed one of the crucial pillars of white supremacy—the idea that the white man was superior in body and mind to all the darker peoples of the earth."

More people listened on the radio to Joe Louis knocking out Max Schmeling in the first round of their June 22, 1938, rematch than had listened simultaneously to anything before in the history of the world. That night was the first time that many people heard a black man referred to simply as "the American."

Millions upon millions of people carried the historic first fight between Muhammad Ali and Joe Frazier in their hearts. Writing in advance of that March 8, 1971, encounter, Mark Kram declared, "This is THE international sporting event of our age, one of the great dramas of our time. The thrust of this fight on the public consciousness is incalculable. It has been a ceaseless whir that seems to have grown in decibel with each new soliloquy by Ali, with each dead calm promise by Frazier. It has cut deep into the thicket of our national attitudes and it is a conversational imperative everywhere."

Mayweather-Pacquiao pales in comparison with these celebrated encounters and others like them in terms of its social impact. With Johnson-Jeffries, Louis-Schmeling, and Ali-Frazier, the combatants represented opposite sides of a supervening socio-political issue. Here, Pacquiao represents the Filipino people. And Floyd is either admired for his ostentatious lifestyle or disliked for his treatment of women.

With Johnson-Jeffries, Louis-Schmeling, and Ali-Frazier, depending on who fans were rooting for, the outcome affected their mood like the death of a friend or the birth of a child. One week after Mayweather-Pacquiao, the result will matter to the Filipino people. Beyond that, a handful of insiders will be counting large sums of money and the rest of the world will have moved on.

Indeed, Mike Tyson had a much bigger impact on the American psyche than Mayweather or Pacquiao. Tyson's celebrity status exploded out of control. Everyone knew who he was. When Tyson crashed his car, got into a street fight, appeared on *Barbara Walters*, or was tried and convicted in Indiana, it was on the front page of newspapers across the country. When Mayweather was arrested and went to jail, it was on boxing websites and TMZ.

Because Mayweather-Pacquiao lacks the historical gravitas of boxing's most socially important encounters, it will be remembered in direct correlation to how good a fight it is. It could be similar to Mayweather's outings against De La Hoya and Canelo Alvarez, which were hugely successful economic ventures but contributed little to boxing lore. Or it could be something more.

In a best-case scenario, Mayweather-Pacquiao will be similar to Sugar Ray Leonard's first fights against Roberto Duran and Thomas Hearns. Those fights captured the imagination of sports fans in advance and, more important, delivered on their promise. They were epic battles.

But Leonard-Duran III (which came almost a decade after their "no mas" rematch) and Leonard-Hearns II (separated by eight years from its predecessor) are best forgotten. The fighters were too old by then.

So let's give the last word to Ray Leonard, who recently observed, "Mayweather is 38 and Pacquiao is 36. They have looked good in their fights, but you notice them slowing down and getting hit more."

Then Leonard added, "This fight here is more important than any fight in their life, career, everything. This fight is about bragging rights. This fight is about legacy."

Mayweather-Pacquiao was a huge financial success. On every other level, it was a disappointment.

Planet Floyd

Walt Disney captured the imagination of children everywhere with Disneyland. Harry Potter theme parks dot the globe. Fantasy destinations such as Neverland (created by J. M. Barrie as the home of Peter Pan) have long occupied a niche in the public consciousness.

With that in mind, welcome to Planet Floyd, a land that combines reality with make believe, where sense has become nonsense, where worth is measured in terms of money rather than good deeds, dignity, or respect.

In 2014, scientists identified what they called "the largest living organism on Earth"—a parasitic fungus growing in the northeast quadrant of Oregon that measures 2.4 miles in diameter. The fungus sprouts *Armillaria* mushrooms, while decaying and killing the root systems of trees that stand in its path.

That was Floyd Mayweather vs. Manny Pacquiao. If you prefer a different analogy, one might liken the promotion to a giant steamroller crushing everything before it.

Still not satisfied? How about referencing Jimmy Cannon, who wrote long ago that boxing is the red-light district of professional sports.

There were times when Mayweather-Pacquiao seemed like a high-class bordello operated by Mayweather Promotions, Top Rank, and the rest of the Las Vegas establishment. Floyd and Manny were the call girls. The media was pimping for tips. Ticketholders and pay-per-view buyers were the Johns.

"I love you, baby. That feels so good. I'm doing this just for you, baby, because you want it."

The fight was all about money. But the promotion told us that from the start, didn't it? The publicity for Mayweather-Pacquiao was never about what a great fight it would be as much as it was about how much money it would generate.

For over a hundred years, boxing helped drive communications technology and what is now know as "media." The sport was a significant factor in generating newspaper and magazine sales in the 1800s and the sale of radios and televisions in the succeeding century. It was also on the cutting edge of closed-circuit and pay-per-view technology.

Now communications technology in the form of social media is playing a significant role in driving boxing. Social media has transformed what we understand a major event to be. The economics of Mayweather-Pacquiao were propelled by social media, which turned the event into an exercise in wish fulfillment with all the puffery and spin control of a national political campaign.

Let's start by summarizing some often cited numbers.

The previous record live gate for a fight was the $20,003,150 engendered by Mayweather vs. Canelo Alvarez on September 14, 2013. Initially, it was announced that tickets for Mayweather-Pacquiao were priced as follows: $10,000 (1,100 tickets), $7,500 (2,500 tix), $5,000 (2,500 tix), $3,500 (4,000 tix), $2,500 (2,500 tix), and $1,500 (2,500 tix). That would have come to a live gate of $66,250,000. Then there was a reallocation of tickets within categories. Ultimately, a live gate of $72,198,500 was reported to the Nevada State Athletic Commission.

Tecate bid an unprecedented $5.6 million to become the lead sponsor. Total sponsorship revenue was reported as $13,200,000. There were record-breaking international television rights sales in the neighborhood of $40,000,000.

And most significantly, there was pay-per-view. The previous domestic-pay-per-view-buys record for a fight was 2.5 million, established when Mayweather fought Oscar De La Hoya in 2007. Mayweather-Alvarez held the record for PPV receipts with $152 million.

Mayweather-Pacquiao shattered these numbers by a wide margin. Best estimates at present are that it engendered well over 4 million buys. Moreover, the pay-per-view price was $99.95 ($89.95 for those who were willing to forego high definition). That's $25.00 more than the previous high charged for Mayweather-Alvarez.

The typical split between the content provider of a pay-per-view fight card and the entities disseminating the telecast (multi-system cable operators, DIRECTV, and others) is approximately fifty-fifty. Here, the split was roughly sixty-forty in favor of the promotion.

Once expenses are paid, the remaining revenue will be divided 60 percent to Team Mayweather and 40 percent to Pacquiao and Top Rank (Manny's promoter). Based on these numbers, Mayweather will earn more than $200 million. Putting that amount in perspective, *Forbes* reported that the previous record for earnings by an athlete (including endorsements) in a single year, adjusted for inflation, was the $125 million that Tiger Woods earned in 2008.

Don King once declared, "A good hustler knows that he can't hustle by himself. He needs someone working with him."

The powers-that-be behind Mayweather-Pacquiao formed alliances that maximized their return.

Only a handful of tickets were made available to the general public. The rest were distributed 30 percent to Al Haymon (Mayweather's business advisor) and Mayweather Promotions; 30 percent to Top Rank and Pacquiao, and 40 percent to the MGM Grand.

The MGM earmarked most of its tickets for high rollers. But Top Rank CEO Bob Arum later alleged that the company had a side deal with Haymon that enabled the entrepreneur to purchase roughly 2,000 tickets from the MGM's allotment at face value.

Haymon and Top Rank made a substantial profit by selling many of their tickets to brokers and others on the secondary market.

The MGM Grand's contract with the promotion blocked non-MGM properties on the Las Vegas strip from showing the fight in ballrooms, bars, and even in guest rooms on pay-per-view. That limited viewing to MGM Resorts properties. After the bout, MGM Resorts chairman and CEO Jim Murren told Bloomberg that MGM had sold 46,000 tickets to watch the fight on closed circuit, generating $9 million. The "drop" at the casinos before and after the telecast was considerably more.

Numerous press releases regarding the live gate and other income streams were issued by the promotion. There was no announcement regarding how large the site fee was, giving rise to the belief in some circles that a portion of it might have been subject to particularly creative deal making.

On April 16, it was announced that, as a form of crowd control, there would be a ten-dollar admission charge and assigned seats for members of the public who attended the weigh-in (which would be held at the

MGM Grand Garden Arena). All proceeds were to be donated to the Susan G. Komen for the Cure Foundation and Lou Ruvo Center for Brain Health. Less than forty-eight hours after going on sale, tickets for the weigh-in sold out. Thereafter, they were resold for as much as $150 a seat, giving rise to the question of who was pocketing the difference.

No stone was left unturned in the pursuit of profit. After weighing in on Friday, Manny Pacquiao (who was being nicely compensated by Butterfinger) ate a Butterfinger peanut butter cup on stage.

Room rates for five-star hotels on the nights of May 1 and 2 were running $700 above the average Friday and Saturday-night rates.

Imagine a smile on a serpent's face. That's what some Mayweather-Pacquiao insiders looked like during fight week. The event was boxing's ultimate cash machine.

ESPN.com senior writer Tim McKeown described the proceedings as a "weeklong descent into absurdity." Reni Valenzuela wrote on Philboxing.com (a leading boxing portal in the Philippines), "Mayweather-Pacquiao is exclusive for elite millionaires. The fans are left out or set to become bait for sharks that lurk in shallow waters. The boxing contest is not about boxing anymore, much less about the fans."

It would have been better for boxing if the fight had been contested in Cowboys Stadium with 100,000 fans and longtime members of the boxing media (many of whom were shut out by the promotion) able to attend. But the prevailing ethos was to bleed every dollar out of the promotion. If smoking ruins were left behind, so be it.

The fight captured the attention of mainstream media worldwide. Studios A and B at the MGM Grand (which normally serve as the "media center" for big fights) were rechristened the "broadcast center" and reserved for dozens of television and radio networks conducting a week-long vigil. Just outside the hotel, a huge tent was set up for print and Internet media.

The media tent was beset by an infestation of moths, which gave rise to the question of whether locusts, frogs, lice, and other Biblical afflictions would follow. Elsewhere in the hotel, a huge display case (thirty feet long and twelve feet high) in the MGM Grand lobby showcased twelve of Mayweather's championship belts in addition to the gloves, robes, and shoes that Floyd had worn in seven of his fights.

There were so many turf wars (Top Rank vs. Mayweather Promotions and HBO vs. Showtime, to name two) that one half expected a flurry of drive-by shootings to break out.

Bob Arum has been down the super-fight road many times. In order to finalize Mayweather-Pacquiao, Arum made some remarkable concessions: most notably (1) if there were a dispute between Top Rank and Mayweather Promotions, the issue would be resolved by CBS Corporation CEO Les Moonves (CBS is Showtime's parent company, and Showtime has a long-term contract with Mayweather), and (2) the Mayweather side of the promotion was given complete control over contract negotiations with the MGM Grand.

By April 23, Arum was so disgruntled that he announced Pacquiao would not participate in the "grand arrival" of the fighters at the MGM Grand (which traditionally takes place on the Tuesday of fight week) and would enter the hotel only for the final pre-fight press conference, weigh-in, and the fight itself.

"We're not going to go there any more than we have to," Arum told the media. "We know the way they've been acting, and we're not welcome."

When Arum did enter the MGM Grand for fight-related events, he passed through the complex like a head of state being escorted through hostile territory.

"I'm eighty-three years old," Arum said on Wednesday afternoon in the media tent. "And this has been the most hellish time of my professional career."

Thereafter, Arum added that he had gotten along reasonably well with Mayweather Promotions CEO Leonard Ellerbe. But he had less than kind words for Mayweather advisor Al Haymon, who he called "a truly evil man." And he referenced Showtime boxing tsar Stephen Espinoza as "a contrary son-of-a-bitch who's impossible to work with" before declaring, "I don't like him."

Presumably, those sentiments were returned in kind.

Meanwhile, Showtime (Mayweather's network) and HBO (which has a contract with Pacquiao) were also at odds. Showtime was the lead producer on what was to be a joint telecast. As fight week progressed, HBO personnel complained of not being informed when schedules changed. Worse, the commentating team still hadn't been finalized, although it was known that Jim Lampley (HBO) would handle blow-by-blow duties with Al Bernstein (Showtime) at his side. The allocation of other on-air talent wasn't finalized until late Thursday night. Paulie Malignaggi (Showtime) learned that he would be on the fight-night host desk with James Brown (Showtime) and Lennox Lewis (HBO) when he read a tweet posted by Chris Mannix of SI.com on Friday morning.

The promotion had a toxic aura. But instead of poison wafting through the air, the ka-ching of cash registers sounded and the silent swipe of credit cards whizzed by.

There were the usual big-fight rituals, although on a larger scale. Mayweather's "grand arrival" took place in the MGM Grand Garden Arena instead of the hotel lobby and was heralded by the Southern University marching band. The final pre-fight press conference was held in the KA Theatre rather than the David Copperfield Theatre to accommodate the media horde.

A who's-who of boxing royalty was on hand to promote the event. Evander Holyfield, Bernard Hopkins, Shane Mosley, Julio Cesar Chavez, and Juan Manuel Marquez were in the broadcast center at various times.

As the week progressed, the MGM Grand was overrun by fans aggressively seeking photos with and autographs from virtually anyone who was recognizable. Jim Lampley needed assistance from hotel security after the weigh-in to get to his room.

"I've been a prisoner in my room since I got here," Lampley said on Saturday morning. "I've now ordered dinner from room service three nights in a row."

There wasn't a lot of passion among boxing insiders in the media tent and broadcast center. Many seasoned observers were there simply because it was their job. The fight didn't inspire the same energy level among them that previous super-fights such as Lennox Lewis vs. Mike Tyson and the classic encounters between Ray Leonard, Thomas Hearns, Marvin Hagler, and Roberto Duran had.

First timers who had never been to a fight before and might never go again seemed to be enjoying it all.

Throughout fight week (as it had earlier in the promotion), Team Mayweather called most of the shots.

"This fight happened because of me," Floyd had said at the March 11 kick-off press conference. "We had to chose an opponent for May 2nd, and I chose Pacquiao."

The fight posters and other promotional material were designed so that the eye was drawn to Mayweather's name and image before Pacquiao's. Manny himself acknowledge that he was the "B-side" of the promotion. "It's better to do that," he explained, "or there is no fight."

Pacquiao's trainer, Freddie Roach, countered with the thought that, in this instance, "A" stood for "asshole." But Team Mayweather was in charge, and everyone knew it.

Mayweather's appeal is a stick in the eye to the establishment. It's as if he's saying, "I do what I want. I treat people, including women, the way I want. If you don't like watching me count my money, I don't give a fuck."

That morality play has been coupled with incessant bragging about being "TBE" (the best ever) and pronouncements like, "God only made one thing perfect: my boxing record."

On Monday of fight week, Mike Tyson appeared in the media center and said of Mayweather, "This guy is going around saying he's better than Ali. I don't want to hear that shit."

"When Mike Tyson is the voice of reason in a room," one boxing scribe noted, "the room has a problem."

Meanwhile, for much of the week, Pacquiao seemed intent on bearing witness to the glory of God.

At a sit-down with writers just prior to Wednesday's final pre-fight press conference, Manny declared, "I cannot imagine that a boy who is sleeping on the streets, starving, looking for food, is where I am today. God raised me up from nothing to where I am today. I want people to know that."

At the press conference itself, Manny added, "I hope that, after the fight, I can have a conversation with Floyd, sharing my faith in God. There is God, who can raise something from nothing. Jesus is the name of the Lord."

That message continued during a satellite interview tour on Thursday, when Pacquiao proclaimed, "I am trusting in God for this fight. There is nothing for me to worry about. I have peace of mind. I'm confident.

The Lord is with me. I am hoping that, after the fight, I can talk with Floyd about God, and it will bring a change in his life. I want Floyd to know God."

Fighters who rely on The Almighty to bring them victory don't necessarily prevail. Pacquiao was trusting in the Lord. Mayweather was trusting in himself.

As fight week progressed, it became clear that the number of pay-per-view buys would be astronomical. But behind the scenes, turmoil reigned. Thursday and Friday were hectic. All the things that had been put off by the promotion for "later" had to be done "now."

Also, the market for ticket prices and hotel rooms was taking a downward turn.

The handling of tickets had been chaotic. As of April 20 (twelve days before the fight), physical tickets still hadn't been delivered or formally gone on sale, prompting Bob Arum to declare, "This is not acceptable. This is a worldwide event that the city of Las Vegas is involved in. It's one of the craziest things I've ever seen."

Two days later, there were still no tickets. By the time they were available (on Wednesday evening), reality was setting in.

Many of the early online listings for Mayweather-Pacquiao tickets had carried the feel of shill bids at an auction. But Las Vegas ticket brokers (who are usually pretty savvy) had invested heavily, buying early at premium prices from the promotion. By mid week, most brokers simply wanted to break even. By Friday, they were trying to cut their losses, and tickets could be bought below face value.

Meanwhile, some would-be customers had cancelled trips to Las Vegas because of delays in the distribution of tickets and the fear that they wouldn't be able to see the fight live or even on closed-circuit. Hotel rooms at the MGM Grand for Friday and Saturday night were available online for as little as $190 a night (well below the normal week-end price and far below the $1,600 rate that had been quoted during the height of the feeding frenzy).

On Friday afternoon, there was a huge turnout for the weigh-in. The fighters walked to the scales in the manner of fighters going to the ring for a big fight. Mayweather was introduced as "the world's highest-paid athlete."

There was a lot of gamesmanship at the Nevada State Athletic Commission rules meeting that followed. The Mayweather camp objected to Pacquiao's gloves and protective cup, while Team Pacquiao raised questions about Floyd's gloves.

Mayweather was a 2-to-1 betting favorite, although Bob Arum reminded people that the last time Pacquiao had been an underdog was in 2008 when he destroyed Oscar De La Hoya.

"If you had to design a fighter, a style that could beat Mayweather," Bruce Trampler (Top Rank's Hall-of-Fame matchmaker) told the *Los Angeles Times*, "you're going to come up with a left-hander who's good with lateral movement, side to side, shifty, can punch with either hand. That's not a guarantee that Manny is going to win the fight. But he's got the best chance of anyone to take away the '0' on Floyd's record."

But everyone who follows boxing knew that this wasn't the Manny Pacquiao who blew away Oscar De La Hoya, Ricky Hatton, and Miguel Cotto six years ago. One can attribute his decline to age. One can link it to what Manny did, or didn't, put into his body (legal or illegal, just as Mayweather seems to have benefitted from all of the advanced training methods that are at his command).

Also, even under the best of circumstances, Mayweather is a hard mountain for an opponent to climb.

"Floyd may be an ass," Freddie Roach said. "But he's still a great fighter."

Mayweather-Pacquiao was the thirty-first fight that Roach and Pacquiao had prepared for together. Freddie is widely recognized as a great trainer and also a great guy. His heroic battle against the ravages of Parkinsonism remains an inspiration. When asked during fight week about dealing with his condition, Roach responded, "The first thing is to not lay down and die."

But Roach is a hands-on trainer. And his declining physical condition, which was compounded by back and hip problems, made readying Pacquiao to fight Mayweather a more difficult task.

Meanwhile, Roach's counterpart in the Mayweather camp was extremely confident. Among the thoughts that Floyd Mayweather Sr offered were:

★ "Too many fighters today, especially young ones, aren't in shape. Or if they are in shape, they think conditioning is more important than technique. Floyd has both."

★ " Floyd is as well-rounded a fighter as there has ever been. But he's really still here because of his defense. It's his great defense that has kept him on top for so long."

★ "Once you get hit like Pacquiao did [by Juan Manuel Marquez] and your ass goes to sleep, it doesn't take too many more for it to happen again."

★ "Whatever it is will be one-sided. To be honest with you, I don't think it will be much of a fight."

Las Vegas has long been considered a terrorist target. It's on the Department of Homeland Security short list after Washington, DC, and New York.

On Friday and Saturday, the National Guard was patrolling McCarren International Airport. MGM Resorts CEO Jim Murren later said that Mayweather-Pacquiao broke the record for private planes parked at McCarren. The old record had been 350 private aircraft. After 500 private planes landed in advance of the fight, officials began diverting new arrivals to North Las Vegas.

On fight night, Department of Homeland Security personnel mingled with local police and fire-fighting personnel at the MGM Grand. Nine explosive-sniffing dogs were in and around the arena.

Many of the people who attended the fight weren't boxing fans. They were people with money and connections who wanted to be at the big happening. A press release from the promotion stated that the celebrities in attendance included Robert DeNiro, Clint Eastwood, Denzel Washington, Michael Keaton, Beyoncé, Jay Z, Sean Combs, Sting, Michael Jordan, Tom Brady, Magic Johnson, Andre Agassi, Steffi Graf, Charles Barkley, Reggie Miller, Ben Affleck, Christian Bale, Mark Wahlberg, Bradley Cooper, Michael J. Fox, Jake Gyllenhaal, Don Cheadle, and Claire Danes.

Inside the arena, it felt like any other big Las Vegas fight when the pay-per-view telecast began at 6:00 p.m. Most of the seats were still empty. The fans in attendance were subdued.

Mayweather-Pacquiao was a chance for boxing to put its best foot forward, impress the largest pay-per-view audience in boxing history, and show the world that there are fighters beyond Mayweather and Pacquiao who are worth watching. But the promotion gave viewers two predictably awful undercard fights.

Vasyl Lomachenko (a 20-to-1 favorite) scored a ninth-round knockout over a not-very-game Gamalier Rodriquez. Then Leo Santa Cruz (a 30-to-1 favorite) whitewashed Jose Cayetano 100–90 on each judge's scorecard.

That set the stage for the main event, which was a massive disappointment. The crowd was overwhelmingly pro-Pacquiao. But the crowd can't fight.

There was a noticeable size differential between the fighters. Thirty hours after weighing in, Floyd looked like a full-fledged welterweight in the ring with a lightweight.

Brin-Jonathan Butler of SB Nation described what followed as "a game of tag that only accidentally elevated into the realm of a glorified sparring session."

Prior to the bout, there had been a record number of Internet "hits" related to the fight. In the ring, the hits that mattered most were few and far between. According to CompuBox, Mayweather landed eight punches in round one and Pacquiao landed three. By round twelve, things had improved to the point where Mayweather landed eight punches and Pacquiao landed four. The rounds in between weren't much better.

For most of the fight, Mayweather dictated the distance between the participants with his footwork, jab, and lead right hands. Pacquiao had trouble getting inside. When he did, more often than not, Floyd tied him up.

Mayweather fought a safety-first fight. Also, safety-second and safety-third. Good defense is admirable. Freddie Roach has said, "I don't know anyone who gets hit on purpose." But "hit and don't get hit" doesn't mean "run and be boring." An action sport should have some action in it.

Pacquiao was strangely passive throughout the bout and unable to score effectively even when Mayweather backed into a corner. If it had been an undercard bout instead of "Mayweather-Pacquiao," viewers at home would have seen it as an ideal time for a bathroom break. If it had been two guys on ESPN, channel surfers would have watched for a minute and resumed surfing.

Adam Berlin summed up the end of the contest as follows: "Most nauseating was how round twelve began. Instead of the customary glove-touching, these two supposed warriors went one step further. Floyd Mayweather and Manny Pacquiao embraced. Their slow dance in the middle of the ring wasn't one of fatigue and pain and spirit spent. It was a money dance. Some calculations put the pay-out per second of fight time at $130,000. This seven-second embrace, worth about a million bucks, was, like too many greed-inspired ventures, built on the backs of suckers. These precious seconds should have been filled with boxing action. That's what the ringside crowd had paid exorbitant prices to see. That's what viewers at home who'd shelled out ridiculous pay-per-view dollars had paid to see. Round twelve was a farce. For all the fighting Mayweather and Pacquiao did in the twelfth, they should have just been honest. The two boxers-turned-businessmen should have sat down on a couple of deck chairs. They should have lit up a couple of expensive cigars. They should have cracked open a bottle of Glenmorangie, aged 25 years. They should have touched glasses. And then, Floyd Mayweather and Manny Pacquiao should have leaned back and looked into the horizon, not a gold horizon of boxing glory but a green horizon of capitalist greed. The round bell wasn't a call to arms. It was Wall Street's 9:30 AM signal that the market was open for business."

The fighters were paid well over a million dollars for each punch landed.

Hampered by what we now know was a torn rotator cuff in his right shoulder, Pacquiao was able to land only eighteen jabs during the entire fight. That comes to an average of 1.5 jabs per round.

The judges favored Mayweather by a 118–110, 116–112, 116–112 margin.

Fans often cry "robbery" after a bad decision. They were crying it after Mayweather-Pacquiao because they felt ripped off. This was boxing's ultimate money grab. It made what happened in Shelby, Montana, when Jack Dempsey fought Tommy Gibbons in 1923 look like a charity show.

Throughout the promotion of Mayweather-Pacquiao, boxing fans were told that it was a one-of-a-kind event. The impulse now is to say,

"That's good." But apart from to its economic success, the fight was a one-of-a-kind event in another way not intended by the promotion. It was oddly detached from the rest of boxing. This wasn't a fight like Sugar Ray Leonard vs. Thomas Hearns or Oscar De La Hoya vs. Felix Trinidad, which seemed an organic part of boxing. Mayweather-Pacquiao was never going to take the sport to a new level. It was a one-off.

Boxing's biggest events engender the most talk in advance. But the best fights are ones that people talk about with reverence afterward. On the phone, around watercoolers at work on Monday morning, and long after when the narrative has become a treasured part of boxing history.

Mayweather-Pacquiao fell woefully short of that standard. As Bart Barry wrote, "No Mayweather victory is a victory for anyone but Mayweather. Figures like that do not live on as legends. They are either forgotten in time or become cautionary tales."

Under normal circumstances, Bobby Haymon would be little more than a few lines in boxing record books. But Bobby has a younger brother named Al. And that changed everything.

Bobby Haymon

Al Haymon has said that one of the factors that motivated him to get involved with boxing was the less-than-satisfactory experience that his brother, Bobby Haymon, had as a fighter.

Bobby Haymon lived in Cleveland and fought for most of his career as a welterweight. He turned pro on March 31, 1969, with a fourth-round knockout of Sam Ivory (whose record was 1-17-1).

Don Elbaum was the promoter, matchmaker, or booking agent for nineteen of Haymon's thirty-one professional fights.

"Bobby could fight," Elbaum says. "He wasn't much of a puncher. But he was a good boxer and he had a good chin. His manager, a guy named Dominick Polo, was also his trainer. Polo brought him to me, and I thought Bobby was a prospect. I promoted his fight against Sam Ivory. Then Dominick took him to the Washington, DC, area for three fights, which wasn't too smart because Bobby lost two of them and got a draw in the third."

Haymon returned to Elbaum for his fifth pro outing, a four-round decision over 1-and-9 Joey Blair. Then Polo took him back to Washington, DC, where he lost again.

"Dominick was overmatching Bobby," Elbaum says. "Bobby wasn't ready for that level of competition. Finally, after three losses, Dominick realized it wasn't working and put the choice of opponents in my hands."

Under Elbaum's guidance, Haymon won ten consecutive fights during an eighteen-month stretch, most of them against sub-500 competition.

"He was a good main-event fighter for a club show and a good undercard fighter for a bigger show," Elbaum recalls. "He wasn't a runner. He made good fights. And he was a nice guy. He had a pleasant personality. I liked him."

Then, on May 26, 1971, Elbaum matched Haymon against 11-6-3 Ralph Correa.

"Correa was a good tough club fighter, that's all," Elbaum remembers. "Before that fight, I thought that Bobby had a chance to become a legitimate contender. But Correa kept the pressure on all night, started nailing him, wore him down, and Bobby folded. I hadn't expected that. When Bobby lost that one, I realized he wasn't going to go as far as I thought he would."

After losing to Correa, Haymon took nine months off from boxing. Then Elbaum brought him back for a sixth-round knockout of Jesus Alicia (who had 8 wins in 31 fights). Hall of Fame matchmaker Bruce Trampler picks up the narrative from there.

"I saw a few of Haymon's early fights because I was in college at Ohio University and went to as many fights as I could," Trampler recounts. "I was at the Joey Blair fight, and Bobby's wins over Gene Masters [1969] and Al Bashir [1970]. I also saw the Ralph Correa fight, although that was after I graduated from college and moved to Miami to work with Chris and Angelo Dundee. It was on the undercard of Floyd Patterson against Terry Daniels. Haymon got massacred. Correa brutalized him."

In late 1972, Trampler moved back to Ohio.

"That's when I actually met Bobby," Bruce recalls. "He trained at the Olympic Gym on East 55th Street in Cleveland. Dominick was a disciplinarian where training was concerned. He emphasized conditioning and a fighter knowing how to work on the inside. Bobby was a competent boxer, a good technical fighter. But my strongest impressions of him were as a person. I think he was a [meter reader for a utilities company] back then. And he was a nice guy. Bright, quiet, easy-going, always friendly with a big smile."

Trampler was the matchmaker for three of Haymon's 1972 fights: ten-round decisions over Sammy Rookard and Hector Perez, and a fourth-round disqualification victory over Terry Hayward.

"I also promoted the Hayward fight," Bruce recalls. "Al Haymon was at that one. It was the first time I met him. Al came by the Top Rank office a few years ago. I took out my scrapbook with some clips from that fight, and we talked about what we remembered from it."

In mid-1973, Trampler suggested to Russell Peltz that he match Haymon against William Watson (a young prospect from Philadelphia) on an August 31, 1973, card that Peltz was promoting at The Spectrum.

"I thought Watson would win easily," Peltz recalls. "He was doing well at the time. It was scheduled for ten rounds, and it was a terrific fight. Watson got cut pretty badly in the first round, but he knocked Haymon down twice in the second."

"From that point on," Russell continues, "Watson was pretty much in control, but Haymon made a fight of it. Then, in the sixth round, Haymon tripped over Watson's leg, fell out of the ring, and hit his head on the press table. He was hurt badly enough that they carried him from the ring on a stretcher. Since it wasn't a punch that knocked him out, the fight was called a no contest."

"I don't think Elbaum and Dominick Polo were getting along so well at the time," Peltz adds. "There's a story that Polo hired someone to put a bomb under the hood of Elbaum's car."

"Not true," Elbaum responds. "It was under the bottom of my car, not the hood. And it wasn't Polo. What happened was, there was a hit man named Danny Green who killed a lot of people. They made a movie about him. You can look him up on Wikipedia. He exploded something like thirty-five bombs in cars before some people killed him the same way. Anyway, someone offered Danny five thousand dollars to kill me. But Danny had come to some of my fights, and we'd had drinks together. So he said he wouldn't kill me for five thousand dollars, but he'd warn me for free. I had a Cadillac, and Danny blew it up with dynamite. Fortunately, I wasn't in the car at the time. I knew some wise guys and spent a couple of weeks trying to find out who was behind it. Finally, someone told me who it was and said, 'It's over. You do nothing.' The guy who hired Danny is still alive. I won't tell you who it is because I don't want to piss him off."

Elbaum was also feuding at the time with Dean Chance (who'd won the Cy Young Award as the best pitcher in baseball in 1964 and promoted one of Haymon's 1973 fights). Elbaum challenged Chance, who towered over him, to a fist fight.

"I won't fight you," Chance countered. "But I'll throw baseballs at sixty feet."

Meanwhile, Peltz wanted to promote a rematch between Haymon and William Watson, but Haymon retired instead. Four years later, he returned to the ring with knockout victories over three opponents who finished their careers with a composite record of 16 wins in 94 bouts. That set up Haymon's final fight, a knockout defeat at the hands of Sugar Ray Leonard at the Capitol Centre in Landover, Maryland, on April 13, 1978.

"I was the one who got him the Leonard fight," Trampler recalls. "I was friendly with Mike Trainer (Leonard's attorney) and suggested opponents from time to time. On that one, I put Bobby's name in through Eddie Hrica, who was a matchmaker in Baltimore, and Hrica passed it on to Trainer. Obviously, Bobby was the underdog. But it was a payday for him, and it was only Ray's tenth pro fight."

Leonard-Haymon was contested before 15,272 fans, breaking the record for an indoor fight in Maryland set two years earlier by Muhammad Ali versus Jimmy Young. Leonard knocked Haymon down one minute fifty-five seconds into round three. Then, simultaneously with the bell ending the round, he stunned Bobby with a hard right and followed up with a left hook that left Haymon draped over the ropes. Television replays clearly showed that the final punch was thrown after the bell.

Haymon's handlers dragged him to his corner. He was unable to come out for the fourth round. Dominick Polo later complained, "I talked to the officials, and they said they couldn't do anything about it. That's because they had fifteen thousand people here, and they didn't have the guts to do anything about it."

An Associated Press article the following day was headlined "Tainted Victory for Sugar Ray." A fight report in *The Afro-American* noted, "Leonard finished him off at the end of the round—and shortly after it."

"Most likely, Bobby would have been knocked out anyway," Trampler notes. "That last punch saved him from taking worse punishment later in the fight."

Leonard-Haymon was Bobby Haymon's final fight. He retired as an active fighter with a ring record of 21 wins, 8 losses, 1 draw, 1 no contest, 9 knockouts, and 2 KOs by. His brother, Al, is carrying the Haymon banner today. That's more of a legacy than most fighters have.

There were times when Wladimir Klitschko's fights were evocative of Teofilo Stevenson's glory days as a three-time Olympic gold medalist; a giant playing with smaller, less-talented men.

Wladimir Klitschko vs. Bryant Jennings

There was a time when the public at large stopped to watch, read, and listen whenever the heavyweight champion of the world entered the ring. Those days are long gone. But it's still worthy of note when the man presumed able to beat anyone else on the planet in a boxing match defends his crown.

At Madison Square Garden on April 25, 2015, Wladimir Klitschko put his championship on the line against Bryant Jennings.

Klitschko, age thirty-nine, is an anomaly among fighters. A highly educated man, he transitions easily from Russian (learned in his native Ukraine) to German (the language of the country where his professional career bloomed) to English (he now lives in the United States with actress Hayden Panettiere).

Klitschko's ring ledger shows 64 wins, 3 losses, and 54 knockouts. He has won 22 consecutive fights over the past eleven years. At present, he's the longest reigning of three champions from the old Soviet Union who stand atop three of boxing's traditional glamour divisions. Sergey Kovalev (175 pounds) and Gennady Golovkin (160) are the others.

In a different era, Klitschko would have been regarded as a living legend by the American public. But boxing in the United States has been in decline for a long time. And Wladimir plies his trade mostly in Europe.

"For our business model," Bernd Boente (Klitschko's primary business advisor) states, "America is not the center of the world."

Prior to facing Jennings, Klitschko had fought at Madison Square Garden three times. The first was a second-round knockout of David Bostice on the undercard of Lennox Lewis's April 29, 2000, annihilation of Michael Grant. That was followed by a seventh-round stoppage of Calvin Brock on November 11, 2006, and a desultory twelve-round decision over Sultan Ibragimov on February 23, 2008.

One of the problems that Klitschko has faced in seeking to prove his greatness since then (and erase the memory of knockout defeats at the hands of Ross Puritty, Corrie Sanders, and Lamon Brewster earlier in his career) has been a lack of inquisitors.

Dominance is one thing. Greatness is another. Since last appearing in New York, Wladimir had defeated the likes of Alex Leapai, Francesco Pianeta, Marius Wach, and Jean-Marc Mormeck. His most recent opponent, Kubart Pulev, evinced the skill and finesse of a Bulgarian circus strongman.

Jennings (a 15-to-1 underdog) wasn't expected to pose much of a threat. His team kept referring to Buster Douglas's monumental upset of Mike Tyson, which occurred almost twenty-five years to the day before the February 4 Klitschko-Jennings kick-off press conference. But Douglas was a well-schooled fighter with victories over Oliver McCall, Trevor Berbick, and Greg Page to his credit when he dethroned Tyson. Jennings had a meager amateur background. And his 19-and-0 (10 KOs) pro record had been compiled against pedestrian opposition.

At the kick-off press conference, Jennings had the look of a man who would be happier once the fight was over. And not because he thought that he'd be champion when the fighting was done.

Klitschko, by contrast, seemed happy and relaxed as the festivities unfolded.

"Let us, Bryant and me, entertain you," Wladimir told the media. "He has the quality of Rocky Balboa. From Philadelphia."

Nothing on Jennings's resume suggested that he was a credible opponent for Klitschko. The bout shaped up as a performance rather than a competitive fight.

Team Klitschko controls its environment as completely as possible. In the case of Klitschko-Jennings, that included a contract clause mandating a smaller-than-usual, eighteen-by-eighteen-foot ring.

When fight night arrived, a crowd of 17,056 sat in relative silence through an abbreviated undercard. But it came alive with Ukrainian flags waving when Wladimir entered the ring.

At 6-feet-6-inches, 242 pounds, Klitschko was three inches taller and fifteen pounds heavier than his opponent.

Jennings retreated in the early going, looking to survive rounds rather than win them. That allowed the Klitschko to dictate when and where there was violence. On the few occasions when Bryant came forward, he found it hard to work his way past Wladimir's jab and the right hand that lay in wait behind it.

Then, in round four, Jennings became more aggressive, lunging forward with punches (which seemed to be asking for a counter) and pumping his free hand to the body when Klitschko tied him up on the inside.

In round six, the performance turned into a fight with hints of Klitschko's 2004 loss to Lamon Brewster wafting through the air. In that long-ago encounter, Wladimir scored multiple knockdowns in the first few stanzas before collapsing from exhaustion at the end of round five. But this is a different Klitschko, stronger and more confident than the Klitschko of eleven years ago.

Jennings won the sixth round. But in round seven, Wladimir recalibrated the distance between them and regained control, moving around the ring as though he were playing chess, fighting a patient, cerebral, methodical fight.

Jab . . . Straight right . . . An occasional hook up top . . . Minimal body punching (to avoid exposing his chin). Tie Jenning up whenever the smaller man got inside and push him back with superior strength.

In round nine, Klitschko suffered a small cut under his left eye. Referee Michael Griffin deducted a point from Wladimir in round ten for excessive holding. But not much else went in Jennings's favor. Bryant fought as well as he could. But Klitschko was too big and strong for him.

This writer scored the bout 118–109 in Klitschko's favor. The judges saw it 118–109, 116-111, 116–111. Wladimir didn't look as sharp as he has in recent outings. Perhaps age is creeping up on him. Or maybe Jennings is better than Kubrat Pulev and Alex Leapai.

One can (and should) argue that Lennox Lewis and Hasim Rahman were the legitimate heavyweight champions when Klitschko wore the WBO crown from October 2000 through March 2003. And brother Vitali was the more credible champion for part of Wladimir's current reign, which began in 2006.

That said; Klitschko is now the best heavyweight in the world. His size and ring skills would have made him competitive in any era. The eighteen consecutive successful title defenses in his current run place him third in the heavyweight division behind Joe Louis (25) and Larry Holmes (20) in that category.

And Bernd Boente said recently, "As long as Wladimir is motivated and healthy, he will continue to fight. I know it is in the back of his mind that, if he is still champion on December 21, 2017, he will beat Joe Louis's record [of eleven years, eight months, and eight days] for the longest reign by a heavyweight champion."

So what comes next?

At present, the most interesting challengers Klitschko could face are Tyson Fury and Deontay Wilder.

It's unlikely that Wilder will fight Klitschko. More likely, Deontay will avoid Wladimir and try to move in after Klitschko has departed from the scene. Fury might take the fight. Contested in England, Klitschko-Fury would be a huge event. Beating Fury wouldn't do much for Wladimir's legacy. Losing to him would hurt it.

Miguel Cotto has said, "I want to be remembered as a warrior." He will be.

In Celebration of Miguel Cotto

Miguel Cotto entered his dressing room at Barclays Center on the night of June 6, 2015, at 8:25 p.m.

He was casually dressed, wearing faded blue jeans, a well-worn gray T-shirt, a blue leather jacket, and loafers with no socks.

There was a time when winning a world championship was boxing's equivalent of a mobster becoming a made man. No more. In an era characterized by multiple sanctioning bodies and more than a hundred world "champions" at any point in time, only a handful of fighters matter to the public.

Miguel Cotto matters.

There has been a premium in the new millennium on trash-talking and glitz. That's not Cotto's way.

Miguel has always respected the sport of boxing and its practitioners. "I am where I am in boxing because I work hard instead of complaining," he says. "I don't ask for anything I didn't earn."

He would have been respected as a fighter in any era.

Cotto's journey through boxing began in 1992.

"I was a chubby child," Miguel recalls. "I weighed 162 pounds at age eleven. My sport was to sit in front of the TV and eat. I started boxing to lose weight and fell in love with it."

Cotto has been fighting professionally for fourteen years. At his peak, he was a destructive force, devastating good fighters like Zab Judah, Carlos Quintana, and Paulie Malignaggi and outpointing great ones like Shane Mosley. He burnished his English skills to improve his marketability and be able to communicate directly with English-speaking fans. Then something bad happened.

On the morning of July 26, 2008, Cotto had a 32-0 record and was ranked in the top five on most pound-for-pound lists. That night, he stepped into the ring at the MGM Grand in Las Vegas to face Antonio Magarito and suffered a horrific beating. The weight of the evidence strongly suggests that Margarito's gloves were "loaded" that night. His license to box was suspended for one year.

But Cotto was no longer the same fighter. On November 14, 2009, Miguel absorbed another beating, this one at the hands of Manny Pacquiao. He fought sporadically after that, earning victories over Yuri Foreman, Ricardo Mayorga, and Margarito (in a rematch) before being outpointed in back-to-back losses to Floyd Mayweather and Austin Trout.

After the loss to Trout, Cotto's days as a star attraction seemed to be over. On October 5, 2013, he scored a third-round knockout over Delvin Rodriguez. But Rodriguez has won only four of eleven fights dating back to 2008, so that didn't count for much in the eyes of the boxing establishment.

Then, on June 7, 2014, Cotto challenged Sergio Martinez for the middleweight championship of the world.

Cotto knocked Martinez down three times in the first stanza. The fight was stopped after nine lopsided rounds. But it was an open issue as to whether Miguel had looked good or Sergio (who'd undergone extensive knee surgery prior to the fight and would require more surgery afterward) looked bad.

The victory over Martinez brought Cotto's record to 39 wins against 4 losses with 32 knockouts and gave him renewed bargaining power. In January of this year, he signed a lucrative three-fight contract with Roc Nation that included a substantial signing bonus, a contribution by the promoter to Miguel's charity in Puerto Rico, and an agreement between Roc Nation and Cotto Promotions to co-promote a series of boxing cards and rock concerts on the island.

In the aftermath of the signing, there were harsh words from Todd DuBoef of Top Rank (Cotto's former promoter). At a February 5, 2015, luncheon to formally announce the deal, a reporter asked Gaby Penagaricano (Miguel's attorney) about DuBoef's negative comments.

"I am going to be the only one to talk about it," Miguel interrupted. "We had a fight by fight deal with Top Rank. I expect respect, and a lot of people I knew from the beginning of my career didn't show that."

Later, when asked if there was any lingering bitterness between him and Top Rank, Miguel answered, " If they want to say hi to me, they have my number."

Cotto's opponent at Barclay's Center was Daniel Geale.

Geale (31-3, 16 KOs) had been competitive in past outings against fighters like Darren Barker, Anthony Mundine, and Felix Sturm. But when last seen in New York, he'd been knocked out by Gennady Golovkin in three rounds in a fight that evoked images of a bug flying into the windshield of a eighteen-wheel truck on an interstate highway.

"I didn't come here for a holiday," Geale said of his impending confrontation with Cotto. "I came here to fight."

But Geale (a 5-to-1 underdog) had been brought in on the assumption that he would lose. He was a respectable but "safe" opponent. Not too fast, not too skilled, not a big puncher. He wouldn't bring anything to the table that Cotto couldn't deal with.

Furthering Cotto's advantage, the fight was to be contested at a catchweight of 157 pounds although Miguel's 160-pound title was at stake. But the belt was of secondary importance. In a world inundated with phony belts and make-believe champions, this was a Miguel Cotto fight.

Barclays Center is the home of the NBA Brooklyn Nets. Cotto was treated like visiting royalty. Geale had been given an ordinary dressing room. Team Cotto was ensconced in the Nets suite.

The dressing area was a spacious enclosure, thirty-six feet long and thirty feet wide with a twelve-foot-high ceiling and recessed lighting above. A white Brooklyn Nets logo was woven into plush black carpet. There were twelve separate dressing stations, each one with its own vertical closet, sliding drawer, and swivel chair. The last name and number of a Nets player was on a placard affixed to the wall by each station. The rest of the suite consisted of a lounge, lavatory, shower room, whirlpool room, and medical area.

For the first two hours after Cotto's arrival, well wishers came and went. Family members and friends, sanctioning body officials, representatives of Roc Nation. Through it all, the core group remained the same. Trainer Freddie Roach, assistant trainer Marvin Somodio, cutman David Martinez, strength and conditioning coach Gavin MacMillan, and Bryan Perez (Miguel's closest and most trusted friend).

Former New York Yankees great Bernie Williams (who'd been asked by Miguel to walk him to the ring) sat quietly to the side.

The mood was relaxed, almost festive.

Cotto doesn't smile often in public. He's self-controlled and gives the impression of being on guard at all times. One might describe him as stoic. He endures hardship and pain without complaint and rarely shows his true feelings. But Miguel has expressive eyes that, depending on the moment, can be soft, hard, thoughtful, happy, lonely. His smile is genuine and warm.

Cotto smiles more in the dressing room on fight night than he does at press conferences and other media events. As time passed, he chatted casually with Perez, Somodio, and others as though he were circulating at a cocktail party. Other times, he sat alone with his thoughts or paced wordlessly with his arms folded, sipping from a bottle of water.

There were the normal pre-fight rituals supervised by New York State Athletic Commission inspectors George Ward and Sue Etkin. Referee Harvey Dock gave Cotto his pre-fight instructions. Miguel applied underarm deodorant before putting on his boxing gear and checked his smart phone for messages.

At 9:00 p.m., the salsa music of Ismael Miranda wafted through the air, adding to the festive aura.

Trainer Freddie Roach stood off to the side. Cotto-Geale was the third fight that he and Miguel had prepared for together.

In an earlier incarnation, Roach compiled a 39-and-13 ring record as a combatant. He's still every bit as much a fighter as the men he trains. But now he's fighting a different kind of battle, against the ravages of Parkinson's syndrome.

Cotto calls Roach "the best thing that ever happened to my career" and says, "Freddie brought confidence back to me. He comes every day to the gym and gives his best. The only way you can pay a person like that back is to give your best."

Now Roach was reflecting on the time he has spent with Cotto.

"Miguel has a great work ethic," Freddie said. "Once he's in the gym, it's all work. He's one of the most disciplined fighters I've seen in my life. He's very quiet. Every now and then, he tells a joke. He's a pleasure to work with."

"The biggest thing when I started with Miguel," Roach continued, "was, I said to him, 'When you were an amateur, you were a boxer. Why are you throwing every punch now like you want to kill the other guy?

It's not enough to have skills. It's not enough to have heart. You have to fight smart.' And Miguel listened. He tries to do what I tell him to do. You'll see that tonight. I don't know if Geale will come at us and try to impose his size or run all night. Either way, he'll keep his hands high. That's what he always does, so we'll attack the body."

Roach went down the hall to watch Geale's hands being wrapped.

Cotto began stretching his upper body and leg muscles.

At 9:30, Marvin Somodio started wrapping Miguel's hands, right hand first.

Cotto whistled in tune with the music as Somodio worked.

"Miguel loves fight night," Bryan Perez said. "He's enjoying the moment."

Roach returned.

"Geale got a terrible hand wrap," Freddie announced. "I don't think his guy knows how to wrap hands. The way he did it, there's not much protection or strength."

That led to Roach reminiscing about an oddity that occurred years ago when he was training Virgil Hill.

"I went in to watch the opponent getting his hands wrapped, and the guy who was wrapping had no idea what he was doing. Finally, the fighter said, 'Freddie, will you wrap my hands?' I said, 'I can't. You're fighting my guy.' He said, 'Please!' So I did it."

At 9:50, Cotto lay down on a towel on the floor, and Somodio began stretching him out.

Miguel shadow boxed briefly.

Somodio gloved him up.

At 10:27, Cotto began hitting the pads with Roach; his first real physical exertion of the night. Four minutes later, they stopped.

At 10:40, a voice sounded: "Okay, guys."

It was time to fight.

This was Cotto's first fight at Barclays Center after having fought in New York nine times at Madison Square Garden and once at Yankee Stadium.

Geale had a decided size advantage. One day earlier, Miguel had weighed in at 153.6 pounds while Daniel tipped the scales at 157. During the ensuing thirty hours, Geale had gained approximately twenty pounds. He weighed 182 in street clothes on fight night. But size was his only edge.

Cotto-Geale was a craftsman versus an ordinary fighter. It was clear from the start that Miguel was faster and the better boxer.

For the first three rounds, Cotto piled up points with his jab and scored points in addition to doing damage with hard hooks to the body. Thirty-two seconds into round four, a picture-perfect left hook up top smashed Geale to the canvas and left him on his back with his upper torso stretched beneath the bottom ring rope.

Geale rose on unsteady legs at the count of nine and managed to stay upright for another thirty seconds before a barrage of punches punctuated by a short right hand deposited him on the floor for the second time.

Once again, he beat the count.

"Are you okay?" referee Harvey Dock asked.

Geale shook his head.

"No," he said.

Dock stopped the fight.

There was joy in Cotto's dressing room after the fight. It wasn't that he'd beaten Geale as much as the way he beaten him that impressed.

"Miguel boxed very well tonight," Roach said. "The angles were good. He got off first and went to the body a lot." Freddie smiled. "It's a lot easier when the fight happens the way you planned it."

As for the future; Cotto isn't one of the kids anymore. He's much closer to the end of his ring career than the beginning.

"I said that I would be out of boxing by the time I am thirty," Miguel noted recently. " I am thirty-four now."

How many fights he has left will depend in large measure on how much punishment he takes in them and, to a lesser degree, how much each training camp takes out of him.

Meanwhile, June 6 was one more performance to be treasured. But in some ways, it was just another fight. Cotto showered and put on the same faded jeans, gray T-shirt, blue leather jacket, and loafers without socks that he'd worn earlier in the evening. He looked like a factory worker getting ready to go home after an honest night's work.

One might say that Emile Griffith was born a half-century too soon.

A Man's World:
The Double Life of Emile Griffith

Emile Griffith had his first professional fight on June 2, 1958. Less than three years later, at age twenty-three, he was welterweight champion of the world.

Over the course of his nineteen-year ring career, Griffith had 111 fights and boxed the staggering total of 1,122 rounds, 337 of them in championship competition. That's 51 more championship rounds than Sugar Ray Robinson. His final record was 85 wins, 24 losses, and 2 draws. Many of those losses came long after he should have stopped fighting.

Griffith beat Luis Rodriguez three times, Benny Paret twice, Nino Benvenuti, Benny Briscoe, and Dick Tiger. He's on the short list of the greatest welterweights of all time.

He was gay.

A Man's World: The Double Life of Emile Griffith by Donald McRae (Simon & Schuster) is the biography that this complex man deserves.

Griffith was welterweight champion in an era when, in McRae's words, "boxing still carried profound meaning." There were only eight champions on earth at any given time. He won the title by decision over Benny Paret in their first encounter. Before their second bout (which Paret won by decision), the challenger alluded disparagingly to the champion's sexuality. That set the stage for March 24, 1962.

At the weigh-in for their third fight, Paret openly derided Griffith as a "maricon."

"Maricon," McRae writes, "was the worst and deadliest insult in Hispanic culture."

That night, Griffith beat Paret to death in the ring. For the first time ever, a man was killed on live national television. The horror of it led to calls in state legislatures to abolish boxing. A *New York Times* editorial declared, "The question everybody is asking is whether this fight was allowed to go on too long. A better question might be whether it or any other professional prizefight should be allowed to start."

Griffith was haunted by Paret's death. Although he fought for fifteen more years, he was never the same fighter again. And he suffered outside the ring too. The guilt that he felt over killing a man was compounded by the societal taboo against homosexuality.

McRae recounts the tenor of those times:

"The onslaught against homosexuality ran deep and wide. The state and the church and the courts, the police and the doctors, the newspapers and the magazines, the rich and the powerful, the poor and the illiterate, were united in their condemnation of men like Emile Griffith. A homosexual, to them, was sick and cowardly. He was depraved and absurd."

There's more:

"Most of America believed that homosexuality was a disease-spreading curse that needed to be cut out like a cancer. Gay sex in 1964 was still illegal in forty-nine out of America's fifty states. On December 17, 1963, the *New York Times* printed a 5,000-word feature beginning on the front page, which explored 'the homosexual problem.' In a story headlined 'Growth of Homosexuality in City Provokes Wide Concern,' the *Times* complained, 'Sexual inverts have colonized three areas of New York. The city's homosexual community acts as a kind of lodestar, attracting others from all over the country. The old idea, assiduously propagated by the homosexuals, that homosexuality is an inborn incurable disease has been exploded by modern psychiatry. In the opinion of many experts, it can be both prevented and cured.'"

"Amid such oppression," McRae concludes, "the idea of Emile coming out in public as a gay man would not just have invited disbelief. It would have been a criminal act which could have resulted in his imprisonment. It felt forbidden to give voice to his true self."

Thirty-six hours after Griffith-Paret III, Griffith's manager (Howie Albert), trainer (Gil Clancy), and other members of his team met with the press and sought to dispel rumors about Emile's sexuality . . . "It just takes one malicious guy to spread false rumors. This stuff about Emile is so far from the truth . . . This boy is a normal boy. There's nothing wrong with him."

Did they know?

Of course, they did. But as McRae writes, "Emile remained nailed to his cross of silent denial. The idea of calling himself a 'homosexual' seemed impossible once he became such a public figure. The mystery of Emile Griffith was buried tight inside him. He still could not bear to voice the truth out loud, which meant he lived an essentially melancholic life studded by moments of outrageous happiness. It was impossible to live a balanced and serene life."

But Griffith's life as a gay man wasn't as closeted as most people think it was. Yes, there was a concerted effort to keep references to it out of the media. But Emile frequented gay bars on a regular basis and had several long-term live-in lovers.

"He felt no shame or guilt in holding a man, in kissing him and doing much more," McRae reports. "He did not tell himself that he needed to change and stick to a straight and narrow life. And so, even as a new world champion, he was back in Times Square, laughing and dancing with the hustlers and strippers, the young Hispanic gay crowd and the old drag queens. Emile still insisted on walking through the front door of his favorite bars."

The paradox of Griffith's life was crystalized in words that Emile spoke to his friend Ron Ross: "I kill a man, and most people forgive me. However, I love a man, and many say this makes me an evil person."

The words flow well in A Man's World. McRae's writing always does. With the exception of Griffith's 1966 victory over Dick Tiger to claim the middleweight crown (a fight that's barely mentioned), the major fights are well told. McRae, as he did in an earlier book about Joe Louis, re-creates Griffith's private life and demons well.

There are some nagging factual errors in the book. For example, McRae says that Joe Frazier knocked Muhammad Ali down in round eleven of their first fight. It was in round fifteen. Also, McRae attributes the phrase "No Viet Cong ever called me nigger" to Ali. I've never seen a contemporaneous source for that, although it has been incorrectly cited so many times that it has become part of many Ali chronicles. The words were first spoken by Stokely Carmichael. Ali might have spoken them later. He certainly didn't say them on the day he was reclassified 1-A by his draft board and proclaimed "I ain't got no quarrel with them Viet Cong."

That said; McRae is a very good writer. And *A Man's World* is a very good book. The amount of information that it offers regarding Griffith's personal life (including the intimate details of several long-term relationships with gay partners) is particularly impressive and tastefully reported.

The end game for Griffith was sad. Brain damage sustained during his long career as a fighter was exacerbated by a horrible beating outside a gay bar called Hombre in July 1992. His last years were spent in a hellish dementia so severe that he could not speak. By then, McRae recounts, "Emile resembled a man in a waking coma" living in "a shadowy world of silence and sleep."

He died on July 23, 2013, at age seventy-five.

How important was Emile Griffith?

Two voices answer that question.

"Emile," McRae writes, "gave gay men, especially gay black men, belief that the world might start to regard homosexuality in a different light. Every time news spread that the world champion had arrived at Bon Soir or Dr. Feelgood or Telstar or any of the other gay joints, a jolt of courage surged through the clubbers like electricity. Emile made everyone feel just a little stronger. They knew that no one would yell 'faggot' if they came face to face with Emile and recognized him. He did not fit the stereotype of a homosexual man. Emile Griffith broke the mold and, for his courage, he was celebrated. He was cherished. He was loved. He gave them all hope amid the suffering oppression."

Freddie Wright (one of Emile's closest friends for decades) is in accord and told McRae, "Emile lived in two worlds. He was a great fighter, and they loved and respected him in boxing. In his other world, in my world, he made gay people feel so proud, especially because he was a world champion. Emile might not have shouted out his sexuality, but he stayed true to all of us. He lit a fire in so many people. We not only respected and liked Emile. We loved him."

2015, like most years, saw a mix of fights, some of which were good and some bad.

Fight Notes

On January 9, 2015, Roc Nation Sports made its long-awaited boxing debut in The Theater at Madison Square Garden.

The driving force behind Roc Nation is rap impresario Shawn Carter aka Jay Z.

Jay Z's entry into the world of boxing began inauspiciously last year when Roc Nation won the purse bid for Peter Quillin's mandatory WBO title defense against Matt Korobov with a bid of $1,904,840 (more than twice market value). Roc Nation then advised the boxing community that the bout would be contested at Barclays Center in Brooklyn on November 1.

There were two problems with that. First, soon after the bid, New York State Athletic Commission executive director David Berlin advised Roc Nation that the NYSAC would not license Korobov because of a congenital brain condition. Then, while alternative sites were being explored, Quillin gave up the title at the direction of his manager (the ubiquitous Al Haymon), rather than take the fight.

Here, the thoughts of rap artist and vitamin-water mogul Curtis Jackson aka 50 Cent are instructive. Last month, Fiddy observed, "When you come into the sport of boxing and have money, you're steak. To a lot of people, you look like dinner."

There's only one chance to make a first impression, so January 9 was important to Roc Nation. Two days before the reconfigured event, its COO for boxing Dave Itskowitch told writer Tom Gerbasi, "We want to make the in-arena experience more appealing to fans. We want to really amp up the fan experience. I know the fights should do the talking. But there will be other bells and whistles that are going to make things even more enjoyable for fans and keep the fans engaged."

When fight night arrived, radio personality Angie Martinez was the in-ring hostess. There were a lot of celebrities in attendance. Jay Z,

Rihanna, Jake Gyllenhaal, C. C. Sabathia, Victor Cruz, DJ Mustard, and Carmelo Anthony were there. Rap artist Fabulos performed for ten minutes before the main event.

The attendance was announced as 4,235, but the house was papered. And rather than give those freebies away as comps, Roc Nation took the unusual step of purchasing them before giving them away. That meant it had to pay an MSG facility fee as well as state and city taxes on each one.

As for the fights; they were essentially club fights.

The six undercard bouts were a mix of bad mismatches and competitive but boring contests. The most notable undercard moment came when light-heavyweight prospect Jerry Odom whacked Andrew Hernandez with two crushing blows. Unfortunately, those blows landed while Hernandez was on the canvas, having taken a knee to recover from a body shot. Odom was appropriately disqualified.

The co-featured fight of the evening pitted sloppy aggression (Tureano Johnson) against all-out retreat (Alex Theran). Sloppy aggression won when the ring doctor stopped the bout after the fifth round.

The main event saw Arthur "Dusty" Hernandez-Harrison against Tommy Rainone. Harrison, a twenty-year-old from Washington, DC, is being groomed and protected. Rainone lacks power and came into the bout with 4 knockouts in 28 fights. Four months ago, Tommy fought to a draw against a boxer with a 1-and-2 record. His most recent loss was to an opponent whose record was 2 and 6. Harrison prevailed on the judges' scorecards by a 100–90, 99–91, 99–91 margin.

Roc Nation lost a lot of money on the show. It costs six figures to open The Theater. Fighters have to be paid, and there were other heavy promotional expenses. Was it an effective loss leader?

The marriage of music and boxing hasn't been successful in the past. Think HBO's ill-fated *KO Nation* and promoter Cedric Kushner's money-hemorrhaging *Thunderbox*. It's not enough to have a ten-minute performance by a popular rap artist before the main event. The fights have to be entertaining too.

★ ★ ★

Deontay Wilder vs. Bermane Stiverne, contested on January 17, 2015, was seen going in as an entertaining match-up between two guys with questionable chins who could punch. Even better, it was unclear who would win.

Stiverne came in at 239 pounds with some extra weight around his waist. For most of the night, he plodded forward without letting his hands go often enough. Wilder used his considerable advantage in height and reach well. Even though Deontay moved away for most of the night, he did so as the aggressor, firing jabs with occasional right hands mixed in. His jab was effective as both an offensive weapon and a defensive shield. The right hands stunned Stiverne at the end of round two and again in round seven.

Wilder had never gone more than four rounds before. By mid-fight, it was clear that Stiverne needed a knockout to win. The only open issues were Deontay's stamina and his chin. Bermane didn't do much to test either. Instead, he kept plodding forward, taking punishment and failing to cut off the ring. On the few occasions when he landed something promising, Wilder fired back. The judges' scores of 120–107, 119–108, and 118–109 were a bit generous to Deontay, but close to the mark.

With his victory, Wilder claimed the bogus WBC heavyweight belt. The real champion is Wladimir Klitschko. But by besting Stiverne, Deontay established himself as a legitimate contender. He looked better against Bermane than a lot of people thought he would.

Wilder is entertaining to watch. He has the potential to excite people. There's a big payday waiting for him against either Klitschko or Tyson Fury. Wladimir would be a decided favorite over Deontay. Fury would not.

Let's hope than Wilder opts for Klitschko or Fury in his next fight and not Bozo the Clown.

★ ★ ★

The January 24, 2105, rubber match between Brandon Rios and Mike Alvarado shaped up at best as an entertaining club fight. The two men had combined to lose five of their previous seven outings over the past thirty-three months, with their only victories coming against each other. There was an effort to brand the trilogy as the second coming of Arturo Gatti vs. Micky Ward. That had no more credibility than likening Harry Connick Jr to Frank Sinatra.

In the weeks leading up to the fight, there was a widespread belief that, at best, Alvarado wasn't training properly. At the start of round one, he looked like a man who didn't want to fight. Then he morphed into a human punching bag. His only moment of serious aggression came toward the end of the second round, when he walked away from the action, then turned and whacked Rios in the testicles. In round three, Brandon pounded away without mercy. Following that stanza, the fight was stopped.

HBO commentator Jim Lampley acknowledged afterward, "It was a one-sided annihilation by a well-prepared Brandon Rios against a stunningly unprepared Mike Alvarado. Basically, he wasn't there."

"He had nothing, zero," promoter Bob Arum added.

Boxing fans were spared comparisons with Gatti-Ward in the post-fight analysis.

★ ★ ★

HBO's March 14, 2015, telecast started poorly with Isaac Chilemba vs. Vasily Lepikin and Steve Cunningham vs. Vyacheslav Glazkov. The main event—Sergey Kovalev vs. Jean Pascal—was worth watching.

Kovalev came into the bout with 26 wins, 23 knockouts, 0 losses, and a technical draw that should have been recorded as a win. Four months ago, he solidified his credentials as the best 175-pound fighter in the world with a 120–107, 120–107, 120–106 whitewash of Bernard Hopkins.

Pascal (29-2, 17 KOs) was regarded as a good measuring stick for Kovalev.

Kovalev was the aggressor in the early going and fought at a brisk pace. In round three, Pascal decided to fight with him and wound up being saved by the bell after a hard right hand draped him over the ropes and led to a correctly called knockdown. It was the first knockdown scored against Pascal in his pro career.

Pascal rallied to win rounds five and six, but tired noticeably in round seven. In round eight, Kovalev unloaded, leaving Jean on wobbly legs. Referee Luis Pablon stopped the bout at the 1:03 mark with Pascal pinned in a corner but still standing.

It was the first stoppage loss in Pascal's career. He can take solace in the fact that Kovalev never knocked him off his feet. After the bout, Jean told television viewers and the crowd at the Bell Centre in Montreal, "I don't know why the referee stopped the fight. It's not hockey."

Kovalev showed a good chin and an improving left hook to go with his power. The fact that he outlanded Pascal 122 to 68, indicates an effective delivery system for his arsenal. He got hit with too many solid punches, but that makes for exciting fights.

★ ★ ★

Al Haymon's Premier Boxing Champions venture is a marathon, not a sprint. The latest installment of the race was run on Saturday, April 11, 2015, when NBC showcased Danny Garcia vs. Lamont Peterson and Andy Lee vs. Peter Quillin at Barclays Center in Brooklyn.

Lee came to Barclays with a 34-and-2 record, 24 KOs, and the WBO 160-pound belt by virtue of his sixth-round stoppage of Matt Korobov last December. On the negative side of the ledger, Andy has been knocked out by Julio Cesar Chavez Jr and Brian Vera and seems to have passed his prime.

Quillin (31-0, 22 KOs) has been protected for most of career, fighting opponents who either were past their prime or never had one. His signature victories were against Hassan N'Dam N'Jikam, Gabriel Rosado, and a very old Winky Wright.

Quillin failed to make weight for Lee-Quillin, following in the footsteps of too many fighters who have skirted their contractual obligations recently and, in the process, gained a competitive edge. A deal was struck whereby Peter paid $125,000 of his $500,000 purse to Lee, raising the latter's total to $625,000. The fight was also reclassified as a non-title bout.

It's not often that a "champion" enters the ring as a 3-to-1 underdog, but that was the case here. Those odds seemed short at the 2:30 mark of round one, when Quillin landed a lead right and deposited Lee on the canvas. Andy rose on shaky legs but survived the round. He visited the canvas again in round three, when Quillin scored with another lead right while standing on Andy's right foot (which referee Steve Willis mistakenly ruled a knockdown).

Adding to Lee's miseries, he emerged from the third stanza with a cut above his left eye. But Andy exacted a measure of revenge and scored a knockdown of his own with a crisp right hook in round seven.

After that, the action slowed considerably. The fight was there for the taking by Quillin. But Peter fought cautiously; too cautiously. And Lee showed heart. This writer gave the nod to Quillin. The judges called it a split-decision draw: 113–112, 112–113, 113–113. Lee kept his title, but didn't look particularly good doing it.

Danny Garcia (WBC and WBA) and Lamont Peterson (IBF) each held 140-pound belts but contracted to fight at 143 pounds.

Garcia had a 29-and-0 (17 KOs) record with signature victories over Amir Khan and Lucas Matthysse. But he'd fought only twice during the preceding nineteen months, winning a dubious majority decision against Mauricio Herrera and knocking out a pathetically overmatched Rod Salka.

Peterson entered the ring with a 33-2-1 (17 KOs) record highlighted by a razor-thin split-decision triumph over Amir Khan. But Lamont had been stopped in the third round by Lucas Matthysse and dominated by Tim Bradley en route to a near-shutout decision loss.

Like Quillin, Garcia was a 3-to-1 betting favorite.

Garcia-Peterson was a strange fight. For the first seven rounds, Lamont didn't do much of anything except circle away (the operative word being "away"). It frustrated Garcia, who was unable to cut off the ring. And it frustrated the fans, who had come to Barclays with the expectation of seeing a fight. There was sustained booing. And worse from Peterson's point of view, he dug himself into a hole on the judges' scorecards that he was unable to climb out of.

In round eight, Peterson began to fight. From that point on, he was the dominant fighter. But it was too little too late. Garcia prevailed on a majority decision: 115–113, 115–113, 114–114. Lamont could have won the fight. But he gave it away by cycling for seven rounds before fighting for five.

* * *

Boxing is in the midst of a remarkable run that has seen major fights on HBO, Showtime, CBS, NBC, and/or Spike virtually every week.

April 18, 2015, brought more of the same with HBO and Showtime competing directly against each other.

The HBO card featured two fights with four different promoters: Ruslan Provodnikov (Banner Promotions) vs. Lucas Matthysse (Golden Boy) and Terence Crawford (Top Rank) vs. Thomas Doulorme (Gary Shaw Productions).

Crawford had compiled a 25-0 (17 KOs) record and earned recognition as the best lightweight in the world with a ninth-round stoppage of Yuriorkis Gamboa last year. This was his first fight at 140 pounds.

Doulorme (22-1, 14 KOs) was considered a prospect until Luis Carlos Abregu exposed his deficiencies and knocked him out thirty months ago. Since then, Thomas had carefully picked his opponents.

Thirty seconds into round six of Crawford-Doulorme, Terence's skills and Thomas's limitations coincided. A straight right wobbled Doulorme, who appeared to take a knee rather than be put down by two errant punches that followed. Thomas then went into survival mode, but failed to survive. Knockdowns #2 and #3 ended the bout at the 1:51 mark of the sixth stanza.

Crawford looks like a complete fighter. It wasn't just that he beat Doulorme. The way he beat him was impressive.

Provodnikov-Matthysse brought to mind the words of Jay Larkin (the architect of Showtime's boxing program). Larkin had a simple way of describing his job. "It's not rocket science," he'd say. "It's boxing on television."

In other words, a fight that looks good on paper is more likely to look good in the ring than a fight that shapes up on paper as a dud.

Provodnikov-Matthysse didn't look good on paper. It looked great.

Provodnikov (24-3, 17 KOs) had lost narrow decisions to Mauricio Herrera and Chris Algieri (a split verdict) as well as a one-point defeat at the hands of Tim Bradley. But the latter bout (honored as 2013's "Fight of the Year") saw Bradley out on his feet twice and on the canvas once. In his next outing, Provodnikov battered Mike Alvarado into submission.

Matthysse (34-3, 34 KOs) had suffered one-point split-decision losses to Zab Judah and Devon Alexander and a two-point defeat at the hands of Danny Garcia. But 32 of his 34 wins had come by knockout and, two years ago, he brutalized Lamont Peterson en route to a third-round stoppage.

Matthysse and Provodnikov can be outslicked. Neither of them out-slicks opponents. They bludgeon their foes. One day before the bout, Jimmy Tobin summed up the anticipation when he wrote, "The ring in the Turning Stone Resort and Casino will have a diamond set in it on Saturday night when Lucas Matthysse and Ruslan Provodnikov reveal what beauty can be wrought from pressure and heat. It is impossible to imagine these men leaving the ring unchanged by the other's mischief."

Provodnikov–Matthysse lived up to expectations. Matthysse has better boxing skills than Provodnikov. And he can whack. Worse from Ruslan's point of view, in the opening minute of round two, an acci-dental clash of heads opened an ugly gash on his left eyelid that bled throughout the fight.

There are fighters who crumble and fighters who don't. Earlier in the evening, Doulorme had crumbled. Provodnikov didn't.

Ruslan lost five of the first six rounds and took a pounding in most of them. But he came on strong at the end of each round and gathered steam as the fight wore on. Instead of calling him "the Siberian Rocky," one might refer to him simply as "the Siberian Rock." His face was a bruised, battered, bloody, swollen, mess. It must have been a shock for him to look into a mirror after the fight. But he showed incredible resolve and heart.

Matthysse had enough in his arsenal to emerge victorious by a 115–113, 115–113, 114–114 margin.

Showtime's card was an Al Haymon venture. In the opening bout, twenty-four-year-old super-lightweight Amir Imam (18-0, 14 KOs) fought Walter Castillo (25-2, 18 KOs), who'd been imported from Nicaragua as a measuring stick. Iman won a clear-cut 100–90, 99–91, 98–92 decision. That set the stage for Showtime's main event: Julio Cesar Chavez Jr (48-1, 32 KOs) vs. Andrzej Fonfara (26-3, 15 KOs).

Chavez (marketed as "son of the legend") has his father's DNA in his chin. He turned pro in 2003 and amassed a 48-1 (32 KOs) record while frustrating fans with an often-slovenly work ethic and inattention to such matters as making weight. Indeed, there were times (particularly prior to fighting Brian Vera in 2013) when Chavez seemed to be rewriting weight clauses in contracts to fit his eating and exercise habits rather than the other way around.

But Chavez is a ratings magnet. Also, over time, he became a legitimate contender, beating opponents like John Duddy, Andy Lee, and Marco Antonio Rubio, in large measure because of his superior physical gifts.

In theory, Chavez also briefly held the WBC middleweight championship after the sanctioning body shamelessly lifted Sergio Martinez's crown to accommodate Julio. But Martinez ended that fiction by winning eleven of twelve rounds en route to a unanimous-decision triumph over "son of the legend" three years ago.

Fonfara (a natural light-heavyweight) had been chosen as Chavez's opponent on the theory that Andrzej is there to be hit, doesn't hit too hard, and would make Chavez look good. Also, Julio hoped that the 172-pound contract weight would add to Fonfara's limitations by depleting Andrzej's strength.

Chavez didn't look to be in particularly good shape when Chavez-Fonfara began; a suspicion that was confirmed as the bout wore on. His technique (which has never been particularly good) fell apart. And his body work didn't have the same effect on Fonfara that it has had on smaller men in the past.

By round six, there was bruising and swelling beneath both of Julio's eyes, and he was only fighting in spurts. Fifty-five seconds into round nine, Fonfara (an orthodox fighter) shifted position and threw what in effect was a straight left that put Chavez on the canvas for the first time in Julio's career. At the end of the round, Chavez went back to his corner, where trainer Joe Goossen asked, "How do you feel?"

"Stop it," Chavez told him. "Stop the fight. I'm done. Stop it. I want it stopped."

Fonfara had an 89–80, 88–81, 88–81 lead on the judges' scorecards at the time of the stoppage and outlanded Chavez by a 285-to-118 margin.

After the bout, Chavez put the blame for his defeat on fighting at a contract weight of 172 pounds. "The guy is too heavy for me," he said. "172 is too much for me."

Question: Whose fault was that?

Answer: Julio's.

That said; Chavez is still marketable. He's a good fighter with an aggressive ring style and defensive deficiencies that make for entertaining fights. And he still has his name, although Saturday night tarnished it a bit.

When Chavez lost to Sergio Martinez, he was treated in some circles as though he'd won because of a dramatic last-round effort that saw him floor Martinez twice. After losing to Fonfara in abysmal fashion, Julio will be treated as though he lost.

★ ★ ★

On September 30, 2014, when Saul "Canelo" Alvarez attended a luncheon at HBO to announce a multi-fight contract with the network, his red hair and green pullover shirt gave the impression of an early Christmas present.

One reason Canelo signed to fight on HBO was that he didn't want to play second fiddle to Floyd Mayweather at Showtime. Beyond that, he's a key puzzle piece in HBO's desire to continue its appeal to Latino subscribers and Golden Boy's attempt to maintain its standing as a major promoter.

"My focus is Canelo, one hundred percent," Golden Boy president Oscar De La Hoya (Alvarez's promoter) told reporters at the luncheon. "Whatever he asks, I have to do."

At age twenty-four, Alvarez has established himself as a marketable commodity within the boxing community. He's not a crossover star in the United States. Nor is he an elite fighter. In ESPN's most recent pound-for-pound poll, not one panelist gave him a top-ten vote. And let's not forget what happened when Canelo fought Floyd Mayweather two years ago.

That said; with Julio Cesar Chavez Jr imploding and Juan Manuel Marquez on the verge of retirement, Alvarez is Mexican boxing's most promising hope for the future. He engenders good ratings. He has amassed a 45-and-1 (32 KOs) ring record against increasingly credible competition. And there have been times (most notably against Erislandy Lara and Austin Trout) when he went in tougher than he had to.

On May 9, 2015, Alvarez entered the ring for the first time pursuant to his new contract with HBO. Bart Barry summed up the impending confrontation as follows:

"A week after Pacquiao-Mayweather, Mexican Saul 'Canelo' Alvarez will fight Texan James Kirkland at Minute Maid Park in Houston before a crowd that should be about three times the MGM Grand's crowd. 'But oh,' cries a passel of aspiring businessmen from their parents' couches. 'They won't make as much money.' First of all, why the hell are you so excited about strangers making money? Second of all, three times as many aficionados and potential aficionados will have a chance to see a major event in a sport you care about, which is better for your sport in every single way.'"

Kirkland entered the ring with a 32-and-1 (28 KOs) record. James has granite hands but a bit of glass in his chin. He came out punching at the opening bell. Canelo weathered the storm, mixed effective body punching with solid shots to the head, hurt Kirkland with a hard right to the body, and knocked him down with a straight right up top.

There was 1:20 left in round one. Kirkland was in trouble but survived the onslaught that followed, including a barrage that left him all but out on his feet at the close of the stanza.

Round two was marked by exciting back-and-forth action.

In round three, Kirkland was clearly tired and Alvarez seemed to be wearing down. Both fighters dug deep. A right uppercut put James on the canvas at the 1:50 mark. He rose. There were more punches. Then Canelo wound up an overhand right from so far back that everyone in Houston except Kirkland could see it coming. The blow landed flush on James's jaw and knocked him out.

Last week, Evander Holyfield complained, "I've attended the three biggest fights of the year so far: Deontay Wilder vs. Bermane Stiverne, Wladimir Klitschko vs. Bryant Jennings, and now Mayweather vs. Pacquiao. And you know what I've seen? Not much boxing. In 36 total rounds, I saw zero knockdowns. I saw a lot of holding and hugging and a lot of running. I saw three twelve-round unanimous decisions. What I didn't see were punches being thrown and landed. No fighter in any of the three fights was ever threatened or even in trouble. I didn't even see a fighter with a cut or a bruise after the fight. Everyone was just playing defense, trying not to get hit. How can you have a boxing match if guys aren't throwing and landing punches? The answer is, you can't."

Evander has been going to the wrong fights.

★ ★ ★

Six hours before Alvarez-Kirkland, Hildago, Texas, (300 miles southwest of Houston) hosted a Premier Boxing Champions doubleheader on CBS.

In the opening bout, England's Jamie McDonnell (25-2, 12 KOs) survived a third-round knockdown to score a hard-fought 114–113, 114–113, 114–113 decision over Japan's Tomoki Kameda (31-0, 19 KOs). The final round (when McDonnell dug deep and Kameda didn't) was the difference.

But the real story of the evening was referee Laurence Cole and three judges, who administered a dose of Texas injustice to Scotsman Ricky Burns (37-4, 11 KOs) in his fight against local favorite Omar Figueroa (24-0, 18 KOs).

Prior to the bout, Figueroa (who was moving up from 135 pounds) showed a lack of professionalism by weighing in 1.5 pounds over the 140-pound contract weight. But the day's most relevant number might have been "22" (the number of miles that Figueroa lives from Hidalgo).

As early as round two, CBS commentators Mauro Ranallo, Paulie Malignaggi, and Virgil Hunter were commenting on Cole's conduct of the proceedings.

"Cole has become a big factor in this fight," Hunter noted. As the fight wore on, Virgil added, "Laurence Cole continues to pull Ricky Burns's arm away [in clinches], putting him in a dangerous situation ... Right now, you see Figueroa holding and hitting, and he's not being warned. Let's have a fair fight here."

When Figueroa led with his head (which he did often), Cole warned Burns for pushing Omar's head down.

"I don't like that warning," Malignaggi said on one such occasion. "I'd like to see Cole warn Figueroa as well." After a similar warning later in the fight, Hunter objected, "You have a right to protect yourself. The head is a dangerous weapon."

"He [Cole] continues to inject himself unnecessarily," Ranallo opined.

In round eight, Cole deducted a point from Burns for "holding," prompting Malignaggi to observe, "When both guys are jockeying for position like that, it's not even holding." In round eleven, Cole deducted another point from the Scotsman.

It was an exciting fight. Figueroa is a volume-punching, come-forward brawler, and Burns obliged him. But the bout was marred by the refereeing and also by the nagging suspicion that Ricky would be jobbed by the judges when it was over.

That's what happened. I thought that, even with Cole's intercession, Burns won. The judges ruled otherwise, scoring 117–109, 116–110, 116–110 in Figueroa's favor. To say that Burns won only three or four rounds was frivolous.

It's no accident that every time there's questionable officiating in Texas, it favors the house fighter.

Figueroa is an exciting fighter. But he gets hit too much. If Omar faces a big puncher, not even Texas refereeing and judging will save him.

★ ★ ★

The May 29, 2015, fight between Amir Khan and Chris Algieri at Barclays Center surprised a lot of people.

Khan made his mark in boxing as a seventeen-year-old silver medalist for the United Kingdom at the 2004 Olympics. He turned pro in 2005 and was being groomed for stardom when reality intervened in the form of a first-round-knockout loss at the hands of Breidis Prescott in 2008.

Amir rebounded from that defeat with eight consecutive wins, including impressive victories over Paulie Malignaggi, Marcos Maidana, and Zab Judah. Then back-to-back losses to Lamont Peterson (on a razor-thin split decision) and Danny Garcia (KO by 4) derailed him. More recently, Khan scored a unanimous-decision triumph over Devon Alexander. His record going into the Algieri fight stood at 30 and 3 with 19 KOs and 2 KOs by.

Algieri brought a 20-and-1 (8 KOs) ledger into the contest. His biggest win was a controversial split-decision verdict over Ruslan Provodnikov at Barclays on June 14, 2014. In his only fight after that, Chris was knocked down six times by Manny Pacquiao en route to a lopsided decision loss.

The assumption going in was that Khan could do everything Algieri could do and do it better.

"I take every fight seriously," Amir said in a May 5, 2015, teleconference call. "I've fought some fights that I thought were going to be a walk in the park. I got hurt; I lost the fight. I can't take this fight lightly and think it's going to be easy and lose my fight. Then all my dreams are shattered."

That said; Khan was a 12-to-1 betting favorite.

It was a spirited fight. Algieri surprised by coming out hard, forcing a fast pace, and fighting aggressively for most of the night. Khan spent a lot of time counterpunching in retreat, which he did with increasing effectiveness as the bout progressed.

The refereeing of Mark Nelson (an import from Minnesota) left a lot to be desired. Algieri kept trying to work on the inside, and Khan kept putting him in a headlock (seven times in the first three rounds alone). Also, there were many times when Amir held onto Chris's left arm in a clinch but Algieri was still scoring effectively to the body with his right, and Nelson broke them.

By round nine, the area around Algieri's left eye was bruised, swollen, and starting to close. Round ten was Khan's best of the fight, highlighted by a brutal hook to the body that caused Chris to wince and slowed his advance.

It was a hard bout to score. Many of the rounds could have gone either way. I thought it was even. The judges favored Khan by a 117–111, 117–111, 115–113 margin.

There's a school of thought (to which I subscribe) that the judges were kinder to Algieri than they should have been when he fought Provodnikov at Barclays Center last year. Perhaps the judges in Khan-Algieri were trying to avoid that mistake and over-compensated in the opposite direction.

★ ★ ★

The recent deluge of fights on television has taken on the feel of an all-you-can-eat buffet. That means boxing fans are going to start making choices and become more selective in their viewing.

June 12 and 13, 2015, saw three telecasts of note. One on HBO, one on Showtime, and one on Spike. Let's take a look at what viewers saw.

HBO featured four undefeated fighters in two match-ups from The Theater at Madison Square Garden: Felix Verdejo (17-0, 13 KOs) vs. Ivan Najera (16-0, 8 KOs) and Nicholas Walters (25-0, 21 KOs) vs. Miguel Marriaga (20-0, 18 KOs).

Hall of Fame matchmaker Bruce Trampler once noted, "There's a difference between a learning-curve record and a padded record."

Verdejo has the former. He's a twenty-two-year-old lightweight from San Juan, who Top Rank hopes will be its next Puerto Rican star.

Felix has a sparkling personality, a flashy fighting style, and he's good. He's also *f-a-s-t.*

Najera was tough and game. He tried to turn the fight into a brawl. But Verdejo's punches were too sharp and his defense too good.

Ivan got dropped by a left uppercut in round five and a left hook in round seven (lightning strikes that seemed to come out of nowhere). Each time, he got up fighting but his cause was hopeless.

Verdejo took the tenth round off and still won it on two of the judges' scorecards en route to a 100–88, 100–88, 99–89 triumph. After the fight, he told his fans, "Continue to support me, and you will have Felix for a long time."

That sounds like a good deal. Let's see if his promise is fulfilled.

Nicholas Walters turned heads last October with a sixth-round knockout of Nonito Donaire, and was considered by some to be the best featherweight in the world. Miguel Marriaga was a largely unknown opponent from Colombia.

Walters-Marriaga disappointed.

For starters, Walters weighed in initially at 127.4 pounds, couldn't get lower than 127, and was forced to vacate his 126-pound title.

Add to that the fact that a lot of the energy in the arena dissipated after Verdejo-Najera, giving Walters-Marriaga the feel of a walk-out bout.

Worse, Walters-Marriaga was a boring fight. Miguel fought cautiously, and Nicholas was content to outbox him. There were moments of heated engagement but not many. When it was done, Walters had outlanded Marriaga by a 279-to-165 margin and bested him 119–108, 118–109, 117–110 on the judges' scorecards.

In the course of an hour, Walters went from must-see viewing to it all depends on what else is on TV tonight.

WBC heavyweight belt holder Deontay Wilder (now 34-0, with 33 KOs) stepped up in his last fight and answered some questions about his ring skills with a unanimous-decision triumph over Bermane Stiverne. But Wilder's performance against Eric Molina in Showtime's main event on Saturday night (June 13) left a lot to be desired.

Soft touches aren't unheard of in heavyweight title matches. But few fighters less qualified than Molina have fought for a heavyweight belt. Team Wilder hyped the fact that it was bringing a "championship" fight to Deontay's home state of Alabama. But Molina had as much chance of winning as Charleston Southern does when it journeys to Tuscaloosa to face the Crimson Tide on the gridiron. Yes, Eric had a 23-2 record. But he'd never beaten a quality opponent and had been knocked out twice in the first round.

Wilder was an 35-to-1 favorite. The conventional wisdom was that Molina (who weighed in at a blubbery 239 pounds) wouldn't make it past the first round. Wilder knocked him down once in round four, twice in round five, and delivered a finishing right hand in round nine. But he looked sloppy and failed to impress.

Spike's June 12 telecast offered viewers one interesting fight and one awful one. Let's start on the plus side.

Artur Beterbiev is a thirty-year-old Russian now living in Canada, who's making waves at 175 pounds. After a 300-fight amateur career, he turned pro in 2013 and scored eight knockouts in eight fights before facing Alexander Johnson on Friday night.

Johnson was a 50-to-1 underdog. Nothing on his record suggested that he would be competitive with Beterbiev, and he wasn't. Artur put him on the canvas twice in round five; the first time with a short stiff jab that came from an awkward angle, and the second with a right uppercut. He also turned southpaw from time to time, which added to Alexander's troubles.

Johnson fought largely to survive, which he did until round seven when a straight right to the temple ended matters.

Beterbiev is entertaining to watch and very good.

Beterbiev-Johnson was followed by Erislandy Lara (20-2-2, 12 KOs) vs. Delvin Rodriguez (28-7-4, 16 KOs), which was a dreadful match-up.

Lara is a quality junior-middleweight. Rodriguez had won four of his last eleven fights dating back to 2008, which explained why Erislandy was a 40-to-1 favorite.

Lara-Rodriguez was a drab one-sided beating with no entertainment value. Lara had a 233-to-63 edge in punches landed and won 120–107 times three on the judges' scorecards.

Meanwhile, while other fighters were in the spotlight this past weekend, local fan favorite Seanie Monaghan scored his twenty-fifth victory in twenty-five fights with a ninth-round stoppage of Fulgencio Zuniga in an undercard bout at Madison Square Garden.

Monaghan didn't turn pro until age twenty-eight. Five years later, he's ranked in the top-ten at 175 pounds by each of the four major sanctioning bodies. His best assets are a Spartan work ethic, iron resolve, and a good chin. His most significant liability is that he's slow for a boxer. Speed and quickness can't be taught.

Zuniga, age thirty-seven, turned pro in 2001 and now has a 27-11 (24 KOs) record. In recent years, he has become an opponent, losing to Gilberto Ramirez, Hassan N'Dam, James DeGale, Tavoris Cloud, Lucian Bute, Kelly Pavlik, and others.

Monaghan got hit more than he should have against Zuniga, particularly with left hooks up top. But he scored well to the body, moved inexorably forward, and willingly engaged in trench warfare. The end came at 2:10 of round nine, when Zuniga took a knee after one final body shot, signaling to referee Danny Shiavone that he'd had enough.

"I'm not the most polished boxer in the world," Monaghan acknowledged afterward. "But I come to fight, I fight hard, I win my fights, and the fans have a good time."

"Right now, we're waiting for a title shot," trainer Joe Higgins added. "The guy we have our eye on is [WBA belt holder] Juergen Braehmer [of Germany]. Sooner or later, Seanie will get his chance. When it comes, he'll be as ready as he can be."

★ ★ ★

There was a time when Adrien Broner (30-1, 22 KOs) sought to position himself as the successor to Floyd Mayweather. No undersized punching bag was safe when Adrien was on the loose. His formula was to potshot opponents until he knew they were danger-free and then go after them. He had (and still has) prodigious physical gifts.

"At lightweight, where he was able to exploit his size," Jimmy Tobin writes, "Broner walked opponents down and banged them out. His mediocre defense was masked by his ability to handle a lightweight punch. His struggles to transition between offense and defense were hidden by the fact that Broner never needed to take a backward step."

But as Broner moved up in weight and the caliber of opponent improved, his limitations as fighter became evident. He won a narrow split-decision victory over Paulie Malignaggi at 147 pounds in 2013 and, later that year, was exposed in a unanimous-decision loss at the hands of Marcos Maidana.

Broner claimed that he wanted a rematch against Maidana. But as Carlos Acevedo observed, "Not only was Broner thrashed by Maidana, he was humiliated. He rose like a man suffering from Jake Leg after being knocked down in the second round, tried to buy a disqualification by writhing on the canvas like a two-year old in a Wal-Mart after Maidana butted him, hit the deck again in the eighth, was the victim of a revenge humping, and then fled the ring under a gauntlet of beer cups. Another loss to Maidana might have put an end to the Broner hype once and for all."

So instead of fighting a rematch against Maidana, Broner went down in weight to 140 and fought three overmatched opponents. Then, on June 20, 2015, he squared off against Shawn Porter (25-1, 16 KOs) at the MGM Grand in Las Vegas at a catchweight of 144 pounds.

Porter's resume had a unanimous-decision victory over Devon Alexander on it and also a majority-decision loss to Kell Brook. As a point of further comparison with Broner, Shawn wiped out Paulie Malignaggi in four rounds last year.

Porter was a 6-to-5 betting favorite. Broner has better natural gifts, but the feeling among those in the know was that Adrien is soft. Broner can trash-talk with the best. But it has become increasingly clear that he can't back it up. Against Porter, he didn't even try to.

Boxing maven Charles Jay has opined, "I hate it when a guy talks like a monster before the fight and then comes out and fights like a little lamb. I've seen it too many times, and it shows disrespect for the sport itself."

That was Broner on Saturday night.

There's a difference between fighting cautiously and stinking out the joint. Against Porter, Broner ran all night. Whenever Shawn got inside, Adrien tied him up. As the fight progressed, hugging and holding evolved into forearms to the throat. Then Adrien added headlocks to his repertoire. By round four, Steve Smoger (who was commentating for NBC) noted, "All we've seen so far is four rounds of fouls and forearms."

Porter tried to make it more of a battle. But he couldn't figure out how to do damage while coming in. And whenever he got inside, Broner tied him up. Adrien simply didn't want to fight. And Shawn didn't know how to fight a guy who didn't want to fight.

Referee Tony Weeks let Broner continue to hold and foul until round eleven, when he belatedly deducted a point. It was one of the few times in memory that the crowd has roared its approval when the referee took a point away from a fighter.

Early in round twelve, Porter got sloppy and Broner landed a hook up top that put Shawn on the canvas. But when Porter rose, Adrien went back to holding and hugging rather than going for a knockout (which he obviously needed to win).

Porter prevailed by a 118–108, 115–111, 114–112 margin on the judges' scorecards and had a 149-to-88 advantage in punches landed.

Thereafter, Broner nonsensically proclaimed, "I'm okay. It's okay. It don't matter. I'm a real animal. I came to fight today and I didn't get the decision. But at the end of the day, everyone here will take my autograph and my picture."

Broner isn't as good as he says he is. Boxing fans figured that out a while ago.

★ ★ ★

Andre Ward (now 28-0, 15 KOs) hasn't joined the federal witness protection program. But he's no longer in the thick of things either.

Ward rose to prominence with victories over Mikkel Kessler, Arthur Abraham, and Carl Froch in Showtime's "Super Six" 168-pound tournament. But contractual problems, injuries, and a general disinclination to fight credible opponents limited him to two ring appearances in the forty-two months that followed.

Earlier this year, Ward signed a promotional contract with Roc Nation, which tried unsuccessfully to land a date for him on HBO or Showtime. The problem was that Andre wanted big-fight money for a tune-up bout. His excuse was that he hadn't fought since November, 19, 2013, and needed a soft-touch opponent to work off the ring rust.

Here, one might note that Sugar Ray Leonard had been out of action for three years when he returned in 1987, went up two weight classes, and fought Marvin Hagler. Vitali Klitschko came back after four years of inactivity and faced WBC heavyweight champion Samuel Peter in his comeback fight.

Eventually, Ward got his soft touch. On June 20, 2015, in his hometown of Oakland, he squared off against England's Paul Smith (35-5, 20 KOs).

Smith, a likable man who has never beaten a world-class fighter, was a 30-to-1 underdog. He simply didn't have the tools to challenge Ward on any level.

Ward fought a safety-first fight. After three dreary rounds, he had a 72-to-10 edge in punches landed. The rest of the bout was no different. During the seventh stanza, blow-by-blow commentator Barry Tompkins observed, "It's been the same dance since the opening round." The seventh round also saw Smith cut above the left eye (which has been a problem for him in recent outings). In round nine, Ward broke Smith's nose; blood began to pour; and Paul's corner stopped the fight. Andre won every minute of what looked like a one-sided sparring session.

Fights like this might help Ward's bank account. But they don't help the Roc Nation brand. Meanwhile, Andre's status in boxing is best understood when one compares him to Miguel Cotto.

Ward is undefeated. When last in action, he was rated #2 on most pound-for-pound lists. Both Ward and Cotto are signed to Roc Nation. Each man fought a B-level opponent this month. But Cotto fought on HBO and Ward needed a time buy on BET to get his comeback fight on television.

There are two opponents of note outside of the Al Haymon universe that Ward could fight next: Gennady Golovkin at 168 pounds and Sergey Kovalev at 175. No other foreseeable Andre Ward fight matters.

★ ★ ★

It was a stretch to call the August 1, 2015, fight at Barclays Center between Danny Jacobs and Sergio Mora a "championship" fight.

Jacobs (29-1, 26 KOs) had fought one world-class opponent in his career (Dmitry Pirog) and was stopped in the fifth round. Mora (28-3-2, 9 KOs) has spent much of the last ten years living off the name recognition that came from a successful run on *The Contender*. But Jacobs and Mora are professional fighters. And their fight was a good one while it lasted.

Mora is a ring stylist who tends to avoid all-out action. This time, he had a different plan in mind.

"I take a good punch," Sergio told this writer the day after the fight. "I don't think Danny does. I was ready to go all out from the start."

Midway through round one, Mora hooked to the body, waited for a receipt, and got one in the form of a straight right hand that landed flush on his jaw, depositing him on the canvas. Sergio rose and backed into a corner. Jacobs followed, stopped to admire his handiwork with his hands down, and . . .

Boom! A left hook up top from Mora returned the knockdown favor.

The action continued in round two.

"I knew the first four rounds would be tough," Mora said on Sunday. "And then it would be a war of attrition. I've been there and won those kind of fights. The one time Danny was there, he got knocked out."

Then the unthinkable happened.

"I was fighting low against the ropes," Sergio recounted. "I'm comfortable in that position. I've made a career of defending myself that way. Danny hit me on the back of my head or neck with a grazing punch. He put his weight on me. We both lost our balance. I went down. My right leg was bent under my body, but I was okay. Then he stumbled over me. I heard a loud pop and felt an incredible pain in my ankle. I got up. And as soon as I put my weight on the ankle, it confirmed what I already knew. My ankle was broken."

"Are you ready to go?" referee Gary Rosato demanded.

"No," Sergio responded. "My ankle."

The fight was stopped and ruled a knockout victory for Jacobs at 2:55 of the second stanza. But was that the right ruling?

It's unclear from the camera angles aired by ESPN whether or not Mora visited the canvas as the consequence of a legal punch. Unless footage to the contrary exists, the ruling of the referee on that point has to stand.

But there's a second issue: Was Mora's broken ankle caused by a legitimate boxing move (the knockdown) or by an accidental foul that followed?

A look at one of the ESPN replay angles appears to show the following: Mora is on the canvas with his right ankle bent backward. As Jacobs stumbles forward over Sergio's body, Danny's right thigh pushes against Sergio's torso with the force of his momentum and weight, pinning Sergio's already-turned ankle under the weight of both bodies. It's at this point that Sergio heard the "pop" and a look of unspeakable pain crossed his face.

The New York State Athletic Commission has used video replay in the past to overturn fight results.

In 2007, Terrance Cauthen was ahead of Raul Frank on the judges' scorecards when he was accidentally head-butted on the chin and knocked woozy. Referee Ricky Gonzalez didn't see the head butt, stopped the fight, and declared Frank the winner by knockout. After a hearing, the result was changed to "no contest."

That same year, the NYSAC used video review to change the result of a fight between Delvin Rodriguez and Keenan Collins. The bout was originally ruled "no contest" after Collins suffered a fight-ending cut above his left eye that referee Eddie Claudio ruled was caused by an accidental clash of heads. A review of the video showed that the cut was caused by a punch. The result was changed to a second-round knockout in Rodriguez's favor.

Fundamental fairness requires a hearing on Jacobs-Mora if Sergio follows the proper legal procedures and brings the matter to the attention of the NYSAC.

"I don't need another loss on my record," Sergio says. "And it's not fair that I should have one."

★ ★ ★

Styles make fights. Danny Jacobs vs. Peter Quillin at Barclays Center on December 5, 2015, shaped up as an entertaining fight.

Jacobs entered the ring with a 30-1 (27 KOs) record against pedestrian opposition. In 2010, he'd stepped up in class and was knocked out in the fifth round by Dmitry Pirog. The only other quality fighter on his resume was a faded Sergio Mora. That fight, which was unfolding as a good one, was cut short when Mora suffered a broken ankle in round two.

Quillin (32-0-1, 23 KOs) had fought better opposition than Jacobs. But he gave up a bogus middleweight belt last year rather than defend it against mandatory challenger Matt Korobov. Now he was challenging for Jacobs's bogus crown.

Jacobs and Quillin are known for having questionable chins with Danny's being the more questionable. Each man has been kept away from punchers. Jacobs is the better boxer. Quillin has more power, which made Peter a 7-to-5 betting favorite.

Danny was the sentimental favorite. He's a likeable young man with an engaging personality, whose comeback from cancer is an inspirational story. It's hard to root against him.

The widely held view of the fight was that whichever man landed the first hard punch would have a decided edge.

Jacobs landed first. Forty-six seconds into round one, he staggered Quillin with a straight right to the temple. A barrage of punches followed, punctuated by a thudding right to the body, a sharp right to the top of the head, and a another right hand to the temple that sent Quillin reeling and wobbling around the ring. At that point, referee Harvey Dock stepped in and stopped the contest. The bout lasted 85 seconds.

There were scattered complaints about the stoppage. But Quillin wasn't among the complainers. And after watching a replay, Showtime analyst Paulie Malignaggi noted, "At first, I thought it was a quick stoppage. But looking at Quillin's eyes, he was kind of very much out of it."

When Dock ended matters, Quillin was struggling to simply maintain his balance and was in no condition to defend himself. Jacobs landed twenty-five "power punches" during his assault, and more would have followed. As WBC heavyweight belt holder Deontay Wilder told the media at a pre-fight sit-down, "The head isn't meant to be hit."

"That's why Harvey Dock is a great referee," Lou DiBella (who promoted Jacobs-Quillin) said afterward. "I had a great vantage point to look at Peter, and he didn't know where he was. He was out on his feet."

This article was written before Ronda Rousey's fall. When I called UFC publicist Tom Gerbasi to set up an interview with Rousey, he asked if I'd become one more in a long line of writers who "has the hots for Ronda."

"Tom," I told him, "not only am I too old for Ronda; I'm too old for Ronda's mother."

Ronda Rousey

Ronda Rousey has been in the news a lot lately. The 28-year-old UFC women's 135-pound champion and consensus choice as best female MMA combatant in the world has been featured in myriad publications ranging from *Time Magazine* and *The New Yorker* to *Maxim* and the *Sports Illustrated* swimsuit issue. Her autobiography—*My Fight, Your Fight*—was published recently by Regan Arts. Movie-goers have seen her on-screen in *Entourage* and *The Expendables 3*.

More recently, Rousey was chosen over Floyd Mayweather as "Best Fighter" at the 2015 ESPY Awards, after which she stuck it to Mayweather with the declaration, "I wonder how Floyd feels being beat by a woman for once."

Rousey stands at the complicated intersection of sex and violence. First and foremost, she's a fighter with a fighter's instincts and a fighter's mentality. She won gold medals in judo at the 2004 and 2006 Junior World Championships and the 2004 and 2005 Pan Am Games before capturing a silver medal at the 2007 World Championships. She was a 2004 Olympian and earned a bronze medal in judo at the 2008 Beijing Olympics, becoming the first American woman ever to win an Olympic medal in that sport.

Rousey is now the face of women's MMA. It's a pretty face. With long dirty-blonde hair that extends below her shoulder blades. she looks at times like a model rather than a fighter. The camera is her friend. She's photogenic and telegenic. She has charisma.

She's also smart, verbal, cocky, and energetic with an instinct for finding the spotlight and knowing what to do when it's shining on her.

She's never boring.

On the surface, Rousey has an upbeat personality. But there seems to be a fair amount of anger bubbling not far beneath the surface.

"I'm complicated," Ronda says. "Too complicated to be understood."

Rousey's mother was the first American woman to win a World Judo Championship; a feat she accomplished in 1984 at age twenty-six. She now has a PhD in educational psychology.

Ronda was born in 1987. "I come from a family of very empowered women," she notes.

She also comes from a dysfunctional family that makes the average dysfunctional family look functional. Her father committed suicide in 1995 after suffering complications relating to Bernard-Soulier syndrome (a bleeding disorder). Ronda suffered from a speech impediment as a child and was unable to speak in full sentences until age six. She had a tortured adolescence highlighted by a love-hate relationship with her mother, who believed in tough love with emphasis on the tough.

"I was very shy," Rousey recounts. "I wore baggy clothes all the time. I had a lot of evolving to do."

Meanwhile, judo was "the family business." Ronda began learning the craft at age eleven and was obsessed with it as she grew older. She also became bulimic in her constant struggle to make weight. She was determined to pay any price necessary to succeed.

"I was raised with the mentality that, if you're going to do any-thing, you're going to do it to be the best at it," Rousey told writer Tom Gerbasi. "The self-confidence that people see in me now has developed over time. It came mostly from doing well in sports. I felt that, if I was amazing in something, I'm actually a cool person and I should think more of myself. It's something about medals, having a tangible thing to hold in your hand. It's like, 'Oh, look; I'm awesome.'"

After the 2008 Olympics, Rousey spent a year abusing her body in a different way. In *My Fight, Your Fight*, she acknowledges, "I had my Olympic medal. And I quickly realized how little happiness it brought me. I had endured so much to get to the Olympics. All along the way, I told myself that the result would be amazing; that it would be all worth-while. But the truth was, it hadn't been worth it. I got back from Beijing with a bronze medal and no home, no job, no prospects. I finally found a bartending job. I camped out in the car for a couple of nights before I got paid. I deposited my money in the bank and set out on my mission to find a non-automotive home. My first apartment was a twelve-by-twelve-foot first-floor studio. The only sink was in the bathroom and it constantly fell out of the wall. On more than one occasion, sewage would come up out of the toilet, and I'd come home from work to an apartment filled with shit."

"Building up my body and chasing the Olympic dream had made me unhappy," Rousey continues. "I wanted to have a normal life. I wanted to have a dog and an apartment and to party. From the end of 2008 well into 2009, my plan involved drinking heavily, not working out, and cramming everything I thought I had missed into as short a time as possible. I started my morning with a smoke on the way to work. When I got to Gladstones [the bar where she worked], I would go behind the bar and mix dark and light ingredients that tasted like delicious iced mocha with vodka in it. I would sit and drink that all morning. On Sundays, these two hip-hop producer dudes would order surf-and-turf and Cadillac margaritas. They tipped me thirty dollars in cash and enough marijuana to get me high for several days. During the week, one of the regular bar patrons sold Vicodin to servers and would slip me one or two for passing the cash and pills between him and the waitstaff without our boss knowing. I spent that whole year lost."

Then Rousey found salvation in mixed martial arts. She returned to the gym, resumed training, and had three amateur fights, winning them all via armbar submission in a total of 104 seconds. More on Rousey's armbar later. That was followed by four professional bouts (two with KOTC and two with Strikeforce) that lasted a total of 138 seconds. At the same time, to make ends meet, she was working as a veterinarian's assistant at an animal clinic, on the graveyard shift at 24-Hour Fitness, and as a judo instructor.

On August 18, 2012, Rousey ran her MMA record to 6-and-0 with a fifty-four-second demolition of Sarah Kaufman. Three months later, UFC president Dana White (who'd stated publicly that UFC would never promote women's competition) announced that the organization had signed Ronda as its first woman fighter.

UFC then created its first weight class for women—135 pounds—for Rousey. She might not have "saved" UFC. But she was certainly a key component in reversing what appeared to be stagnation if not a down-ward trend in the organization's popularity. That was evident at a press conference I attended at the Beacon Theatre in New York two years ago.

The press conference was part of a national tour designed to pro-mote a series of UFC pay-per-view events. Jon Jones, Georges St-Pierre, Cain Velasquez, Alexander Gustafsson, Johny Hendricks, and Junior dos Santos were in attendance. But the spotlight shone brightest on Rousey, who was readying for her second fight under the UFC banner: a rematch of an earlier conquest of Miesha Tate.

The fighters were seated onstage at the Beacon Theatre. Dana White made a brief opening statement. Then fans (the event was open to the public) were invited to ask questions from the audience.

Rousey was wearing a short fitted red skirt, five-inch heels, and a black top that was notable for its décolletage.

"Your fight is stealing all the heat, all the headlines," she was asked. "Is this a conscious effort on your part? Are you trying to outshine the guys?"

"It's not like I'm purposely plotting all this out," Ronda answered. "But if the opportunity is there, I'm going to play it up. The girls have to fight for attention. I can't say it's a bad thing that all everyone is talking about is the chicks."

Asked if she hated Tate, Rousey replied, "I don't use the term 'hate.' But I've learned more about her personality and I haven't seen anything I like. I would compare being around her to chewing tin foil."

When the Q&A ended, the combatants moved to the front of the stage to sign autographs. Eighty percent of the fans lined up for Ronda. The six men and Tate split the other 20 percent.

Rousey has good people skills. When dealing with the public, she's affable and patient in answering questions and signing autographs. She has a ready smile that seems sincere.

But don't push the wrong button.

Several months earlier, in an interview with Jim Rome on ESPN, Rousey had discussed the pros and cons of having sex before a fight.

"For girls, it raises your testosterone," Ronda had said. "So I try to have as much sex as possible before I fight. Not like with everybody. I don't put out a Craigslist ad. But if I've got a steady, I'm going to be like, 'Yo! Fight time is coming up.'"

Now, as Rousey signed autographs, one of the fans in line shouted out, "Ronda; how many times do you have sex before a fight?"

"Get the fuck out," Rousey responded.

"I'm just asking," the fan pressed.

"I don't give a fuck. If your mother was standing behind you and heard you ask that question, what would she say? I'm serious. Get the fuck out."

At Rousey's direction, the fan was escorted by security from the theater.

I stood on the stage beside Rousey and talked with her for over an hour as she signed autographs.

Ronda is a writers' fighter. She says what she thinks and is a veritable sound-bite machine.

Some of our conversation revolved around the changes that her newfound fame had brought to her life.

"Training is still my number-one priority," Rousey said. "The difference now is that I used to have time between fights to chill out. Now there's no break in the media attention. That's just the way it is. Fortunately, I have a great team that helps me coordinate everything. It's a trade-off, really. Instead of working odd hours at different jobs and fitting it around my training schedule, I have more media obligations. What's happening now is better and more profitable."

In the hour that followed, Ronda discoursed on a wide range of subjects:

★ "Women's eating disorders are a cause for me. The presentation of what a woman's body should look like is all wrong. I'm in a weight-division sport, so watching my weight is part of my life. But when it come to things like women's models, we're presented with a false and even unhealthy ideal."

★ "I had a lot of hope with Obama. In some ways, I've been disappointed. I was expecting more change than we've seen. In politics now, what we're given is an illusion of choice. But I was able to get my teeth fixed because of Obamacare. And I still like him."

★ "The world would be better if people said what was on their mind all the time."

★ "I try to be nice to people when they're nice to me. But I wasn't born to smile like an idiot and be polite no matter what. 'Thou shall be polite' is not a fuckin' commandment."

★ "No one has the right to touch you without your consent."

★ "They wrestled naked in Greece."

★ "I didn't get to where I am by being dumb."

★ "I'm single right now, so my relationship success rate is zero."

That latter comment leads to a less than satisfactory facet of Rousey's life. As catalogued in the pages of *My Fight, Your Fight*, her love life has been marked by an endless stream of failed relationships with loser guys (who, let's not forget, she chose as boyfriends).

One of Ronda's live-in boyfriends was a heroin addict.

"We would break up, but it always felt like the universe kept pulling us back together. The day he stole my car was the low point."

A more recent boyfriend took nude photos her without her knowledge. Ronda found them on his computer, erased his hard drive, and waited for him to come home, at which point she "slapped him across the face so hard my hand hurt, punched him in the face with a straight right, then a left hook, kneed him in the face, and tossed him aside on the kitchen floor."

"Time does not always heal all," Rousey writes. "Sometimes, it just gives you more time to get pissed off."

"The problem," her mother told her, "is, you set the bar with your first boyfriend. After Dick, you could bring home a gorilla and we would be like, 'Hello, sir. So nice to meet you. Can I offer you a banana?'"

Miesha Tate became the first opponent to last past the first round against Rousey when they met in their rematch. Ultimately, she tapped out at 58 seconds of the third stanza. Three more victories followed. Rousey vanquished Sara McMann in 66 seconds. Alexis Davis and Cat Zingano lasted 16 and 14 seconds respectively. Those are staggering numbers.

Rousey's professional record is now 11 and 0 with ten of her victories coming in the first round and seven in the first minute. She is 5 and 0 in UFC competition. Because she fights under the UFC banner only twice a year, her struggle with bulimia is in the past. "For about four hours a year, I weigh 135 pounds," she says. "My actual weight is closer to 150."

Rousey's success in the octagon is built on rigorous disciplined training.

"No one is easy until after you beat them," she notes. "Anything can happen. Anybody can push you the distance, and it could be the person you least expect. So I assume that every single person is a danger to me and every single person is trying to beat me and hurt me, and I'm going to be prepared for every single person, no matter who it is. I want training to be the hard part and competing to be the easy part. I'm not going to train less and make competing harder. The knowledge that everything can be taken away at any second is what makes me work so hard. You have to be prepared to win on your worst day."

Ronda's good looks are a marketing plus, but they don't help her once a fight starts. The fights aren't a fantasy video game or scripted WWE extravaganza. They're real.

Rousey writes left handed but fights in an orthodox mode.

"I'm extremely hard to prepare for," she says, "because I don't walk out with a set game plan. I always walk out to improvise and be creative, and that's hard to prepare for as opposed to someone who has a very rigid and predictable style. I see the other girl [in the octagon before the fight starts]. I lock in on her. I always try to make eye contact. Sometimes, she looks away. I want her to look at me. I want her to stare me in the eye. I want her to see that I have no fear. I want her to know that she stands no chance. I want her to be scared. I want her to know that she is going to lose."

"I'm emotionless when I'm out there," Rousey continues. "I see all the options and I look to finish. I try to always be the first one to engage. That way, they're reacting to me more than I'm reacting to them. It's easier to predict because I know, with every single thing that I do, there's only so many right ways that they can react to it. I've memorized every single reaction that they could possibly have, and I have an answer to every single reaction that they have. So it's not being able to see several steps ahead. It's being aware of every single possible scenario and knowing how to deal with every scenario."

Referring to a thirty-nine-second triumph over Julia Budd early in her MMA career, Rousey observed, "It only looks easy because that throw I used, I've done that throw probably thirty thousand times in my life. When you actually master something, it becomes easy. But getting to the point where you master it so it's effortless for you, that's the hard part."

And there's more.

"I dissociate from pain," Rousey explains, "because I am not the pain that I am feeling. I refuse to allow pain to dictate my decision-making. Pain is just one piece of information that I'm receiving. I can choose to acknowledge that information or I can choose to ignore it."

Rousey's fights are not for the squeamish. She has a killer instinct and goes after opponents the way Mike Tyson did when Tyson was in his prime. And she damages opponents.

The Green Bay Packers of the 1960s had their famed end-sweep. Opposing defenses knew it was coming. But it was so well executed that they couldn't stop it. The same is true of Rousey's armbar.

An armbar involves locking an opponent's arm in, leveraging it, and hyperextending the elbow in a way that causes ligament damage and, if the opponent does not submit, dislocates the elbow.

"When people say that I'm a one trick pony and only have the one armbar," Rousey told Tom Gerbasi, "they don't realize that I have so many setups to that armbar that I don't even know them all. When you're watching boxing and you see somebody knock someone out with a right hand every time, you're not like 'Oh, they're a one trick pony.' No. They have a billion different setups for that right hand. Just because it ended with a right hand on the face, it doesn't mean it's the same thing every time. So many people are unfamiliar with grappling and they just see the armbar ending and they assume the setup is the same. But if you look back at all those fights, I've jumped into that armbar from many different positions. It ends the same way, but the setups are always different."

"When you do the armbar," Rousey writes in *My Fight, Your Fight*, "the aim is to put so much pressure on the person's arm that you pop the joint out of the socket. You can feel it when it pops. It's like ripping the leg off a Thanksgiving turkey. You hear it pop-pop-pop, then squish."

Then, describing her use of an armbar against Miesha Tate, Rousey recounts, "Pulling her arm straight, I arched back until I felt the squish, her ligaments snapping between my legs. She was still trying to escape. I grabbed her hand and pushed it over the side of my hip, forcing her elbow to go more than ninety degrees in the wrong direction. I ripped off muscles from her bone and tendons. With a vice on her injured arm, I sat up to punch her in the face with my other hand. With her elbow fully dislocated, there was nothing holding her in that position anymore except the pain and her fear of me."

"I try to win every fight in a way that my opponent never wants to see me again," Ronda says. "After I win, for a little while, everything is right in the world. Winning feels like falling in love, except it's like falling in love with everybody in the room all at once."

Without fighting, where would Rousey be?

Meanwhile, whether or not one likes mixed martial arts, it's clear that Ronda Rousey is happening at the moment. The mainstream media has seized upon her. She has been on the cover of numerous magazines and featured on television offerings as diverse as *Conan* and HBO's *Real Sports*. Type her name into Google, hit "search," and it brings up 14.5 million results.

Will she become a mainstream superstar? Will what's happening now stick? Will the wave of publicity she's currently surfing fade away or will there be bigger waves in the future to surf?

And who can beat her in the octagon? Rousey isn't like boxer Mia St. John, who was promoted largely on the basis of her looks and could fight a little but was far down on any honest list of fighters ranked on the basis of their ring skills. Rousey is the most dominant woman fighter in the world today.

In the past, Ronda has said, "I think the style of fighter that I would have a problem with would be a very high quality striker with very good footwork and takedown defense."

She has never been punched clean by a hard striker. How good is her chin? What happens if she gets taken deep into a fight?

The woman who most people in the industry think would be the most competitive opponent for Rousey is Cristiane "Cyborg" Justino, a Brazilian currently living in California, who competes at 145 pounds. Justino was sidelined in 2012 by a one-year suspension after testing positive for the anabolic steroid stanozolol. That fight is ten pounds away and maybe further.

For the moment then, there are two obvious answers to the question, "How do you beat Ronda Rousey?" ... (1) "You have to get to her before she gets to you," and (2) "You don't."

"When I came into MMA, I wanted to make money," Rousey says. "But it was more important to me to be the best and most exciting competitor in the world at what I do. Not everybody is going to like me. I live a life of exposure. People are going to see pretty much how I am all the time. I'm not going to be on a first date with everybody all the time. Everything is out there. Whatever people think is what they think. Any mistake I make is going to be scrutinized. That's why I'm apprehensive about accepting the term 'role model.'"

It has been a strange journey. More twists and turns lie ahead. Rousey could be a very special vessel. And not just for MMA. MMA might be a platform for more important things. But what?

"The purpose of Garcia-Malignaggi," Bart Barry wrote, "was to welcome Danny Garcia to the welterweight division with a knockout win over a savvy veteran." Malignaggi experienced it differently.

Paulie Malignaggi: It's Over

It began in Brooklyn and it ended in Brooklyn.

Fourteen years ago, on a perfect summer night, a young man named Paulie Malignaggi made his professional boxing debut at Coney Island's KeySpan Park with a first-round knockout of Thadeus Parker. Like all young fighters, Malignaggi harbored dreams of glory. Some of those dreams came true; others didn't. On August 1, 2015, at Barclays Center (an arena that didn't exist when Paulie turned pro), those dreams came to an end.

Malignaggi fought the odds throughout his career and had championship runs at 140 and 147 pounds. Unlike most "name" fighters today, he really would fight anyone. His final ring record—at least, one hopes it's final—shows 33 wins and 7 losses. His biggest fights (against Miguel Cotto, Ricky Hatton, Amir Khan, Adrien Broner, Shawn Porter, and Danny Garcia) ended in defeat. But pivotal victories over Zab Judah, Vyacheslav Senchenko, Juan Diaz, and Lovemore N'dou brightened the mix.

Through it all, Paulie spoke his mind and did it his way. "I'm the kind of guy who doesn't dip his toe into the pool," he says. "I'll jump in to see if it's cold."

Part of his appeal was that he wore his emotions on his sleeve. In and out of the ring, he appeared vulnerable.

"When you win in front of millions of people," Paulie noted, "it's an incredible high. And when you lose in front of millions of people, it hurts. But in the end, it's not about the number of people watching. It's about yourself. I cried after every loss I had as an amateur. And I cried after I lost to Miguel Cotto and Ricky Hatton. Then I stopped crying after losses, but they still hurt."

As Paulie aged, the term "elder statesman" didn't quite fit. Rafe Bartholomew put his finger on one of the reasons why when he wrote,

"Malignaggi's hairstyles have run a gamut unlike any other in a sport where hideous coiffures are common. We've seen Malignaggi go from Pauly D blowout to spiked frosted tips to a peach-fuzz baldie decorated with constellations of shaved-in swirls. The undisputed high point of Malignaggi's follicular odyssey came when he fought Lovemore N'dou with a head full of braided extensions that made him look like the Italian-American love child of Milli Vanilli and Medusa. When he entered the ring with simple cornrows or a red-tinged faux-hawk, it was interpreted as a sign of mature veteran stature."

But Paulie kept on being Paulie.

"The media doesn't know crap about boxing," he told veteran writer Ron Borges. "There are a few exceptions. But they watch every week and don't know what they're doing. If I spent that much time watching something and wrote and said what they do I'd feel very ignorant. I'd feel stupid."

By that time, Paulie had joined the media as a commentator for Showtime Boxing and was carving out a niche for himself as one of the best in the business.

On April 19, 2014, Malignaggi suffered what many people, including Paulie, thought was a career-ending fourth-round knockout loss at the hands of Shawn Porter.

"I was hurt pretty bad," Malignaggi acknowledges. "Porter went off like a grenade. I went from the ropes to the canvas to the hospital. I'd never been hurt like that before."

Thereafter, David Greisman wrote, "Paulie woke up every morning with nausea. It seemed as if he needed to shake cobwebs out of his head before his day could begin. Even then, there would be bad headaches that came unexpectedly. He would sit ringside during broadcasts, see a heated exchange between fighters, and think, 'I'm glad I'm not there.'"

"I never said officially that I was retiring," Paulie noted earlier this year. "But I told the people I was close to that I thought I was done."

Then, to the dismay of family and friends, Malignaggi announced that he was fighting again; a tune-up fight against untested Danny O'Connor. In a series of interviews, Paulie explained his thinking:

★ "At first, I didn't want to fight again. I would see these fights from close range [as a commentator], see the violence, some crazy exchanges.

'Man, better these guys than me. I'm done.' Then little by little, as I started feeling better, I would focus on the crowd reaction, the adrenaline these fighters are feeling. I was starting to slowly change my thinking. It was starting to slowly become more like, 'I got to feel this again; I got to feel that rush again.' It's something missing in my life. If you're not living a certain way, you're basically dead anyway."

★ "I'd love to win another world title. One more world title would be nice. Sometimes, I think about it and I say 'one more year.' And then I think about, if at the end of the year I'm on the verge of getting a big fight, I'm not going to stop. You don't know when for sure."

And the ultimate excuse:

★ "Before the Porter fight, I hadn't looked bad. I had one bad night."

Malignaggi-O'Connor was cancelled when Paulie suffered a cut in training. Then Paulie was offered and accepted an August 1 fight against a far more formidable opponent: Danny Garcia.

"Everybody has asked me, 'Why would you do this?' Malignaggi told writer Tom Gerbasi. "'It's not like you need money. It's not like you're starving.' But in life, there are other things that make you feel fulfilled besides money. Money's good; trust me. But you can't buy happiness and you can't buy that sense of fulfillment. You fight to be on this grand stage. You do all the hard work through the years. You fight in these little club shows early in your career. You're fighting in gymnasiums as an amateur. And you do it all so you can be on these huge stages one day. That's what you dream of. And the bigger the stage, the bigger the rush."

"That elite level," Paulie told *The Players Tribune*. "When you get declared the winner at the end, it's God-like. It's hard to describe. It hooks you. It's addicting, knowing that only a small percentage of people in this world will ever get to feel that kind of adrenaline, and you're one of them. You crave it. It's like a drug."

"A boxer knows it's time to hang 'em up when he fears getting hurt in the ring more than he fears losing," Paulie continued. "If you're afraid of getting hurt, you have no place in between those ropes. If you're afraid to fail and you're afraid to lose and you'll lay your body on the line and do everything humanly possible to beat the man in front of you, you still got it."

But that's nonsense. Judged by that standard, Muhammad Ali didn't fight too long. Ali always had the will to win. Brain damage shows up over time.

In the days leading up to Garcia-Malignaggi, Danny was a 6-to-1 betting favorite. Fighting mostly at 140 pounds, he'd fashioned a 30-and-0 (17 KOs) record highlighted by a fourth-round knockout of Amir Khan and decisions over Lucas Matthysse and Lamont Peterson.

Paulie hadn't fought in almost sixteen months and had won one fight since a disputed split-decision triumph over Pablo Cesar Cano in 2012. His reflexes had slowed. His legs were no longer what they once were. The fresh young face and optimism of youth were gone.

"I know people are saying this is my last fight, that I'm just taking a payday," Paulie noted during a media conference call. "But you know what? You can't take people's opinions in the ring with you. I keep reading, 'This is Paulie's swan song. It's his last fight.' We'll see."

"I don't know how many more great performances I have left in me," Paulie added at the final pre-fight press conference. "I know I'll have one on Saturday night. I've put my body and mind through so much for this fight. I've been so focused. I'm so sharp. People say I don't hit hard, but I hit hard enough to break Danny's nose. And if I break Danny's nose, he has a problem. On Saturday night, you'll see the best Paulie Malignaggi that I can be."

And there was a special motivating factor for Malignaggi.

"So much hinges on Saturday night," Paulie confessed. "A win could put me in the conversation for the Hall of Fame. I made a list of goals that I wanted to achieve when I started boxing, and I've been checking things off ever since. National amateur champion. Yes. Olympian. No. World champion. Yes. Financial security. Yes. Hall of Fame. That was my biggest long-term goal. If I win on Saturday night, that hope stays alive."

Boxing at the world-class level is a game of centiseconds and fractions of an inch. On fight night, those numbers favored Garcia.

Danny was the aggressor throughout. One arguably could have given rounds two, five, and seven to Malignaggi. There were times when he was able to frustrate Garcia and neutralize Danny's attack with movement, jabs, and a handful of body shots. But for the most part, Garcia was in charge. And when Paulie made him miss, he didn't make him pay.

Malignaggi was cut above the right eye in round three and beneath it in round six, a round in which he tired noticeably. By round eight, Garcia was landing right hands to the body and hooks up top with abandon. The assault continued in round nine with Paulie fighting simply to survive. Two minutes and twenty-two seconds into the stanza, referee Arthur Mercante appropriately stopped the bout.

After the fight, Paulie sat on a chair in his dressing room with his head bowed. There was a large discolored lump on the right side of his forehead. Blood seeped from an ugly gash beneath his right eye and there was a second cut above it. The left side of his body looked like raw beef.

Dr. Avery Browne of the New York State Athletic Commission came into the room for a post-fight physical.

"How do you feel?"

"I've been better," Paulie said. "But I'm all right."

"Do you have a headache?"

"Yeah. But it's not as bad as after the last fight."

Dr. Browne administered the normal post-fight tests with a few extra questions for good measure.

"Who's the president?"

"Come on," Paulie answered. "Obama. Do you want me to say Batman?"

"You'll need stitches," Dr. Browne told him.

"I'm getting used to it."

"I'm giving you a forty-five-day suspension."

"How about forty-five years?" Paulie suggested.

The doctor left.

A period of silence followed. It wasn't just that Paulie had lost the fight. By any rational standard, his career as a fighter was over.

Tom Hoover (the newly installed chairman of the New York State Athletic Commission) entered to check on Paulie's condition.

"It was a good stoppage," Paulie told him. "The doctors were great. Thank you."

Dr. Tony Perkins (a plastic surgeon in private practice) was the next arrival.

Paulie lay down on a vanity table that ran the length of the dressing room beneath a mirrored wall.

Dr. Perkins began to work. While the stitching was in progress, Al Haymon came in and walked over to Paulie.

"I don't have it any more," Paulie said.

Haymon leaned over and whispered words of assurance in Paulie's ear.

"You're okay. You're in the family."

An hour earlier, Haymon had visited Sergio Mora's dressing room and spoken the same words to Mora, who'd been unable to continue after breaking his ankle in the second round of a fight against Danny Jacobs.

Haymon left.

Dr. Perkins finished his work. Five stitches above Paulie's right eye and ten stitches beneath it.

Paulie looked at the people gathered around him. His brother, Umberto; longtime friend and business advisor, Anthony Catanzaro; Pete Sferazza, another friend; Bobby Ermankhah, CEO of Azad, which markets a Magic-Man watch named after Paulie.

"My jab wasn't working the way I wanted it to," Malignaggi said. "There were moments when it seemed like I was taking control, and then Danny took it back . . . I'm not as fast as I used to be. And my legs aren't as good. I adjusted my style the last few years to compensate, but it wasn't enough tonight . . . I can still beat a lot of guys, but I want to be more than the pesky crafty guy who comes up short in big fights . . . I'm not an elite fighter anymore."

A year ago, there was a moment that spoke volumes about Paulie Malignaggi's psyche. On May 31, 2014, Carl Froch scored a dramatic one-punch knockout of George Groves in front of eighty thousand roaring fans at Wembly Stadium in London.

"Right now," Paulie told a television audience that was listening to his commentary, "I wish I was Carl Froch."

Paulie never had his Carl Froch moment. But he has been to the mountaintop.

Several months ago, reflecting back on his championship victories and also his fights against Miguel Cotto, Ricky Hatton, and others, Paulie told David Greisman, "When my career is over, years from now, whether I've won or lost these big fights, at least I'll be able to say I was in the ring with those guys. When people talk about great fighters, I got to share a night with those guys in front of a big crowd, and it was really cool. Whether I won the fight or lost the fight, I had some cool experiences."

Paulie is a smart guy. Fighting again would be stupid.

And a Note from Several Weeks Afterward

One reason that Paulie Malignaggi has fought as long as he has is the hope that a big win at the end of his career would keep alive his dream of induction into the International Boxing Hall of Fame in Canastota.

Is the dream dead?

Not necessarily.

There will be no more big wins for Malignaggi. His ring record as of this writing is 33 wins and 7 losses. Each of his losses to date has been against an elite opponent. One of those losses was to Miguel Cotto, who recently told this writer, "After our fight, I became friends with Paulie. His courage on the night of the fight made me think, 'Someday this person will be a champion. He has the heart of a champion and he deserves to be a champion.' I was happy for him when he became a champion."

Future fights will do nothing to enhance Malignaggi's legacy. But his numbers now are comparable with those of Arturo Gatti (40-9) and Ray Mancini (29-5), each of whom is in the Hall of Fame.

How would Malignaggi have fared against Gatti and Mancini? Hall of Fame matchmaker Bruce Trampler offers the following thoughts.

"Gatti-Malignaggi," Trampler says, "is a great fight. Paulie isn't a puncher, so he wouldn't take Gatti out. He'd have to outbox him the way Ivan Robinson did. Arturo would hit Paulie; no doubt about that. But I don't know who wins."

And Malignaggi-Mancini?

"I like Mancini," Trampler answers. "Ray had better technique than people give him credit for. He would have been too aggressive and too strong for Paulie, but it would have been a good fight. Mancini beats Gatti too."

Gatti retired in 2007 and was inducted into the Hall of Fame in his first year of eligibility (2013). The electors understood that Arturo's ring skills weren't on a par with most previous inductees. But he had something extra going for him. He was a thrilling, fan-friendly, blood-and-guys warrior.

Mancini's last fight was in 1992. He wasn't inducted until 2015. Mancini got a boost in the balloting from his ongoing visibility and popularity.

Malignaggi, like Gatti and Mancini, has "something extra" going for him. He's making a name for himself as one of boxing's best expert analysts on television. And he's "Paulie"—a one-name phenomenon.

Mancini waited twenty-three years to be inducted into the Hall of Fame. If Malignaggi's career as a commentator continues to thrive, it's possible that someday the combination of his ring skills and TV work will land him in Canastota.

Floyd Mayweather's September 12, 2015, fight against Andre Berto was a yawner.

Floyd Mayweather vs. Andre Berto

Floyd Mayweather is one of the most gifted defensive fighters ever and also one of the most polarizing figures in boxing. He was raised by fighters and has compiled an unblemished record of 49 victories in 49 pro fights.

"Floyd knows everything there is to know about boxing except losing," his uncle (former WBA super-featherweight and WBC super-lightweight champion Roger Mayweather) has said.

Mayweather is a fifteen-round fighter in a twelve-round era. He tires less than his opponent as a fight goes on. Ray Leonard (who most knowledgeable observers place comfortably above Floyd in historical rankings) acknowledges, "Mayweather is one of the best conditioned fighters I have ever seen, bar none. You have to give him his credit. Sometimes there's outrageous things he says and does. But when he goes into that ring, he's always in shape. That's what I respect about him."

But there's a downside to the Mayweather saga.

Floyd has a well-documented history of violence against women.

His conspicuous consumption and constant bragging about how much money he makes appeals to some. But given the reality of economic inequality in America today, it turns a lot of people off.

Recently, Mayweather bought a car called the Koenigsegg CCXR Trevita for $4,800,000. In recent years, he has bought more than one hundred luxury cars.

According to the University of Nevada Las Vegas website, the cost of living on-campus and attending UNLV for a full school year is $20,012. That includes tuition, fees, rent, utilities, food, books, other school supplies, transportation, and miscellaneous personal expenses. Instead of adding that car to his collection, Mayweather could have taken the money and gifted 240 full-year scholarships to young men and women in his hometown of Las Vegas.

Where Mayweather's in-ring performances are concerned, the most valid complaint has been his choice of opponents. Mayweather has never beaten an elite fighter in his prime. In recent years, he has avoided the best available competition, preferring to fight ordinary opponents or once-dangerous fighters who've seen better days.

Andre Berto (Floyd's opponent at the MGM Grand in Las Vegas on September 12) fit into the Mayweather-opponent mold.

Berto's father was a Haitian immigrant who competed as a mixed martial artist when Andre was a boy and ran a martial arts academy in Winter Haven, Florida, when Andre was growing up.

"I was exposed to a lot of things early, good and bad," Berto told this writer several years ago. "Winter Haven is a rough town. Drugs, street gangs, AIDS; it's all there. A lot of kids think there's no way out, that there's no way they can be better than what's there. You see guys who could have been superstar athletes who gave in to drugs. I had a vision early that I could be great. In school, I was always a little stronger, a little faster, and a little better than the other kids. I wanted to be one of the ones who stood out. And I was living off the example that my father set for me. Self-respect, hard work, stay straight, stay focused. When I was growing up, my father always told me, 'The saddest thing in the world is wasted talent.'"

Andre played running back for the Winter Haven High School football team and ran the 100- and 200-yard dash in track. But his true love was boxing. "Running the streets" had a different meaning for him. He was doing roadwork. When he came to school with a black eye and puffed-up lip, it was from sparring, not a gang fight.

By the time Berto was a senior in high school, boxing had taken him to twenty-two countries. He was a decorated amateur, compiling a 260-and-12 record. He was knocked down twice in the amateurs but never stopped.

The knockdowns came at the 2002 National Golden Gloves.

"I'd won it the year before and was ranked number-one in the country at 152 pounds," Berto recalls. "I got in the ring with a guy I didn't know named DeShawn Johnson. I thought it would be an easy fight. He knocked me down twice in the first round and won a decision. I wanted to fight him again so bad. And a month later, he got jumped in a club. Some guys stomped him and shot him and he died."

Berto turned pro in December 2004 and was regarded as a superstar in the making. At the close of 2010, he was 27 and 0 with 22 knockouts and the WBC welterweight champion.

"My spirit is to try to be dominant," Andre told the media. "I want to be a superstar. I want to bring it back to the days when Mike Tyson would fight on television, and everybody got off work early so they wouldn't miss it."

But in recent years, Berto has regressed as a fighter. Like many Al Haymon clients, he was maneuvered around tough challenges and failed to develop his full potential. Since 2010, Andre has lost four of seven fights, including a knockout defeat at the hands of Jesus Soto Karass.

"The welterweight division is among the deepest in boxing," Chris Mannix wrote for SI.com after Berto was named as Mayweather's opponent for September 12, 2015. "There are established stars, rising stars, and compelling young talents. So of course, Floyd Mayweather picked one of the least qualified of them all. On the list of recent Mayweather opponents, Berto ranks among the worst."

The match-up was so unappealing that Showtime entered into negotiations with Team Mayweather with an eye toward moving the fight from pay-per-view to CBS. Sources say that the idea failed for a number of reasons. Mayweather was reluctant to give up his contractual guarantee, and CBS-Showtime financial models predicted that advertising revenue would be significantly less than the projected income from even a diminished number of PPV buys. There wasn't enough time to market the event to potential advertisers. And given Mayweather's history of domestic violence, many mainstream advertisers didn't want to be associated with him.

The odds varied widely. But generally, Mayweather was a 20-to-1 favorite.

The announced fight night attendance was 13,395, well short of a sellout. That number included quite a few complimentary tickets in addition to tickets that were sold at a discount.

From the opening bell on, Berto seemed resigned to his fate. He was a challenger who didn't challenge. There were two guys in the ring, but it wasn't much of a fight.

Mayweather isn't a big puncher. But as Oscar De La Hoya has noted, "Every fighter has a punch." Floyd's punches might not stun. But they sting and are hard enough to keep opponents from coming forward with abandon.

Berto looked tight in the opening rounds and befuddled for most of the night. He came forward in a straight line, made zero adjustments, threw few meaningful punches, and fought as though Mayweather's body was off limits.

Indeed, Andre talked more aggressively during the fight than he fought in it. Mayweather, as one might expect, responded to the verbiage. In round ten, referee Kenny Bayless stopped the proceedings briefly and told the fighters to stop trash-talking.

That led Showtime analyst Al Bernstein to observe, "Let's be honest. The most interesting thing about this fight has been the debate."

Blow-by-blow commentator Mauro Ranallo added, "The conversation might be more interesting than what we're seeing in the ring."

Mayweather outlanded Berto by a 232-to-83 margin. This observer gave Andre one round. The judges scored it 120–108, 118–110, 117–111 for Mayweather.

Prior to the fight, Mayweather and his team said repeatedly that this would be his last fight. Afterward, Floyd proclaimed, "My career is over. It's official. You got to know when to hang 'em up. I'm leaving the sport with all of my faculties. I've accomplished everything. There's nothing more to accomplish in the sport."

If Mayweather really doesn't fight again, he deserves credit for standing by his word and leaving at the top (as Lennox Lewis did a decade ago). Most observers, myself included, think that Floyd will fight again.

There have been times in the past when Mayweather's word was suspect. Time will tell whether or not he's telling the truth now.

Pound-for-pound is not a weight class. But in today's fractured boxing world, pound-for-pound rankings have taken on added significance.

Gennady Golovkin and Roman Gonzalez: Pound-for-Pound Showcase

On October 17, a sellout crowd of 20,548 filled Madison Square Garden for a fight card featuring Gennady Golovkin vs. David Lemieux and Roman Gonzalez vs. Brian Viloria. These were fight fans; not high rollers who'd been comped to get them into a casino. They arrived early and stayed late.

Golovkin (who's the consensus choice for #1 middleweight in the world) and Gonzalez (who reigns supreme in the 112-pound flyweight division) are technically sound ring predators. Each man dominates opponents with hard precision punching and a pressure assault. With Floyd Mayweather's retirement, they rank first and second on a wide range of pound-for-pound lists. Lemieux and Viloria (15-to-1 betting underdogs) were brought in as building blocks for the stardom of their presumed conquerors.

Gonzalez entered the ring with 43 wins, 0 losses, and 37 knockouts. He's unknown to most sports fans. But in recent months, there has been a buzz about him in boxing circles.

Roman grew up in poverty on the outskirts on Managua and is Alexis Arguello's successor as "The Pride of Nicaragua."

"I used to fight in the neighborhood and in the streets," Gonzalez told Diego Morilla of RingTV.com. "I was lucky to meet Alexis Arguello when he opened a gym in San Judas. My father's fighting name was 'Chocolate.' He used to fight in his younger years and traveled to Cuba a lot. When we went to the gym for the first time to see Alexis Arguello, there were many kids around. Alexis said, 'So you're Chocolate's son? Then you must be 'Chocolatito.' It stuck after that. When he realized

I had some talent, Alexis placed a lot of attention on me. He took me under his wing during my amateur career."

Gonzalez compiled a reported 88-and-0 amateur record and turned pro in 2005. Now twenty-eight years old, he's 5-feet-3-inches tall. Several times a year, he weighs the flyweight maximum of 112 pounds (about the same as a thoroughbred horse jockey). He has a high-pitched voice and, in street clothes, would blend unnoticed into a crowd.

References to God are sprinkled throughout Gonzalez's conversation. "It is a great pride to represent my country," he says. "I am the only champion that Nicaragua has right now, and that's my biggest motivation to continue training more and more. Hearing my name announced away from my country is an extra motivation. When I hear people say 'Chocolatito' in the streets, I feel that everyone in Nicaragua is watching my fights and sending their blessings."

This is the first time in a long time that boxing fans have paid much attention to the flyweight division. Viloria (36 and 4 with 22 KOs) said all the right things leading up to the fight. "Roman has his accolades for a reason," Brian noted. "But I'm relaxed. I'm confident. I know I'm ready."

If one was looking for a peg that Viloria could hang his hopes on, it lay in the fact that, at a media sit-down two days before the fight, Gonzalez was chewing gum and spitting periodically into a nearby trash can; a sure sign that a fighter is struggling to make weight. The following afternoon, that peg was whittled down considerably when Roman weighed in at 111.4 pounds.

Fighting Gonzalez is like fighting a tornado. But in the ring, there's no storm cellar for sanctuary. Viloria started aggressively, getting off first and winning round one on all three judges' scorecards. He also earned the nod from two judges in the second stanza. But he wasn't landing much of consequence, and one had the feeling that it was just a matter of time before the tide turned.

Gonzalez is a relentless non-stop punching machine, who throws three and four-punch combinations to the head and body with pinpoint accuracy. They're sharp punishing blows. In round three, a chopping right hand put Viloria on the canvas. Brian fought back bravely, but his cause was hopeless. By round six, his punches had lost their sting and the issue was how Gonzalez would end it, not if. Referee Benjy Esteves stopped the beating at the 2:53 mark of round nine. Gonzalez outlanded Viloria by a 335-to-186 margin, including a 315-to-161 advantage in power punches.

Sitting with a handful of reporters before the final pre-fight press conference, Gonzalez had talked about how Alexis Arguello taught him to throw punches in combination. Roman also recounted a conversation he had with his mentor about Arguello's first fight against Aaron Pryon.

Arguello told Gonzalez, 'I hit Pryor with my best right hand. With that hand, I knocked everybody down. And nothing happened. At that moment, I looked to the sky and said, 'Ay, mamita!'"

When Viloria was being pummeled around the ring, he could have been forgiven for saying, "Ay, mamita!"

Gonzalez-Viloria was followed by Golovkin-Lemieux.

Golovkin had compiled a 33-and-0 record with 30 KOs, including knockout victories in his most recent twenty fights. He has never been on the canvas as an amateur or pro.

Outside the ring, Gennady has a gentle demeanor that masks how brutally he practices his trade. During fight week, he appears as relaxed as a man who's readying to play an important tennis match at his country club on Saturday night. In the ring, he's methodical and focused. He has mastered the art of controlling the distance between himself and his opponent. The opponent is always in danger.

"My plan is my plan," Gennady said after beating Martin Murray earlier this year. "It doesn't matter what he is doing. Step by step. Box. Then finish it."

Light-heavyweight champion Sergey Kovalev, who has sparred with Golovkin, told Ryan Burton of BoxingScene.com, "When we had the same training camp, we sparred a lot of times. His punches are not heavy but make you feel pain. Heavy is like a 'boom.' His punches are more sharp, even more than heavy. He is a very hard puncher."

And Freddie Roach, who trains Manny Pacquiao and Miguel Cotto, opined, "Golovkin is a great fighter. He's strong. He has good fundamentals. He cuts the ring off well. I've watched his ring generalship. It's fucking great. Ring generalship is a lost art, but Golovkin has it. Ninety-five percent of the time, he's in the right position. If you do that, you win fights. He's heavy-handed. He's a nice kid. I'm a big fan."

Any doubts that people might have regarding Golovkin's ring prowess are based on fights he hasn't had. To wit, the lack of elite opponents on his ring record. By contrast, Lemieux (34-2, 31 KOs) was shadowed by two abysmal past performances.

There was a time when Lemieux was hailed as the future of Canadian boxing. Then, in 2011, he wilted against journeyman Marco Antonio Rubio and was stopped in the seventh round. In his next outing, he was brought back soft and lost again, this time by decision to Joachim Alcine (who has won only three of eleven fights since December 6, 2009).

The selling point for Golovkin-Lemieux was David's "power." Lemieux had won nine fights in a row after losing to Alcine, including a decision victory over Hassan N'Dam to capture an alphabet-soup championship belt. David was said to have "a puncher's chance." Indeed, the promotion kept likening Golovkin-Lemieux to Marvin Hagler versus Thomas Hearns.

But Hagler-Hearns was a toss-up fight. And as Jimmy Tobin wrote, "Lemieux wields his power with the nuance of child learning to use a spoon. Golovkin may not be the fighter of his mystique. But he would have to fall impossibly short of it to lose to Lemieux."

An honest pre-fight appraisal of Golovkin-Lemieux was "It will be entertaining for as long as it lasts."

"Every boxer has power," Golovkin warned. "The question is, 'How much?' I know my job. I think the knockout streak is not finished yet."

When the fight began, Lemieux fought more cautiously than he usually does, which made sense given the fact that he was fighting the equivalent of a Sherman tank that's firing live ammunition. At times, David tried jabbing. That didn't work. At times, he tried fighting more forcefully to back Golovkin up, which is like trying to back up a brick wall.

Through it all, Golovkin moved inexorably forward.

To again quote Jimmy Tobin, "The ground opponents give Golovkin is usually shoveled onto their graves. Those who fire on Golovkin wind up no better, and very often worse, than those who choose to flee."

In round five, a hook to the body sent Lemieux to the canvas, either as a delayed reaction or, more likely, because David took a knee to compose himself. Gennady then landed right to the jaw while Lemieux's knee was down. Referee Steve Willis should have warned Golovkin for what appeared to be an accidental foul and given David time to recover. He did neither.

Lemieux rose and continued to fight. Those who remember the first bout between Roy Jones and Montell Griffin appreciate how differently David, to his credit, handled the situation. Lemieux fought courageously, but his cause was hopeless. At 1:32 of round eight, with Golovkin battering him around the ring, Willis stopped the carnage. Golovkin won every round and outlanded his foe by a 280-to-89 margin with a 110-to-54 advantage in power punches.

As for the future; Golovkin and Gonzalez will add to their collection of belts. But that's no longer the point. Each man is pursuing stardom.

Madison Square Garden was far and away Gonzalez's biggest stage to date. Team Golovkin is now outfitted by Air Jordan. Gennady is featured in a new commercial for Apple Watch. And the issue of *Sports Illustrated* that hit the newsstands during fight week devoted five pages to him.

As for pound-for-pound; Andre Ward, by choice, hasn't fought a credible opponent since facing a debilitated Chad Dawson three years ago. And given Dawson's dismal ring record since then, one has to go back to 2011 (when Ward bested Carl Froch) to find a true inquisitor.

Gennady Golovkin is #1 on my pound-for-pound list with Roman Gonzalez in second place.

Holly Holm's defeat of Ronda Rousey was the combat sports upset of the year.

Ronda Rousey vs. Holly Holm

Sports, unlike most forms of entertainment, have no script. Sometimes the narrative unfolds as expected. Sometimes it doesn't. Once the competition begins, what an athlete has done in the past isn't outcome determinative. Athletes have to prove themselves anew every time.

Ronda Rousey, age twenty-eight, was at the apex of mixed martial arts. *Sports Illustrated* called her the most dominant athlete in the world today. She'd been on the cover of magazines running the gamut from *Maxim* to *The Ring* and verbally out sparred Floyd Mayweather. People piled their expectations onto her shoulders.

Rousey's armbar was the equivalent of Mike Tyson's one-punch knockout power. Iron Mike devastated his opponents. Always. Until the night he didn't.

Tyson was invincible before he fought Buster Douglas. The invincible Sonny Liston was stopped by Cassius Clay. The unbeatable Joe Louis was knocked out in his first encounter against Max Schmeling.

On Sunday afternoon, November 15, 2015, in Melbourne, Rousey was knocked out in the second round by Holly Holm. Now, once again, combat sports is experiencing the shock of a seemingly invincible fighter losing.

It happens.

Holm, age thirty-four, turned to professional boxing in 2002 after an early stint as a kickboxer and compiled a 33-2-3 record in the sweet science. During that time, she scored only nine knockouts, which speaks to a lack of punching power. But "power" is a relative term when talking about professional boxers.

In 2011, Holm suffered a brutal beating in a seventh-round knockout loss to Anne Sophie Mathis. She figured out what she did wrong and, six months later, fought Mathis again, winning a clear-cut unanimous decision. Holm is a fighter.

Rousey-Holm was fought on Holm's terms. She controlled the distance between Rousey and herself with deft footwork and a stiff jab. That and her southpaw stance enabled her to strike effectively when the combatants were on their feet. And she knew enough MMA to blunt Rousey's counter-maneuvers.

Holm also seemed physically stronger than Rousey; if not at the start of the match, then certainly once Ronda had taken some jabs to the face. As the match progressed, Rousey was reduced to following Holm ineffectively around the ring and walking into more jabs. Holly made Ronda look like an amateur.

Two minutes ten seconds into the fight, Holm scored big with a move that's illegal in boxing. With both fighters in striking position, Holly threw what appeared to be a straight left that fell short by design so her elbow landed flush on Rousey's mouth. It might have been the most damaging blow that Ronda has been hit with in her life. The elbow split her lip. She wobbled, held on, and managed to drag Holm to the canvas. Holly escaped.

Fifty-two seconds into round two, a straight left deposited Rousey on the canvas. She jumped to her feet, and Holm measured her for a left leg kick that landed flush on the neck. That put Ronda down for good, on the verge of unconsciousness and defenseless. Holm jumped on her, landed two more punches to the face, and the referee stopped it.

A dazed Rousey needed help getting to her feet and was taken to the hospital for observation. She got beaten up.

How did it happen?

For starters, Rousey's body looked a bit soft when she entered the ring, and she seemed exhausted at the end of round one. Fighting is a fulltime job. It's possible that Ronda's preparation for the fight was hampered by too many outside interests. During the past year, she has modeled, acted in movies, and lived the celebrity life interspersed with the seemingly never-ending drama of her personal relationships with her boyfriend of the moment and her mother.

Muhammad Ali thrived on chaos. But for most athletes, multiple distractions take away from training and cause them to lose focus. It's an old story. The popular champion gets a bit lazy in the gym and cuts a few corners. The old intensity isn't quite there.

Also, one of the biggest mistakes a fighter can make is to buy into the myth of his, or her, own invincibility. Rousey seemed to have become a believer.

When Mike Tyson comes to the gym and tells you what a good boxer you are, and Oscar De La Hoya wants to promote your boxing career, and you're on the cover of *The Ring,* it's easy to lose sight of reality with regard to the true level of your boxing skills. You start to believe what people are telling you; especially if the boxers you're sparring with aren't well trained in the art of hurting and aren't trying to hurt you.

On top of that, Rousey had a lousy game plan for Holm and fought badly, while Holly had a good game plan and fought well. In the past, Ronda has succeeded by bum-rushing opponents, getting them on the canvas quickly, and ending matters with her armbar. Here, because Holm was able to master the distance between them and jab effectively, the bum-rush didn't work.

Rousey-Holm shouldn't be taken as an indication that boxers are superior fighters to mixed martial artists. An elite boxer spends years developing what is essentially one fighting technique and develops that technique better than any single technique in a mixed martial artist's arsenal. By contrast, a mixed martial artist is like a decathlete who masters multiple disciplines while not necessarily being world-class in any of them.

Further to that point; Rousey started in MMA as an amateur in 2010 after a successful career in judo. She turned pro in 2011. Holm began kickboxing in her teens and took up MMA in 2011. More significantly, the two most damaging blows that Holm delivered during the fight— an elbow to the face in round one and the finishing leg kick in round two—were MMA moves.

As for what comes next . . . Fighters lose. The question now is how Rousey will react to the loss? Will she come back strong like Joe Louis and Muhammad Ali did after their first defeat? Or will she be forever diminished as a fighter, as happened with Mike Tyson after his loss to Buster Douglas?

Most likely, Rousey is feeling tortured now. Her life has always been marked by emotional ups and downs. An emotional roller-coaster ride lies ahead.

A rematch between Rousey and Holm would be the most lucrative event in MMA history. The current plan is for it to be contested in Las Vegas at UFC 200 in July 2016.

What will be different the next time around? Rousey can't beat Holm on her feet. The notion that Ronda had somehow become a world-class boxer in addition to her grappling skills was never realistic. In a rematch, Rousey will have to find a way to take the fight to the ground.

Meanwhile, UFC's biggest star has been defeated. But beating "The Woman" doesn't make Holly Holm "The Woman." Like their first encounter, Rousey-Holm II will be largely about Rousey.

In and out of the ring, Oscar De La Hoya has walked through fire. He's still here.

"I'm the Golden Boy, but I'm also Oscar"

Oscar De La Hoya was exhausted. It was 9:30 a.m. on Thursday, November 19, 2015, two days before the fight between Canelo Alvarez and Miguel Cotto in Las Vegas.

Alvarez is Golden Boy's flagship fighter. Golden Boy was co-promoting the bout with Roc Nation Sports, and De La Hoya had been working non-stop for weeks. One had to go back to the glory days of Don King to find a promoter who'd been as omnipresent and worked harder to publicize a fight.

Now De La Hoya was sitting in Coral Room C at the Mandalay Bay Resort and Casino, which was hosting the event. He'd flown to Los Angeles the previous afternoon because he'd promised his nine-year-old son, Oscar Jr, that he'd attend his son's soccer game that day. By the time he returned to Las Vegas and went to bed, it was 3:00 a.m.

Bleary-eyed, wearing a charcoal-gray suit and white shirt open at the collar, his tie loosened, De La Hoya sipped from a container of coffee. He hadn't shaved for several days. Two hours of satellite-TV interviews lay ahead. That would be followed by interviews with print publications, radio stations, and boxing websites. Then he'd host a one o'clock press conference for the Saturday night undercard fighters. Later in the day, he would fly back to Los Angeles for the world premiere of Sylvester Stallone's new Rocky movie, *Creed*.

"My life has always been boxing," De La Hoya told this writer between satellite interviews. "I started boxing when I was five years old, and I didn't like it. What five-year-old kid likes getting hit? Then, after one of my fights—I was still five—one of my uncles gave me a quarter, and a light went on in my head. I can fight and get money."

De La Hoya, handsome and verbally gifted, was the right man in the right place at the right time. As a 1992 Olympic gold medalist, he was an American symbol. Girls swooned at the sight of him.

And he could fight.

De La Hoya never ducked a challenge. Among the men he fought and their records when he fought them were Rafael Rueles (43-1), Genaro Hernandez (30-0-2), Miguel Angel Gonzalez (41-0), Julio Cesar Chavez (96-1-1), Pernell Whitaker (41-1-1), Ike Quartey (34-0-1), Felix Trinidad (35-0), Shane Mosley (34-0), Fernando Vargas (22-1), Bernard Hopkins (44-2-1), Floyd Mayweather (37-0), and Manny Pacquiao (47-3-2).

There were times when De La Hoya disrespected himself. But he never disrespected boxing. And he was a point of pride for the burgeoning Hispanic-American community. Top Rank and HBO built him magnificently as an attraction. That was his launching pad for the formation of Golden Boy LLC, with CEO Richard Schaefer leveraging Oscar's star power to build a promotional empire.

"I will always need boxing," De La Hoya said during a media teleconference call to promote his 2007 megafight against Floyd Mayweather. "Boxing is what made me. Boxing is what's always going to make me. I owe everything I have to boxing."

Then came the fall.

In 1994, Dr. Margaret Goodman (who later became chief ringside physician for the Nevada State Athletic Commission) performed a prefight physical on De La Hoya, who was twenty-one years old at the time.

"I'm going to be different from other fighters," Oscar told her. "Watch; you'll see. Five years from now, I'll be rich and retired."

De La Hoya was rich at age twenty-six. His ring career extended until two months shy of his thirty-sixth birthday when he was knocked out by Manny Pacquiao. His early years in retirement as a fighter were marked by a series of embarrassing personal revelations. There were stints in rehabilitation facilities in 2011 and 2013 for alcohol and cocaine abuse, and publication of the now-infamous fishnet photos showing Oscar dressed in women's lingerie.

All people are entitled to a zone of privacy in their personal life. Because of De La Hoya's fame, that was denied him. In a 2011 interview with Ring TV, he was asked, "Did you get to the point where you didn't want to keep on living? "

"Yes," Oscar acknowledged. "One of those nights when I was drunk and I was alone again, I asked myself, 'Is it worth it to be alive?' I was feeling like I had nothing. And what is going through your mind are your children, your wife, the people who love you. I thought about it. I'm not capable of doing something like that. But I did think about it."

"You have to get out of boxing," Richard Schaefer told De La Hoya as the two men jockeyed for control of Golden Boy in a battle that Oscar ultimately won. "Boxing will kill you."

"No," De La Hoya countered. "Boxing will save me."

On May 8, 2014, Oscar met with reporters prior to the kick-off press conference in New York for Canelo Alvarez vs. Erislandy Lara. "I won't say I'm back because I don't want to be where I was before," he said. "Let's just say, I'm here."

For most of De La Hoya's life, the ring was one of the few places—perhaps the only place—where Oscar felt that he was in control. He's in control now when giving interviews and conducting press conferences.

As a promoter, De La Hoya is prone to hyperbole. There are times when, talking about a fight, he sounds like a political candidate determined to stay on message. He's good at giving interviewers what they need and also telling people what they want to hear. He's articulate in two languages and media savvy.

On one occasion several years ago, De La Hoya was wearing a track suit while sitting for an interview that ESPN's SportsCenter had scheduled to run in two segments on back-to-back days. "Let me take my jacket off," he said after the first segment was recorded. "That way, you'll have a different look for tomorrow."

Oscar no longer inspires the same passion from the public that he once did. But he can still draw a crowd. When he walks into a room, people know he's there. His personal battles have been as dramatic as any that he ever fought in the ring. They're fought every day; some in public, others in private.

Fifteen years ago, I wrote the captions for a photo essay that featured head-shots of eight fighters. Beneath a photo of De La Hoya, I noted, "Far more complex than most people imagine . . . He bruises easily inside . . . Looking inward to find some answers for the journeys still to come."

Those words hold true today. But Oscar is stripping away the layers of varnish that he applied to protect himself from his emotions; a shield that kept him from knowing and accepting who he was for years.

"If you can't handle the fame, it will destroy you," De La Hoya told this writer after the TV-satellite interviews on November 19 came to an end. "I know all the tricks. I can go to Disneyland and wear sunglasses and a hat and dress a certain way. A few people might look and wonder, 'Is that Oscar De La Hoya?' But no one approaches me. I'm left alone. And other times, I want to be recognized. I want people to crowd around me. I need that validation that day, so I present myself differently. On those days, I'm The Golden Boy."

"The most important thing is that, in rehab, I learned who I am," De La Hoya continued. "That was essential to my being happy because I'd forgotten who I was. Yes, I'm the Golden Boy, I was a champion. I accomplished so much. But I'm also Oscar. Oscar had some dark times. I still have dark moments, but I know now that there's no shame in that. That's part of what makes me a real person. I like the person I see now when I look in the mirror, and that wasn't always so."

I chronicled Miguel Cotto vs. Canelo Alverez through the prism of Miguel Cotto

Miguel Cotto: The Professional

Miguel Cotto has a good life now, but he knows that life can be hard. Training camp and the fights that follow remind him of that reality.

Cotto is on the short list of great Puerto Rican fighters; a list that includes Carlos Ortiz, Wilfredo Benitez, Wilfredo Gomez, and Felix Trinidad. But Miguel views boxing as a fistfight for money, not an allegory for civilization. Asked about the Puerto Rico vs. Mexico rivalry prior to his November 21, 2015, fight against Canelo Alvarez, Cotto responded, "I fight for me, for my kids, for my family. After that comes Puerto Rico."

"All I want," Miguel says, "is to be Miguel Cotto."

Dignity, pride, and respect are constant themes in Cotto's life. There's an aura of solemnity about him. His creed is, "Work hard, don't cut corners, and do the best you can." A soldier going to war would want Miguel fighting beside him. He's respected by all segments of the boxing community.

Cotto has a low monotonal voice that doesn't travel far. It can be reassuring, grave, even gentle, depending on the moment. He's more expressive when speaking in Spanish as opposed to English because the words flow more easily. In media settings, he fully considers each question before framing an answer.

Among the thoughts that contribute to a Cotto self-portrait are:

★ "My father was in the military for twenty-five years. In our house, everything had to be by the rules. But my father also did everything he could for us. He gave us a feeling of family. It was important to him for us to understand that family matters most. He gave us an education. He gave me desire as a fighter. But most important, my father did the best he could to create in me a good human being. Now that I'm a grown man, I understand even more what he did for me. He died on January 3, 2010. I remember the day. We had some unfinished business between us. But he is my biggest hero. If I could have my father back for one day, I would say to him 'thank you.' Those are just words, but I would mean them."

★ "My first language was Spanish. In school, I had a required English class, so I knew some English. Then I started boxing, and I used a translator. People would say to me that I could make more money if I spoke English. But the bigger thing for me was, sometimes when I spoke, the translator would change what I said. That made me want to learn more English, so people would hear my thoughts, not the thoughts of someone else talking for me. The work is non-stop. My English will never be perfect. But I try to improve every day."

★ "The fans don't fully understand what it means to be a fighter. They see the fight, and most don't understand even that. But even fewer understand the sacrifices that a fighter must make, the pain he suffers, just to get to the fight. For myself, I'm not a real big fan of boxing. I just enjoy boxing when I'm boxing."

★ "No matter what my face might say, I am a happy guy. But I am a shy guy. Most people don't realize that. I don't prefer the spotlight."

As an elite fighter, Cotto is frequently in the spotlight. And he was there again during fight week for his bout against Canelo Alvarez.

The World Boxing Council had previously announced that Cotto-Alvarez would be for its "diamond" middleweight world championship belt. But fight week began with the WBC stripping Miguel of his championship and declaring him ineligible to fight for the WBC title because he'd tried to negotiate the organization's $300,000 sanctioning fee down to $125,000 and refused to pay the full amount.

Cotto's logic was clear. If he lost to Alvarez, he'd lose the WBC belt anyway. If he won, he wouldn't need the belt to enhance his marketability. "We have four organizations," Miguel said, explaining his decision. "That means we have four champions in each weight division. That is enough. But they want more sanctioning fees, so they create a new champion every six months. I don't need belts. I have enough belts in my house. I can buy any belt I want. And I can be the champion of whatever I want in my house. Canelo and I will not fight any harder or less hard because of a belt."

There were the usual rituals of fight week with Roc Nation Sports and Golden Boy as co-promoters. At the final pre-fight press conference, Roc Nation Sports president Michael Yormark read the names of

sponsors with gravitas appropriate to the reading of "Best Picture" nom-
inees at the Academy Awards. The Friday weigh-in was a celebration of
Latino culture with dueling mariachi and salsa bands.

Trainer Freddie Roach (who Miguel has credited with reviving his
career) was a magnet for media attention throughout. But Roach was
struggling. In addition to Parkinson's syndrome, Freddie suffers from
multiple hip and back issues. Physical pain is a constant in his life. Fabrice
Gautier (Roach's physical therapist) works with him six days a week
from 7:30 to 9:30 a.m.

"Freddie is the toughest patient I've ever worked with," Gautier says.

"Everything I ask of my fighters, I give to Fabrice," Roach notes.
"It's tough getting out of bed in the morning, but he gets me through
the day."

On Tuesday of fight week, Roach was working the pads with Cotto
at the IBA Gym in Las Vegas when Miguel threw a left hook to the body
followed by another to the chin.

"I called the punch and then I got careless," Freddie explained afterward. "I was looking at the pivot to make sure Miguel did it right. So I
wasn't properly focused and missed the hook up top with my pad and it
landed. My knees buckled for the first time since I got sloppy once when
I was training Tyson."

"I always believe in my heart that my guy will win," Roach said of
the impending fight. "And if he doesn't, I blame myself. I ask myself,
'What did I do wrong, and how can I change it so it doesn't happen
again?'"

Then Roach elaborated on his plan for the fight ahead.

"The keys to Miguel winning are simple. Canelo gets frustrated.
Miguel can outbox him and take him to school. I'd be surprised if that
doesn't happen. This is a boxing match for us, not a fight. Miguel has to
set up his big punches rather than always be looking for them. And he
has to stay off the ropes. Canelo isn't a great boxer, but he's heavy with
the right hand. And he'll land it if Miguel is on the ropes, which would
be a problem. Of course, that's all easy for me to say. When the bell rings,
I sit down and Miguel is the one who has to fight."

Meanwhile, Cotto (who'd lost two fights in a row before uniting
with Roach in 2013) appeared to believe in himself again. The self-doubt
that had crept in with the losses was gone.

"This is the best time of my career," Miguel said. "Part of it is Freddie. Freddie made me work harder than I had ever worked before. He made me feel that I am better as a fighter than ever before. I feel because of Freddie that there is still more in boxing for me to do."

But the questions remained.

Had Roach really halted Cotto's decline and turned him around as a fighter? Could Cotto take Alvarez (45-1-1, 30 KOs) to school? After all, although Canelo began boxing professionally when he was fifteen years old, he isn't a kid anymore. Both Erislandy Lara and Austin Trout had tried to outbox him and couldn't.

On fight night, Alvarez was a 14-to-5 betting favorite. At age twenty-five (ten years younger than Cotto), he intended to add many more chapters to his ring history. Miguel's ring career, by his own admission, was nearing an end.

★ ★ ★

Cotto entered locker room #1 at the Mandalay Bay Events Center on Saturday evening at 5:45 p.m. He was stylishly dressed in burgundy slacks with a black turtleneck and black loafers. Freddie Roach, assistant trainer Marvin Somodio, cutman David Martinez, strength and conditioning coach Gavin MacMillan, Bryan Perez (Miguel's closest friend), and Rob Peters (who handles security for Roach) were with him. Gaby Penagaricano (Miguel's attorney) and Hector Soto (vice president of Miguel Cotto Promotions) joined them.

The room was twenty feet square with a charcoal-gray-and-gold industrial carpet and walls that had once been cream-colored but now had a layer of grime on them. Wood benches were built into the walls on three sides of the room. Ten metal-framed cushioned chairs were scattered around the floor. There were no lockers, only hooks and shelves for clothes and personal belongings. A smaller room with four showerheads and three toilet stalls was off to the side.

Miguel took off his turtleneck and slacks, folded them neatly, and put them in a small suitcase. Salsa music wafted through the air.

Ricardo Jimenez (a friend from Cotto's days with Top Rank) came in to wish him well. Miguel's face lit up and the two men embraced.

Miguel and Bryan Perez stacked seven of the chairs in a corner of the room to increase the open area for warming up later on. Then Miguel stood, arms folded across his chest, and watched as the first pay-per-view fight of the evening—Jayson Velez vs. Ronnie Rios—played on a TV monitor.

Canelo Alvarez was shown on screen arriving at the arena during a break between rounds. Miguel smiled.

At 6:30, Cotto sat on the floor in front of the monitor and stretched briefly. Then he rose, sat on a chair, and watched the conclusion of Velez-Rios while Marvin Somodio taped his hands.

There was more stretching.

Referee Robert Byrd entered and gave Miguel his pre-fight instructions. When that was done, Cotto's attention returned to the TV monitor where Guillermo Rigondeaux vs. Drian Francisco was underway.

It was 7:35 p.m. HBO had instructed the main event fighters to be ready to walk by 7:55.

"There's no way I'm gloving Miguel up now and having him warm up," Roach said. "All he'll do is sit around with his gloves on and have to warm up all over again. We'll be ready when they need us. And if we're not ready, they aren't starting the fight without Miguel."

Cotto sipped from a bottle of Gatorade. Bryan Perez helped him into his protective cup. Miguel put on pink-and-white boxing trunks.

Rigondeaux-Francisco drew to a close.

There was a musical interlude in the arena followed by the last undercard fight: Francisco Vargas vs. Takashi Miura.

Miguel alternated between sitting, stretching, and pacing. At eight o'clock, Somodio gloved him up.

At 8:05, Roach put on protective body padding and mitts and began warming up Cotto, giving instructions as they worked.

"Body shots early . . . Hook off the jab . . . Fight smart . . . He does the same thing over and over again . . . Walk him into shots . . ."

After five minutes, Cotto sat and returned his attention to the television monitor. Somodio gave him a sip of water. From time to time, Miguel rose, circled the room, smiled, and reached out to tap the members of his team on the shoulder.

Roach warmed Miguel up for three more minutes.

"That's it . . . There you go . . . Step to the side . . . Good! I like that a lot . . . Remember, fight smart . . . He'll come right to you . . ."

The national anthems of Mexico, Puerto Rico, and the United States sounded in the background. Cheers were heard as Alvarez entered the arena.

At 8:53, an HBO production assistant entered the room: "Alright, guys. We're ready."

Once a fight begins, the storyline of the fight is the fight. The determining factors in this fight were that Alvarez was bigger, younger, and stronger. One day earlier, Canelo had weighed in at the contractual limit of 155 pounds to Cotto's 153½. Now he outweighed Miguel by at least ten pounds and was the aggressor from the opening bell.

In the early going, Cotto circled and tried to get off first, but was unable to land the punishing body blows that Roach had hoped would tire Alvarez as the fight wore on. More importantly, the differential in hand speed that Team Cotto had expected wasn't there.

At the final pre-fight press conference, Chepo Reynoso (Alvarez's manager) had declared, "Fights are won in the gym. In the ring, they just raise your hand."

One might add, "Fighters don't get old in the gym. They get old in the ring."

Age creeps in.

As Cotto-Alvarez progressed, Canelo was able to find the right distance between them. Early in round eight, there was a heated exchange. Alvarez got the better of it. From that point on, he was the hunter and Cotto was the hunted. Miguel was no longer moving side to side for a better angle of attack as much as he was circling away to escape Canelo's assault. Alvarez was fighting to win, while Cotto was fighting to win and survive.

There were a lot of close rounds that the judges could have scored any way they wanted to. Apparently, they wanted to score them for Canelo. Their final tally of 119–109, 118–110, 117–111 was wide of the mark. This writer scored the bout 116–113 for Alvarez, which was in line with the general consensus that Canelo won but it was a reasonably close encounter.

After the fight, Miguel returned to his locker room and retreated to the shower area, where he sat on a chair while collecting his thoughts.

His family and the members of Team Cotto waited in the dressing area. Only Bryan Perez was with him.

"I'm proud of Miguel," Roach said. "And I thought the judges' scores were ridiculous. Let's just say that it was in the best interests of Las Vegas for Canelo to win. Anything more than that and I'll get myself in trouble."

The door to the dressing room opened, and Canelo Alvarez walked in. One by one, he shook hands with each member of Miguel's family. Then he walked into the shower area where Cotto was sitting, leaned over, and patted Miguel on the cheek.

There was a brief conversation in Spanish. "You will always have my admiration," Canelo told him.

A cut that Miguel had suffered on his right eyelid in the final round was stitched up. There were some abrasions on his nose and bruises on his face but relatively little swelling.

Earlier this year, Cotto acknowledged, "I am thirty-five years old and in the last stage of my career. I want to finish my career in the best way possible and retire myself. I plan to be in boxing no longer than a year from now. "

Miguel has one fight left on a lucrative three-fight contract with Roc Nation Sports. It's likely that he'll fight that fight, possibly at Madison Square Garden the night before the June 12, 2016, Puerto Rican Day Parade.

That would be a good way to end.

Cotto has competed honorably as a professional athlete for fifteen years. In some ways, he evokes memories of another proud Puerto Rican sports hero: Roberto Clemente.

Clemente came up to the major leagues in 1955 and played right field for the Pittsburgh Pirates for eighteen seasons. He was a twelve-time all-star, won four batting titles, twelve gold glove awards, and was honored as the National League's Most Valuable Player in 1971. He died in a plane crash on December 31, 1972, while delivering emergency supplies to the victims of an earthquake in Nicaragua. He was the first Latin player inducted into the Major League Baseball Hall of Fame.

In Clemente's early years with the Pirates, he was socially marginalized because he was black and spoke little English. Many baseball teams still had all-white rosters. Baseball cards referenced him as "Bob Clemente."

As it became clear that Clemente was great, time and again, people likened his play to that of Willie Mays and Hank Aaron. Often, Clemente would respond, "Yes, but I also play like Roberto Clemente."

There have been many great Puerto Rican fighters. But Miguel Cotto fights like Miguel Cotto.

Wladimir Klitschko once said of his brother, "Fighting is in Vitali's blood. He was born a fighter. I became one."

Tyson Fury Upsets Wladimir Klitschko

It's hard to improve on Shakespeare. So let the immortal bard speak to Tyson Fury's upset of Wladimir Klitschko on November 21, 2015, in Dusseldorf, Germany, to claim the heavyweight throne: "It is a tale told by an idiot, full of sound and fury, signifying nothing." (*Macbeth*, Act 5, Scene 5)

Those are harsh words. But Klitschko-Fury was a dreadful fight that came on the heels of an embarrassing promotion that showed how far boxing has fallen.

There was a time when the heavyweight championship of the world was the most coveted title in sports. But those days are long gone. Few people other than hardcore boxing fans now know or care who the multiple sanctioning-body champions are.

Within that environment, Wladimir Klitschko offered a safe harbor of sorts.

Klitschko is a gracious man, who stands 6-feet-6-inches tall and fights at between 240 and 249 pounds. Now thirty-nine, he has been the dominant heavyweight of the past decade. Prior to facing Fury, Wladimir had amassed a 63-and-3 record with 53 knockouts and been unbeaten over the past eleven years. During that period, he successfully defended his various championship belts eighteen times.

"Anybody can become a champion for one fight," Klitschko said at a July 21, 2015, press conference in Dusseldorf announcing his title defense against Fury. "It's really tough to be a champion for a long, long time. It's challenging. It's systematic preparation, plan, and experience."

Fury, age twenty-seven, stands close to 6-feet-9-inches tall and has weighed in as high as 270 pounds. Prior to fighting Klitschko, he was unbeaten in 24 bouts with 18 knockouts but had yet to face an elite fighter. The most notable victories on his ledger were two lethargic decision triumphs over Dereck Chisora.

The second Fury-Chisora fight was particularly disheartening. Tyson entered the ring with flab around his waist and looked like a man who'd spent most of training camp eating bangers and mash. It was a dreadful boring encounter. Fury (an orthodox fighter) was content to stand back and jab from a southpaw stance, which he did for most of the night. Chisora came forward and went backward in a straight line without doing much else. After eleven rounds, Dereck got tired of being jabbed in the face and quit.

Fury's size and reach can be intimidating. But he paws with his jab and brings it back slowly and low, which leaves him vulnerable to right-hand counters. He also stands within hitting range too often with his hands down and chin up.

On the psycholological side, there are times when Fury's mindset evokes images of the man he was named after: Mike Tyson.

Several years ago in a profile for *The Guardian*, Donald McRae wrote of the darkness and depression that are constant themes in Fury's life. His father was a violent man who served time in prison for an assault that cost another man his eye. Among the thoughts that Fury shared with McRae were:

★ "There is a name for what I have where, one minute I'm happy and the next minute I'm sad, like commit-suicide sad. And for no reason; nothing's changed. One minute I'm over the moon, and the next minute I feel like getting in my car and running it into a wall at a hundred miles an hour. I don't know what's wrong with me. I'm messed up. I think I need a psychiatrist because I do believe I'm mentally disturbed. Maybe it was the fact that, when I was a kid, my mother and father were always shouting and screaming and hitting each other. My dad had different women and different kids down the road. My mum had fourteen pregnancies, but only four of us survived. We had a little sister born for a few days and she died. That would affect you."

★ "I love boxing. I can't wait for the moment I step into the ring. I feel calm then. It's like everything has been forgotten. It's just me and him and we're going to go at it old school. But after that, it's back to the reality and feeling angry with life."

★ "I'm British and Commonwealth champion. I'm doing okay. I've got a few quid in the bank. I shouldn't be upset. But I don't feel I've done any good at all. I thought, when the children were born, it would be a top thing. And when I became English champion, I thought there'd be a great feeling. But no. I thought, 'Let me win the British title.' But after I took that off Chisora, there was nothing. At the end of the day, what have I done? I've beaten another man up in a fight. I don't know what I want out of life. What's the point of it all?"

Klitschko-Fury was originally slated for October 24. But on September 25 it was announced that Klitschko had suffered a partially torn tendon in his left calf and the fight was rescheduled for November 28.

Fury expressed confidence in the months leading up to the bout. But there was a touch of lunacy in his comments.

At the initial pre-fight press conference in Dusseldorf, Fury addressed Klitschko as follows: "Ich bin Tyson Fury, the sexy meister from the United Kingdom. I'm a unique fighter, one of a kind. There's never been someone like me before in history. A fighter like me only comes along every one thousand years. It is my mission to rid boxing of you because you're a boring old man. You have as much charisma as my underpants. Zero. None. You're a wrinkled old man with a glass chin, and I am going to make that glass explode like a bottle hitting a wall. You're fucked. I don't care about money. I don't care about my legacy or going down in history. I just want to smash your old face, and I don't give a fuck what anybody thinks because I don't give a fuck about being a role model. This Klit is getting licked on October 24th."

On September 23, Fury attended a promotional press conference in London dressed in a Batman costume, called Klitschko "a clown," and proclaimed, "You fought plenty of peasants. You never fought The King before. You ain't nothing. Whatever you are, I don't know. An army sergeant, it looks like it, or a school teacher. You definitely ain't a fighter. You're getting knocked out. I can't wait for this. Please, God, I wish it was this weekend."

Suffice it to say, it's hard to imagine Joe Louis or Rocky Marciano wearing a Batman costume to a press conference.

At times, Fury conjured images of the demented killer in a Halloween massacre movie. Other times, he sounded like a candidate for the Republican presidential nomination.

On Sunday, November 8, Fury told the *Daily Mail*, "We live in an evil world. The devil is very strong at the minute, very strong, and I believe the end is near. The Bible tells me the end is near. The world tells me the end is near. Just a short few years, I reckon, away from being finished. There are only three things that need to be accomplished before the devil comes home. One of them is homosexuality being legal in countries. One of them is abortion. And the other one is pedophilia. When I say pedophiles can be made legal, that sounds like crazy talk, doesn't it? But back in the fifties and early-sixties, for them first two to be made legal would have been looked on as crazy."

"To be honest with you," Fury continued, "I know Klitschko is a devil-worshipper. They are involved in bigger circles and stuff like that and they do magic tricks and whatever. You can go on YouTube and watch them playing with magic. God will not let him defeat me."

Next, Fury told *Boxing News*, "The only thing I ever regret in life is having sex before marriage. If I could erase that, then my life would be practically perfect. I regret all the filth that you do with people. I must have had sex with over five hundred women, more, I don't know, I've lost count. But it's pure filth and horribleness. I look at that now as pure disgusting."

Then Fury added, "My daughter won't have an education because, our way of life, we don't need one, especially women. They grow up, they get married, and they look after the man. I'd like to give my son an education rather than being a hustler. I don't expect my son to follow in my footsteps. I think he's got to go to school, get a proper education, and go from there."

For good measure, seventeen days before the fight, Fury posted a video on his Twitter account that showed him head butting a watermelon in half and intoning, "This is for you, Wlad. I'm coming for you."

In response, Klitschko declared that Fury had "a brain the size of a walnut" and told him at the press conference in London, "I have got friends from the circus industry. They can give you a job as a clown. Clowns make people laugh. It is their job. And right now, after watching this theater, the screaming, the running and the costumes, it is in your genes."

And on a September 19 teleconference call, Klitschko opined, "We need to go a little bit deeper in Tyson Fury's issues. There's a lot of psychological issues here in Tyson Fury's mind. I think he's bipolar. He's not really knowing what he's going to do next. That speaks to me as a person that is psychologically unstable."

The fight was contested in the ESPRIT Arena with fifty thousand fans in attendance. Fury weighed in at 246.4 pounds, Klitschko at 245.3. Wladimir was a 4-to-1 betting favorite.

It was a stultifyingly, horribly boring fight. Both men fought cautiously and threw a lot of stay-away-from-me jabs rather than punching with conviction. Fury circled and moved side-to-side for most of the night, which kept Klitschko from setting his feet to punch with power. Long stretches of time went by with neither man throwing, let alone landing, a significant blow. Fury fought with his hands down and launched long looping punches that begged for a right-hand counter. But Wladimir seemed content to evade punches rather than throw them.

In round five, Klitschko was cut under the left eye by an accidental head butt. In round nine, another clash of heads opened a cut on the right side of his forehead. There were rounds that were hard to score for either fighter because Fury did nothing and Klitschko, if such a thing is possible, did sub-nothing. At one point, referee Tony Weeks deducted a point from Fury for punching to the back of the head.

As the fight dragged on, one could have been forgiven for thinking about the man who wasn't there: Emanuel Steward.

Steward took over the task of training Klitschko in 2004. In their first fight together, Wladimir was knocked out by Lamon Brewster. He was unbeaten over the next eleven years. Emanuel died in 2012, shortly after being diagnosed with colon cancer that had metastasized throughout his body. Thereafter, Johnathon Banks (who'd assisted Steward) took over the task of training Klitschko.

In a way, Klitschko-Fury was reminiscent of May 10, 1996, when Lennox Lewis fought Ray Mercer at Madison Square Garden. Steward had trained Lewis for three fights, all of them knockout victories. But Mercer was a heavy-fisted brawler with an iron chin. And Lennox considered himself a "pugilistic specialist." The plan that night was for Lewis to outbox Mercer.

Except the plan wasn't working. And in the middle rounds, sensing that the fight was slipping away, Emanuel told Lennox, "Just fucking fight him."

Lewis did as instructed and eked out a narrow decision win.

There were a lot of problems with Klitschko's performance against Fury. Some of them stemmed from the fact that Wladimir seemed poorly prepared to fight a man who had a height and reach advantage against him. But Klitschko can whack. At some point during the middle rounds, he needed Emanuel Steward's voice in his ear, saying, "Just fucking fight him."

When Klitschko-Fury was over, Tyson had landed a meager 86 punches over the course of twelve rounds, while Wladimir landed 52. Klitschko's performance seemed even more passive in light of the fact that all but eighteen of the punches he landed were jabs and he scored with only four body blows.

This writer scored the bout 115–113 (seven rounds to four with one even) in favor of Fury. The judges' scorecards were comparable: 115–112, 115–112, and 116–111. If nothing else, Klitschko-Fury put to rest any lingering doubt as to who would have won a fantasy boxing match between the Klitschko brothers.

After the decision was announced, Fury grabbed a microphone in ring center, accepted the victory "in the mighty name of Jesus," and sang "Don't Want To Miss A Thing," which he dedicated to his wife.

On the fortieth anniversary of Ali-Frazier III, The Ring *magazine asked for a remembrance*

The Thrilla in Manila: Forty Years Later

In 1989, I sat on the sofa in my living room with Muhammad Ali beside me and watched a tape of Ali's historic October 1, 1975, fight against Joe Frazier.

Boxing fans are familiar with what happened on that hot humid morning in Manila.

The early rounds belonged to Ali. He outboxed Frazier, landed sharp clean punches, and staggered Joe several times. Frazier kept coming inexorably forward.

The tide turned in the middle rounds. Ali was tiring. Frazier rocked him with thunderous blows. Muhammad's arms came down, and Joe bludgeoned him against the ropes, pounding, pounding.

Ali regained the initiative in round twelve, wobbled Frazier, and measured him for more. One round later, a jolting left hook knocked Joe's mouthpiece into the crowd. Frazier was shaken, but finished the round.

In round fourteen, Ali resumed his assault. Frazier's left eye was completely closed. The vision in his right eye was limited. He was spitting blood. Ali's punches were landing cleanly. Joe couldn't see them coming.

Frazier's trainer, Eddie Futch, stopped the fight after the fourteenth round.

Associated Press boxing writer Ed Schuyler later recalled, "The Thriller in Manila was the best fight I've ever seen. As it unfolded, everybody at ringside understood they were watching greatness. The pace never eased. It was hell the whole way. I've never seen two people give more, ever."

Jerry Izenberg observed, "What it came down to wasn't the heavyweight championship of the world. Ali and Frazier were fighting for something more important than that. They were fighting for the championship of each other."

I'd watched tapes of many fights with Muhammad sitting beside me prior to our watching Ali-Frazier III. We'd been reviewing his career for a book I was writing, *Muhammad Ali: His Life and Times*.

This was different.

Despite the fact that it was one of his greatest ring triumphs, there was no joy in Muhammad's face as we watched Ali-Frazier III unfold.

In the past, we'd sat together and witnessed Henry Cooper knocking Cassius Clay close to oblivion with a picture perfect left hook. That had seemed to amuse Muhammad.

We'd seen Joe Frazier put Ali on the canvas in round fifteen of their first encounter at Madison Square Garden and Ken Norton break Muhammad's jaw. Those punches were safely ensconced in the annals of history, as were the thudding blows that George Foreman landed in Zaire.

Watching Ali-Frazier III, Muhammad seemed to be re-experiencing the pain. Sitting beside me, he winced as some of Joe's blows landed. When the tape ended, he turned to me and said, "Frazier quit just before I did. I didn't think I could fight anymore."

Joe had his own memories of Manila when he and I talked.

"We were gladiators," Frazier told me. "I didn't ask no favors of him, and he didn't ask none of me. I don't like him but I got to say, in the ring he was a man. In Manila, I hit him punches, those punches, they'd of knocked a building down. And he took 'em. He took 'em and he came back, and I got to respect that part of the man. He was a fighter. He shook me in Manila. He won. But I sent him home worse than he came."

Physically, neither man was the same after Manila. They both won and they both lost.

Forty years later, "The Thrilla in Manila" stands as a symbol of what's best and worst about boxing.

Non-Combatants

I met Ella Fitzgerald in 1992 at a fiftieth-birthday party for Muhammad Ali.

Whitney Houston, Diana Ross, Billy Crystal, Dustin Hoffman, and other A-list celebrities had gathered to perform at a gala celebration. The high-point of the evening for many in attendance came when Joe Frazier and Ken Norton walked Ella Fitzgerald onto the stage.

Ella was three months shy of her seventy-fifth birthday, frail and in declining health. Five years earlier, she'd undergone quintuple coronary bypass surgery. Doctors had also replaced a valve in her heart. Her eyesight was poor and she was suffering from diabetes. After a lifetime on the road, she'd performed in concert for the last time at Carnegie Hall the previous year.

Joe Frazier and Ken Norton receded from view. Ella stood on her own and sang one song: "Too Close for Comfort." A standing ovation and a warm embrace from Ali followed.

After the concert, there was a party. Little Richard, MC Hammer, the Pointer Sisters, and each of the Four Tops mingled with stars more famous than they were.

Ella was sitting with a friend. Two women alone at a table. I approached them.

"Excuse me," I said to Ella. "I'm sure you hear this all the time. But I want to tell you how much pleasure I've gotten from your music over the years. You've created such a wonderful legacy. You've made millions of people all over the world happy."

Ella smiled and told me that, yes, people said that to her a lot but I had said it in a particularly nice way. Then she kissed me on the cheek.

I smile when I think of that moment. I've experienced a lot of good things in my life. One of them is that I was kissed by Ella Fitzgerald.

Ella Fitzgerald: An Appreciation

Ella Fitzgerald was the most celebrated jazz vocalist ever and arguably the most gifted jazz singer of all time. Over the years, she performed a remarkable variety of songs with accompaniment as diverse as swing-era bands, jazz trios, and symphony orchestras.

Ella sang in a way that nobody else could. Music and joy seemed to pour out of her. Her voice was exquisite and instantly recognizable. A listener heard it and knew immediately that it was Ella. Jazz pianist Jimmy Rowles played with Benny Goodman and Tommy Dorsey and also behind Billie Holiday, Peggy Lee, and Ella. "Music comes out of her," Rowles said. "When she walks down the street, she leaves notes."

There was very little public drama in Ella Fitzgerald's life. She was never a social force like Elvis Presley or the Beatles. She wasn't a dominant presence like Frank Sinatra. But over time, she became a living legend and a one-name phenomenon. She was "Ella."

Ella Jane Fitzgerald was born in Newport News, Virginia, on April 25, 1917. Her father, William Fitzgerald, and mother, Temperance Williams, never married and separated soon after her birth.

"My mother had a beautiful classical voice," Ella reminisced decades later. "She used to sing real high. I don't think she ever did much with it. They tell me that my father was a guitar player, but I don't know because I never met him."

After separating from Ella's father, Temperance met a Portuguese immigrant named Joseph Da Silva. They moved to Yonkers (a suburb of New York City), where Joseph was a laborer. Temperance worked in a laundromat and as a household domestic. In 1923, a daughter named Frances, Ella's half-sister, was born.

The most reliable one-stop source for information about Ella Fitzgerald's life and music is Stuart Nicholson's biography, *Ella Fitzgerald: The First Lady of Jazz*.

As recounted by Nicholson, dancing, not singing, was Ella's first love. She started dancing at age eight and, despite being heavy and physically awkward, fantasized about a career in dance. In her early teens, she and a friend named Charles Gulliver rehearsed a routine that they performed in local clubs.

Ella's early training as a singer, such as it was, came from the Bethany African Methodist Episcopal Church in Yonkers. It was a time when music was becoming more accessible to the masses through the medium of radio. Jazz was growing more popular. She particularly enjoyed listening to Louis Armstrong and the Boswell Sisters.

Then life took an ugly turn. In 1932, at age thirty-eight, Temperance died of a heart attack. Ella was fifteen years old. Da Silva began neglecting and sometimes abusing her. Ella's aunt, Virginia, brought Ella to Harlem to live with her. Da Silva died soon after.

In Harlem, Ella dropped out of school and worked as a runner for an illegal gambling operation. She was also a lookout in a bordello. She was arrested, sent to reform school, ran away, and returned to Harlem, where she lived on the streets, danced for tips, and slept wherever she could find shelter each night.

That brings the narrative to November 1934. The Great Depression was ravaging America. Joe Louis had been fighting professionally for four months. Jackie Robinson was more than a decade away from breaking baseball's color barrier. Segregation was law in much of the land.

The Apollo Theater on 125th Street in Harlem had recently begun to cater to the black community. One night each week, Ralph Cooper's Amateur Night followed the regular show. First prize in Cooper's amateur competition (the winner being determined by the audience) was twenty-five dollars and inclusion for one week in the regular production.

On November 19, 1934, Ella auditioned as a dancer for the right to compete on amateur night and acquitted herself well enough that she was invited to perform on November 21. The Edwards Sisters (two dancers wearing slinky sequined gowns) closed the regular show that evening. Ella—overweight, wearing a dirty second-hand dress and men's shoes—was the first amateur scheduled to perform. Fearing comparison with the sisters, she decided at the last minute to sing rather than dance. Two songs: "The Object of My Affection" and "Judy." After a shaky start, she won the audience over and was awarded the twenty-five-dollar first prize. But she was denied the one-week slot on the regular variety show because she was poorly dressed and smelled badly from not having bathed.

She returned to the streets. Then fate took a kind turn.

Chick Webb was a popular jazz drummer and founder of the Chick Webb Orchestra. Charles Linton was Webb's lead singer. Webb wanted to complement him with a female vocalist and asked Linton for suggestions.

Decades later, Linton told Stuart Nicholson, "At the theater, I knew an Italian girl who was in the chorus. I asked her, 'Do you know of a beautiful girl who does swing tunes?' 'No, I don't,' she said. 'But there's that little girl who won first prize at the Apollo. Her name is Ella.' I said,

'All right. Do you have a telephone number?' She said, 'No.' I asked for her address, and she said, 'She doesn't have a place to go. She plays out on 125th Street every day.' So I said, 'When you see her, bring her to me.' If it hadn't been for the Italian girl, we wouldn't have any Ella, because she wasn't in any condition to accept any job any place. She was scuffling and didn't have any place to go."

Ella auditioned for Webb and sang well. But as jazz drummer Hal Austin (a friend of Webb's) recounted, "Chick didn't want her. He said she was too ugly."

She also didn't know the basics of personal hygiene. Saxophonist Edgar Sampson later recalled, "Sandy Williams [a trombonist in the band] took care of her like a father. And I mean take care. She didn't use soap and water. That's what I'm talking about. She was in bad shape."

Linton also stepped into the breach. In addition to advocating for Ella with Webb, he arranged for her to eat at a local diner and live with a German family to take her off the streets during the transition period. Mario Bauza (a trumpet player with Webb) told Nicholson that, after Ella left, "The German people cleaned the room out, burned everything, and painted it, which they had to do, it was so dirty."

Ella Fitzgerald was a private person. As her life progressed, despite her warm ebullient public persona, she rarely gave interviews or talked about her childhood. The most remarkable thing about her hard young life is how little of it made its way into her music.

When Ella began singing with Chick Webb at age seventeen, she was an unpolished diamond in the very rough. But she sight-read music well. She had a gift for memorizing lyrics. And she had a voice.

"I'm grateful for that voice," she said years later. "Because without it, nothing could have happened. It's just what God gave me."

Webb mentored her. "I sing like I feel," Ella said. "I sing what comes out." But Webb helped channel her innate talent.

In 1935, Ella cut her first record—"Love and Kisses"—which was released on the Decca label. Forty-two more recordings followed, most of them with Webb's orchestra.

Then, on May 2, 1938, Ella recorded "A-Tisket, A-Tasket," a song that she herself conceptualized based on an old nursery rhyme she'd known as a child. "A-Tisket, A-Tasket" debuted on the best-seller charts on June 18, 1938. Two weeks later, it was in the #1 slot. More than one million copies were sold. It stayed on the best-seller list for nineteen weeks.

At age twenty-one, four years removed from living homeless on the streets of Harlem, Ella Fitzgerald was one of the most popular female vocalists in the United States. And Chick Webb had one of the most popular swing bands in America.

Then fate took another turn. On June 16, 1939, Webb died at age thirty-four from complications stemming from tuberculosis of the spine. Later that year, the orchestra that bore his name was rechristened "Ella Fitzgerald and Her Famous Band."

Ella lived up to the billing. Her voice was a musical instrument . . . Sweet . . . Melodic . . . Joyous . . . Smooth . . . Pure . . . Innocent . . . Inviting . . . Mellow . . . Soothing.

Like a rainbow.

Relaxing and comforting even when she was swinging.

It had remarkable clarity, and she shaded it in subtle ways.

Her vocal range spanned three octaves.

Even great singers sometimes fail to hit a note head-on and compensate by sliding into it. That didn't happen with Ella. Mel Tormé (a superb jazz vocalist in his own right) later opined, "Ella has the best ear of any singer ever. She's always perfectly in tune. I'm still trying to find an Ella Fitzgerald record where she sings one single note out of tune, and I'm failing."

The range and quality of Ella's voice allowed her to make choices that no one else could make. At times, it seemed to her audience that she wasn't even performing; that this was who she was. She made her singing look effortless. It wasn't. She worked hard at her craft and kept adding to her repertoire.

In scat singing, the voice becomes an alternative to a particular musical instrument with the singer making up the syllables. Scat singing had begun to work its way into the musical consciousness of America in 1926 with Louis Armstrong's recording of "Heebie Jeebies."

Soon after joining Chick Webb, Ella began experimenting with scat. Usually, she started with the straight singing of a lyric. Then she'd use her voice as pure musical instrument, taking a turn with the other musical soloists. Sometimes a horn would play, and Ella would mimic it perfectly. Sometimes she made up her own melodies.

"I stole everything I ever heard," Ella said. "But mostly I stole from the horns."

Her voice was as much an instrument as any other in the band. It pulled people in like a gravitational field. There was an irresistible quality to her music. When Ella sang, one couldn't help but listen.

"At her jazziest," music critic Stephen Holden wrote, "her material became a springboard for ever-changing ebullient vocal inventions, delivered in a sweet, girlish voice that could leap, slide, or growl anywhere within a range of nearly three octaves. Her perfect intonation, vocal acrobatics, clear diction, and endless store of melodic improvisations brought her nearly universal acclaim."

"It's not just that her singing is beautiful," Frank Rich added. "It is also liberating, transporting us into a realm of pleasure beyond all barriers, whether of race and age, of jazz and pop, of high art and low. She could turn any song into an oxygen rush of bouncing melody that reached the listener's ears as pure untroubled joy."

Jazz drummer Louie Belson, who was married to Pearl Bailey for thirty-eight years, said of Ella, "There is no voice like that lady. She has it all."

In 1942, Ella left the band to begin a career as a solo artist. Bing Crosby had pursued a similar course when he left the Paul Whiteman Orchestra in 1931. Frank Sinatra had his first solo studio session in January 1942 and left Tommy Dorsey eight months later to go out on his own.

With the guidance of Decca record producer Milt Grabler—and highlighted by several recording sessions with Louis Armstrong—Ella continued to expand her appeal beyond jazz enthusiasts into the general population. But her personal life was less joyful than her singing.

Ella was a private person. She had a warm welcoming face and was a nice woman. But she was insecure at social gatherings unless surrounded by friends and disliked being interviewed.

"It's hard to find out what Ella is really like," Lena Horne said.

"I always felt that Ella was never a true grown-up," commentator Jonathan Schwartz wrote. "That her dearness came from a child's instinct, which was guileless, serene, even bashful, unalloyed with sexual invitation or the wail of romantic obsession."

Pianist Paul Smith, who worked with Ella, observed, "I always thought of her as a lady that never quite grew up. She always had that little-girl quality about her. Her feelings could be hurt very easily. No matter how successful she was, she always had that little anxiety before she went on about whether people would like her. Every time, she'd look around the curtain and say, 'I hope they like me.'"

"It's a funny thing," Ella acknowledged. "If I'm at a party, I'm very shy. And it's not easy for me to get up in front of a crowd of people. It used to bother me a lot. But now I've got it figured out that God gave me this talent to use, so I just stand there and sing. The moment I hit that stage, it's a different feeling. Maybe it's because it's something I love to do."

In addition to being shy, Ella was plagued throughout her life by her weight. She was a heavy adolescent. Eating regularly—and then some— once she began working with Chick Webb, she got heavier. In 1937, *Down Beat* unchivalrously reported that she weighed 220 pounds.

"Some artists sought release from the inevitable buildup of stress by turning to drink or drugs," Stuart Nicholson recounted. "She turned to eating. She could afford to eat well, and she did. She ate regularly at expensive restaurants and prepared huge meals at home. She ballooned. Although it caused her embarrassment, she simply could not stop eating."

June Norton, perhaps Ella's closest friend, recalled, "She was a heavy woman for most of her life. She hated being overweight. She'd say, 'I was looking at all those small cute girls out there, and look at me.'"

"I know I'm no glamour girl," Ella acknowledged.

Ella's innate shyness and problems with weight left her vulnerable to men. At age twenty-four, she fell in love with Benjamin Kornegay, a con man with a criminal record who attended her performances regularly and ingratiated himself with her. They were married on December 26, 1941, after which revelations regarding Kornegay's criminal past surfaced.

Ella asked for a divorce. He refused. So she sued to annul the marriage on grounds that Kornegay had lied to her about his criminal record and entered into the marriage with criminal intent. In mid-1942, the annulment was granted.

Five years later, while on tour with Dizzy Gillespie's band, Ella fell in love with bass player Ray Brown, a talented musician in his own right. On December 10, 1947, they were married. Ella was thirty years old at the time. Brown was twenty-one.

The newlyweds adopted a boy recently born to Ella's half-sister, Frances, and named the infant Ray Jr. Eventually, the marriage failed;

in part because of the couple's conflicting work schedules and in part because of other differences between them. It ended on August 28, 1953, with a "quickie" divorce in Mexico. Brown left Ella, not the other way around. And she was upset about it.

In 1957, there were reports (quite possibly true) that Ella had secretly married a Norwegian named Thor Einar Larsen. Then it was revealed that Larsen had spent time in prison for stealing money from a previous fiancée, and he disappeared from Ella's life. In 1961, she had another, more public, affair with a young man (blond hair, blue eyes, name unknown) from Denmark and lived for a while in Copenhagen.

"I've had some wonderful love affairs and some that didn't work out," Ella acknowledged late in life. "I don't want to dwell on that."

That said; as noted by Tony Bennett in a 1999 PBS documentary, "She began to rely more and more on her audience for the love that was missing in her life. She was happy when she was singing. When she was onstage, her audience adored her."

"I guess what everyone wants more than anything else is to be loved," Ella told an audience one night. "And to know that you loved me for my singing is too much for me. Forgive me if I don't have all the words. Maybe I can sing it and you'll understand."

A listener never had to strain to hear a lyric that Ella was singing. Every word was clearly sung. If her music lacked anything, it was that, unlike Frank Sinatra (who all but acted out the lyrics when he sang), Ella seemed to regard lyrics as secondary to the musical dimensions of a song.

"I like pretty lyrics," Ella said. "They tell a story."

But as Stuart Nicholson observed, "She did not attempt to impose an emotional dimension on what she sang. In responding more to the inherent musical features of a song than to its libretto, she never became part of a song's inherent drama."

Lena Horne concurred, saying, "In her music, she skirted around the emotion. She didn't seem to be curious about anything that was being said in those songs. She didn't make you sad or angry. She was like a beautiful typewriter with an amazing sense of rhythm."

Stephen Holden noted, "Stylistically, she was the polar opposite of Billie Holiday, who conveyed a wounded vulnerability. Even when handed a sad song, Miss Fitzgerald communicated a wistful sweet-natured compassion for the heartache she described."

Jazz pianist Jimmy Rowles agreed, saying, "Ella never impressed me as being inside a song, like with the feeling of the lyrics, like Lady [Billie Holiday]. That wasn't Ella's strong point."

Indeed, one can hypothesize that one reason Ella's scat singing was so remarkable was that, when scatting, she was unencumbered by words.

In 1949, Ella received another career boost when she met jazz impresario Norman Granz, who was the driving force behind a series of concert tours known as Jazz at the Philharmonic. Prior to their union, Ella's solo performances had been mostly in nightclubs. Grantz, who later became her manager, took her to a new level, moving Ella from jazz clubs to concert halls. He also booked her on television variety shows hosted by the likes of Frank Sinatra, Bing Crosby, and Jimmy Durante.

Ella didn't reduce Sinatra to the role of a back-up singer. But she came close. When they sang together, one could see Sinatra deferring to her.

Granz also sent Ella around the world, which brought her international acclaim. Later, he paired her with symphony orchestras. There were times when she was on the road for fifty weeks a year. It was a brutal schedule, but she loved it. In her mind, she wasn't away from home. Home was wherever she was singing.

Granz brought Ella into the mainstream of American culture. For the first two decades of her career, she'd been under contract to Decca records. It was a mutually profitable relationship that resulted in the sale of 22 million records. Then, in 1955, the contract expired and he signed her to a label that he'd founded: Verve Records.

Long-playing records had been introduced in 1948. By the mid 1950s, they were generating significant revenue and becoming an industry standard. They were also the ideal vehicle for a new venture that Granz had in mind. He wanted Ella to record multi-record sets of songs written by America's greatest popular composers.

"At first, I thought, 'What is Norman doing?'" Ella later reminisced. "He's taking me away from my jazz. Who wants to hear me sing this?' But it was like a new beginning. It was a turning point in my life."

Ella Fitzgerald Sings the Cole Porter Songbook, released in 1956, was the first of eight "songbooks" that Ella recorded. That was followed by Rodgers & Hart (1956), Duke Ellington (1957), Irving Berlin (1958), George and Ira Gershwin (1959), Harold Arlen (1961), Jerome Kern (1963), and Johnny Mercer (1964).

"The songbooks," Nicholson notes, "had great appeal for a whole generation brought up in the era of big bands who were feeling disenfranchised from popular music by successive waves of bop and rock 'n' roll. The songs from the Broadway composers from the late 1920s, the 1930s, and the early 1940s were the music with which they identified."

Putting the venture in further perspective, Frank Rich observed, "In the songbook series, she performed a cultural transaction as extraordinary as Elvis's contemporaneous integration of white and African-American soul. Here was a black woman popularizing urban songs often written by immigrant Jews to a national audience of predominantly white Christians. By the time she had gone through the entire canon, songs that had been pigeonholed as show tunes or jazz novelties or faded relics of Tin Pan Alley had become American classical music."

Ella's songbook recordings were lavishly praised.

"I never knew how good our songs were until I heard Ella Fitzgerald sing them," Ira Gershwin said.

"Whatever she does to my songs," Richard Rodgers declared, "she always makes them sound better."

In truth, the songbooks were not Ella at her best. Many of the orchestrations were pedestrian and unimaginative. Also, as Nicholson states, the songbooks "exposed both Ella's strengths and, on occasion, her limitations. The necessity of cranking out the songs made it impossible to internalize most of the material. The consequent effect in certain songs was to open a gulf between singer and material." Thus, despite the strength of their underlying concept, Nicholson concludes, "The *Songbooks*, for all of the hyperbole that surrounds them, can never be anything more or less than good songs well sung."

That said; the first annual Grammy Awards honoring outstanding performances in the musical recording industry were given out in 1958. Ella won two that year: Best Female Vocal Performance for *Ella Fitzgerald Sings the Irving Berlin Songbook* and (2) Best Individual Jazz Performance for *Ella Fitzgerald Sings the Duke Ellington Songbook*.

And Granz didn't forget Ella's jazz roots. In 1958, Verve released the first in a series of albums that she recorded in front of a "live" audience. Overall, these albums, were of a higher quality than her studio sessions.

Ella fed off of a live audience and the spontaneity of fellow musicians. The live jazz albums highlighted her strengths and confirmed her greatness.

In the late-1950s, Ella moved from New York to southern California. In the decades that followed, she tried at times to cover songs sung by a new wave of recording artists. But it wasn't her music.

"As she got older," jazz pianist Paul Smith recalled, "there was less desire to go out and try to do something new. She did the things that were tried and true, which is what people came to hear. In the last twelve years, I was with her on and off. We didn't do a lot of new material. She realized it was the standards people came to hear her sing. They didn't want a Michael Jackson song."

In the 1970s, Ella became known to a new generation of television watchers as the focal point of a commercial for Memorex audio tape. She performed with Frank Sinatra and Count Basie in a sold-out two-week engagement at the Uris Theatre on Broadway. And she continued touring overseas.

"Some kids in Italy call me 'Mama Jazz.'" Ella reported. "I thought that was cute. As long as they don't call me 'Grandma Jazz.'"

She was often referred to as "The First Lady of Song" or "The First Lady of Jazz." Not just by publicists or fans, but also by her peers.

Inevitably, Ella's arduous touring schedule coupled with her weight took a physical toll. In 1972, she began having vision problems complicated by diabetes. In 1985, she was hospitalized for congestive heart failure. One year later, she underwent quintuple coronary bypass surgery. She feared she might never sing again, but returned to performing in 1987.

Jazz singer Betty Carter, a contemporary of Ella's, observed, "It's unreal how she's working so hard, being as ill as she is. She just wants to do what she loves. She wants to hear the applause. It's her life, her reason for living."

"As long as she could get out there and sing," June Norton later recalled," she didn't care if you wheeled her out in a wheelchair or if you propped her up. She wanted to entertain. That was where her joy was."

Ella's final concert performance was in 1991 at Carnegie Hall. Her last public appearance as a singer came in 1993. Later that year, both of her legs were amputated below the knee because of severe circulatory problems stemming from diabetes.

She had spent fifty-eight years of her life on the road.

Ella's final three years were spent wheelchair bound at her home in Beverly Hills. The official Ella Fitzgerald website recounts, "During this time, Ella enjoyed sitting outside in her backyard and spending time with Ray Jr and her granddaughter, Alice." The same website quotes her as saying, "I just want to smell the air, listen to the birds, and hear Alice laugh."

She died at home on June 15, 1996, at age seventy-nine.

"I don't know whether her love life was what she expected it to be," jazz trumpeter Harry "Sweets" Edison said afterward. "But I know that she had a great life."

Numbers blur when discussing Ella. And numbers don't do justice to her story. But let it be noted that, during her career, she recorded approximately two thousand songs, sold more than forty million albums, and won thirteen Grammy Awards. In 1992, she was awarded America's highest non-military honor, the Presidential Medal of Freedom.

"Ella is the boss lady," jazz composer and pianist Billy Strayhorn (who collaborated with Duke Ellington for three decades) said of her work.

Jazz singer Peggy Lee put matters in perspective best when asked to name the greatest jazz singer of all time. A confused look crossed Ms. Lee's face, and she answered, "You mean, after Ella?"

Ella Fitzgerald had elegance and grace. Her essence was singing.

"The only thing better than singing is more singing," she said.

Eight decades after she stepped onto the stage at the Apollo Theater— an unkempt, awkward, seventeen-year-old girl—Ella remains in a class by herself.

Inspectors are the eyes and ears of a state athletic commission in the dressing room and at ringside.

Ernie Morales: The Inspector

Will Walters sat on a chair in a backstage corridor at B. B. King's Blues Club in New York. Three days earlier, the thirty-four-year-old welterweight had flown to New York from California to serve as an opponent.

Walters had a 2-and-7 record as a professional fighter. In less than an hour, he'd enter the ring to face Peter Dobson, who was undefeated in four professional bouts.

There were eleven fights on the card, which meant that some fighters had been relegated to the corridor rather than sharing one of the small makeshift dressing rooms. It was hot and humid. The corridor had a concrete floor and cinderblock walls. There were no fans and little air circulation. Adding to the discomfort, a door alarm had been blaring for a half hour.

As Walters's hands were being taped, a well-groomed forty-seven-year-old man wearing a navy blue blazer, gray slacks, white shirt, and black tie (all perfectly pressed) watched intently.

Ernie Morales is an inspector for the New York State Athletic Commission. He's 5-feet-9-inches tall, weighs 163 pounds, and over the years has completed fourteen New York City marathons with a best time of 3:42:42. "I'm not in boxing shape," he says. "But I am in shape."

Morales was born on the lower east side of Manhattan on August 2, 1967. "When I was growing up," he recalls, "it was just my mother and me. She had me when she was nineteen years old, and I lived with her until I got married in 1992. I knew who my father was. My name is Ernest Morales III. But it wasn't a strong relationship."

Morales's mother was a dental hygienist. "It was important to her that I grow up right," he says. "And she put that belief in me. But the crack epidemic was in full bloom back then, and she went through several relationships where she got involved with intravenous drugs. She tried to keep it from me, but I knew. I made a promise to myself that I would never get caught in that cycle."

When Morales was five years old, his mother enrolled him in the Boys Club of New York at 9th Street and Avenue A near Tompkins Square Park.

"I was in the gym a lot," he says. "Then, when I was eight or nine, they opened a boxing program. I tried it, liked it, and stayed with it. I was an average fighter, nothing great. I had 74 amateur fights; won 50, lost 24, and had one knockout. That tells you I wasn't much of a puncher. The knockout came at a small show in New Jersey. We got into an exchange, I was scoring pretty well, and the referee stopped it. I had a good jab and I could hit you with a solid straight right. The problem was, I might hurt you with the right but I didn't have the power to finish."

Morales reached the semi-finals of the New York City Golden Gloves twice. The first time was in the novice 118-pound division; the second, in the open division at 125 pounds. He was never counted out during his amateur years, but he was stopped three times.

"I didn't have that much natural ability," Ernie acknowledges. "But boxing was a great experience for me. It kept me away from the streets at a time in my life when a lot of the kids I was growing up with were getting in trouble. I learned about discipline and how to take care of my physical health. I don't drink. I never did drugs. Boxing started me out right."

Morales graduated from Chelsea Vocational High School in 1985. While in school, he ran cross country and clocked a 4:32 mile.

And he had one professional fight. That came at age twenty-one against Rene Pellot (who was also making his pro debut) at Gleason's Arena in Brooklyn on May 26, 1989. There's a backstory on that one.

"Pellot was well-conditioned and tough with a body like Adonis," Ernie remembers. "A year or two before, there had been an amateur show when they wanted to match us and I chickened out. I wouldn't fight him. When it was time to turn pro, Bruce Silverglade (who was promoting the card) gave my trainer, Juan Rivera, five names and said we could choose the opponent. Juan told me 'you choose.' Pellot's name was on the list. I said to myself, 'If I don't face my fear now, I'll never get past it.' So I chose Pellot. He came right at me like I knew he would. And I got cut from a head butt in the second round. But I outboxed him and won a unanimous decision."

Meanwhile, Morales had taken the New York City Police Department qualifying examination. "I'd known from the time I was twelve years old that I wanted to be a police officer," he says.

In mid-1989, Morales was called for duty. Trainees at the Police Academy and in the period immediately after graduation are on probation. During that time, they cannot have outside employment. Professional boxing was considered outside employment. That marked the end of Ernie's ring career.

New York State Athletic Commission inspectors work on a per diem basis and have a variety of "day jobs." Morales has one of the NYSAC's more interesting resumes.

His first assignment with the NYPD was in the 25th Precinct in Harlem, initially in community policing and then in plainclothes anticrime. That was followed by a four-year stint as an undercover officer in the Manhattan North Narcotics unit.

"I was buying drugs in Washington Heights, which was the cocaine capital of America," Ernie recalls. "There were times when I was nervous. But I brought the same mentality to it that I brought to boxing. If you lose that nervous edge, you're going to get hurt."

Morales was promoted to sergeant in 1998 and spent much of the next three years in the 47th Precinct in the Bronx on a plainclothes anticrime detail. Then he was drafted into Internal Affairs (an independent unit that investigates alleged misconduct by police officers).

"I didn't ask for that assignment," Ernie says. "I was told that was what I was going to do next."

After one year with Internal Affairs, Morales was promoted to lieutenant and sent to the 44th Precinct in the Bronx. In 2002, he was selected to attend a three-month advanced-training program in law enforcement at the FBI National Academy in Quantico, Virginia. Then he was assigned to the Bronx narcotics unit as a supervising lieutenant, a role he filled for nine years. He was promoted to captain on October 31, 2011, and transferred to the 34th Precinct in Manhattan, where he served as executive officer (#2 in the chain of command behind the precinct's ranking officer). A similar assignment in the 32nd Precinct in Harlem followed.

Then, on August 18, 2014, Morales was appointed to his present position: commanding officer of Transit District 12 in the Bronx. The district covers eight precincts and forty-two subway stations. "Over a half million people pass through those stations each day," he notes. "We have to make sure they're safe."

In twenty-five years with the NYPD, Morales has never fired his gun in the line of duty. Fourteen of his years on the force have been devoted to fighting drugs.

"Every promotion I've gotten," he says "has felt to me like winning a world title fight."

Morales's work as an inspector with the New York State Athletic Commission flowed naturally from his love of boxing.

"I used to go to shows from time to time," Ernie recounts. "Then I met [former NYSAC chief inspector] Felix Figueroa, who told me about the commission and asked if I wanted to get involved. The idea appealed to me. I was at Madison Square Garden as a fan when Billy Collins fought Luis Resto [on June 18, 1983, the night that trainer Panama Lewis removed padding from Resto's gloves in the dressing room prior to the fight]. That night, a man's life was ruined because of a cheater."

Morales was hired as an inspector on August 4, 2008. On fight night, he arrives at the venue two hours before the first bout. As a general rule, he's assigned to monitor one or two fighters. In the dressing room, he introduces himself to each fighter that he has been assigned to cover and also to the fighter's seconds. During the next few hours, he supervises the gathering of urine samples, wrapping of hands, and gloving up, in addition to making certain that myriad commission rules are followed.

"I try to keep a calm environment," Morales says. "I explain the rules to the fighter and his seconds and tell them how they're expected to conduct themselves. One of the commission's responsibilities is to make sure that, within the rules, the playing field is as level as possible. My job as an inspector is to help implement that policy. If something doesn't look right—a gauze pad, a medication, whatever it is—I don't just say 'no' and give it back to them. I hold onto it until after the show and then decide with the chief inspector what to do with it."

In performing his task, Morales is firm but non-confrontational. He does his best to treat every fighter equally. The fact that he's bilingual is a plus.

When the fighter leaves for the ring, Morales goes with him. In the corner, he watches to ensure that adherence to the commission rules continues. Also, during the bout, he's a link in the chain of safety for a fighter. A good inspector knows when to signal to the referee that a fighter might be laboring between rounds or to suggest to the ring doctor that the fighter needs a closer look.

"I find it all very rewarding," Ernie says. "It's service-oriented and allows me to remain part of the sport I love. Felix was my first mentor. The other person who taught me a lot was [current NYSAC chief inspector] George Ward. George has a lot of experience and he's generous in sharing it. I learned a lot by watching how George does his job."

"Iron Will" Walters vs. "Pistol Pete" Dobson wasn't much of a fight. Walters holds his left hand low and, to make matters worse, brings it back slowly when he jabs. That made him a sitting duck for chopping right hands that Dobson landed throughout the contest. Referee Harvey Dock mercifully stopped the bout with Walters still on his feet at 1:33 of the third round.

Morales sat with Walters in the corridor afterward.

"It's embarrassing," the fighter said.

"Don't say that," Morales told him. "To step in the ring like you just did is never embarrassing. Very few people have the courage and skill to do what you did tonight."

"Thanks for the kind words, man. I appreciate them."

There were six more fights on the card. Dobson-Walters was now history.

"I've lived in a lot of places," Walters said, ruminating on his life as he sat in the corridor. "Moved around a lot when I was a kid. My last job was as a server in a restaurant. Right now, boxing is all I do, but it's a dirty gig. I loved boxing when I was an amateur. The whole community of fight people seemed special to me. But the way they match people up in the pros; I understand it from a business point of view. But in a perfect world, I'd be more evenly matched."

"Probably, I'll have a few more fights. Then I'd like to do something else. My dream would be to be a fireman. Firemen are the real heroes, but those jobs are hard to get. Maybe I could be a paramedic or something like that where I'm helping people."

Walters's purse for fighting Dobson was three thousand dollars. He'd traveled alone to New York and picked up two corner men at the last minute. Richard Schwartz would get a hundred dollars for serving as chief second; cutman George Mitchell, twenty-five.

"I'm bummed out that things happened the way they did tonight," Walters continued. "But that's the story of my life. I always seem to come up short, even if it's just by a little bit. I run marathons sometimes. My goal is to break three hours. My best time so far is three hours and twelve seconds. Think about that. If I'd run each mile a half second faster, I'd have broke three hours."

"I wanted to go the distance tonight. That way, maybe my next fight would be eight rounds instead of six. They pay more for eight-round fights. But what happened happened. It would be cool if Dobson becomes a great fighter some day. Then I could say I fought him way back when."

On that note, Walters's mood brightened a bit.

"I like fighting in New York," he said. "The pay is pretty good and they pay your medical expenses. If I need another MRI, I'll try for another fight in New York. And I liked the inspector. He's a nice guy. He knows what he's doing and where the fighters are coming from."

"Wilt Chamberlain," Jerry West once observed, "was one of those fabulous players who defined sports."

Tom Hoover Remembers Wilt Chamberlain

Tom Hoover was confirmed in June 2015 as the new chairman of the New York State Athletic Commission. That makes him one of the most influential regulators in boxing.

Hoover has enjoyed a long career in private business and public service. But he's best known to sports fans as a basketball player. An All-American at Villanova University in Philadelphia, he was the sixth pick in the 1963 NBA draft. Playing for the New York Knicks, he logged 988 minutes during the 1963–64 season, averaging 5.6 rebounds and 4.8 points per game. After a second year on the Knicks roster, he spent time with the St. Louis Hawks before moving to the rival American Basketball Association, where he suited up for the Denver Rockets, Houston Mavericks, Minnesota Pipers, and New York Nets.

Hoover entered the NBA at a time when the league had stars like Oscar Robertson, Jerry West, Elgin Baylor, and, most notably, Bill Russell and Wilt Chamberlain. Chamberlain played a special role in his life.

"I met Dip in the summer of 1959," Hoover reminisces. "Over the years, he had a lot of nicknames. His favorite was 'The Big Dipper,' so I called him Dip. I'd just graduated from Archbishop Carroll High School in Washington, DC, and was going into my freshman year at Villanova, There was a great basketball tradition back then. Each summer, they had a weekend when teams from Philadelphia and New York would play three all-star games against each other in one city or the other. They rotated the city back and forth from year to year. It was high-school players versus high-school players, college players versus college players, and pros versus pros. I was in the college game."

"At one point," Hoover continues, "I heard someone shouting, 'Come on, Hoov! Block that shot! Box out! Rebound! Come on, Hoov!

Let's go!' I turned to see who was yelling. And 'Omigod! That's Wilt Chamberlain. He knows my name.'"

Chamberlain was twenty-three years old at the time and about to start his first season in the NBA. Prior to that, he'd played two years at Kansas University and a year with the Harlem Globetrotters before being eligible to join the Philadelphia Warriors under league rules then in effect that said a player was ineligible for the draft until what would have been a four-year college commitment expired. He was the most-talked-about, most-anticipated rookie in league history.

"We won the Philly–New York game," Hoover remembers. "Then Dip introduced himself and took me to a club on Broad Street called Pep's, where Dizzy Gillespie was playing. After that, we went around the corner and heard Miles Davis, Cannonball Adderly, and John Coltrane. At the end of the evening, he drove me back to school in his purple Eldorado Cadillac convertible. I have no idea why he singled me out that day, but he did."

Chamberlain—with his unique combination of size, agility, and strength—changed the way basketball was played. He was the NBA's dominant player for fourteen seasons; first with the Warriors (who later moved to San Francisco), then with the Philadelphia 76ers and Los Angeles Lakers. Along the way, he rewrote the record book like no athlete in any sport ever has.

"Dip was head and shoulders above everybody else," Hoover says. "He wasn't fast. He wasn't quick. But he was seven-one, maybe a bit taller, with incredible upper-body strength. He was so much stronger than anyone else in the league. Bill Russell won with the Celtics because he had great teams around him for his entire career. Dip rarely had that. When he did, he won."

Meanwhile, the Chamberlain-Hoover friendship flourished.

"After that first night," Hoover recalls, "I didn't see Dip again until the NBA season started. Then I started going to Warriors games, and he'd drive me back to the campus afterward. We talked about music, politics, women. Wilt liked women, but the numbers you hear are an exaggeration. His parents lived in Philadelphia, and I was in their home for dinner a lot."

Then Hoover's own NBA sojourn began.

Chamberlain kept an apartment in New York when he played in Philadelphia. Hoover played cards there with Wilt, Calvin Ramsey, and a high-school student named Lou Alcindor. Chamberlain took Hoover to Las Vegas and introduced him to Frank Sinatra, Sammy Davis Jr, and other members of the Rat Pack. He and Wilt made a commercial together for a shoe called Easy Walkers."

And there are other memories.

"Dip took me to Atlantic City a number of times," Hoover recounts. "The first time we went, we heard Sam Cooke. I was with the Knicks then. I remember parts of that night very well and other parts are blank. I was trying to drink with Dip, which I never did and which was a mistake. Champagne and Old Grand-Dad. The last thing I remember from that night was sitting in the middle of Kentucky Avenue, very drunk. Dip was laughing at me. The next thing I remember was waking up in my bed in New York. Dip had picked me up, put me in his car, drove me home, carried me into my apartment, and put me to bed. I was six-nine, 235 pounds back then."

"People were always asking Dip for things and looking for him to pay the bill whenever they went out," Hoover continues. "That wasn't my style. I never asked him for anything, and I think he liked that. He was always very generous with me. We never played on the same team in a game. But I went up against him when I was with the Knicks and Hawks. I played center; so when I was in the game, I had to guard him. You're not friends then. Dip wanted me to be successful in the league, but not against him."

Chamberlain's athletic prowess wasn't limited to basketball. He was a magnificent track and field athlete and a first-rate volleyball player. He also came close to trying his hand at boxing.

"Dip was a smart guy," Hoover says. "And he had a good business sense. He knew how to make money."

There was a lot of talk in 1971 about Chamberlain fighting Muhammad Ali. But the discussions had begun in 1967.

"Ali was getting ready to fight Zora Folley," Hoover remembers. "Dip came to me and said, 'Hoov; we're going to make some money. I'm going to fight Muhammad Ali, and you're going to manage me.'"

As for what happened next . . .

"There were conversations back and forth," Hoover recounts. "Then, one day, I went over to Madison Square Garden to watch Ali when he was training for Folley. Ali was sparring. He saw me and shouted, 'That's a Wilt Chamberlain spy.' Then he got out of the ring, came over to me, and started yelling, 'Tell that big guy he can't beat me. He's too slow. I'm too pretty. Here! Take this back to that big guy.' Then he threw fifteen jabs like a machine gun within an inch of my nose. That night, I told Dip, 'We can make some money. But he's going to beat your ass.'"

Years later, Chamberlain told this writer, "I took it seriously. I spent some time training with Cus D'Amato. I believed I was capable of going out there and representing myself in a way that would not be embarrassing. I didn't have to learn how to become a complete boxer. I was going to learn for eight or ten months how to apply my strengths and skills against one person. One of the first things Cus said to me was, 'You're going to learn how to fight one man; that's all. We're going to have all the tapes of Ali. We're going to know all the things you have to do and what you possess to do it with against this one person. There's no way that Ali can train to fight you. He won't know anything about you as a fighter because there's only one of you and no tapes.'"

"That was my edge," Chamberlain continued. "Ali would be coming in blind. He'd have no idea what he was facing, whereas I'd know what to expect. And of course, I had God-given strength, size, and athletic ability. If I'd been the oddsmaker, I'd have made Muhammad a ten-to-one favorite. But I thought a man as great at his job as Ali was might take me lightly. I could see that happening. And because of his nature, he'd want to have fun with this particular fight, which might give me an opening. I truly believed there was a chance for me to throw one punch and take Ali out."

"That sounds great," Hoover says, looking back on that long-ago time. "But it wouldn't have happened."

Hoover's friendship with Chamberlain continued for decades. Then came a tragic day in 1999.

"Dip and I talked on the phone a lot," Hoover reminisces. "He'd usually call around midnight his time, which was three in the morning in New York. I don't know if I could talk with him on the phone for two hours starting at three o'clock in the morning anymore. I'm getting old;

I need my sleep. One night, I called and left a message for Dip around seven o'clock California time, and he didn't call back. The next day, I heard on the radio that he'd died from heart failure."

"Dip was larger than life," Hoover says in closing. "That wasn't supposed to happen; not when he was so young, sixty-three years old. Outside of family, no death ever hurt me as much as his did. He was a beautiful person. He helped me grow to manhood. I still miss him. Write something nice about him. He deserves it."

Michael Buffer has become part of the fabric of boxing.

Some Notes on Michael Buffer

Recently, I had lunch with Michael Buffer, who was reminiscing about a time in his life when he saw Muhammad Ali fairly often.

"We're talking about 1973, 1974," Buffer said. "This was way before I got involved in boxing. There wasn't a thought, an inkling, a clue that I'd be a ring announcer some day. I was just a fan, living in Lansdale, Pennsylvania, working as a Volkswagen salesman."

"Lansdale was a ninety-minute drive from Deer Lake. One or twice a week when Ali was in training, I'd visit the camp. Deer Lake was open to everyone. The crowds got pretty big. But no matter how many people were there, Ali sat down and signed every autograph that every last person wanted after each sparring session."

"Larry Holmes was one of Ali's sparring partners back then," Buffer continued. "He'd drive up from Easton in a 1965 black Lincoln Continental and was always late, so he was always getting speeding tickets. [Former lightweight champion] Ike Williams hung around. He was broke. Ali would ask him questions about boxing to make him feel important and slip him a few dollars. He gave money to a lot of people."

"After a while, Ali got used to seeing me around," Buffer recalled. "Usually, I drove a Volkswagen to the camp. Occasionally, I rode my motorcycle [a Suzuki 550]. One time when I was there, Ali hopped on the bike, rode off, and was gone for an hour. Angelo [trainer Angelo Dundee] was furious at me for giving Ali the motorcycle. He was gone so long, they thought he'd been injured in an accident."

"And there's another memory I have that's special," Buffer said. "Ali had a couple of magazine covers with his picture on them taped to the wall of the gym. He'd been so nice to me that I wanted to do something for him. So I took the covers off twenty-or-so boxing magazines that I had with his picture on them and brought them to Deer Lake. Ali and I put them up together on the wall. When I think back on that, it's pretty cool. Me and Muhammad Ali, taping magazine covers to the wall of the gym at Deer Lake. And now I'm in the Hall of Fame. Go figure."

★ ★ ★

When Floyd Mayweather and Manny Pacquiao met in the ring on May 2, 2015, "those in attendance and the millions of people watching around the world" knew that something was wrong. Michael Buffer (the real "TBE") could barely talk.

The promotion of Mayweather-Pacquiao was marked by turf wars at every turn. The division of ring-announcing duties was no exception. Buffer is identified with HBO. Jimmy Lennon is Showtime's guy. After extensive negotiation, a narrative was scripted that divided announcing duties between them as evenly as possible.

Then, on the morning of the fight, Buffer woke up and his voice was gone. Too many interviews during fight week had robbed him of his magical powers.

The original plan had been for Michael to open the show by welcoming viewers at the start of the pay-per-view telecast. He'd also been slated to read the introductions and results for Vasyl Lomachenko vs. Gamalier Rodriguez. Those chores were reassigned to Lennon.

Meanwhile, Buffer spent the day drinking tea with honey and communicating by e-mail only. By fight night, his voice had recovered to the point where he was able to introduce the Filipino national anthem, call Manny Pacquiao to the ring, and intone his iconic, "Let's get ready to rumble!"

But his voice was noticeably hoarse.

Michael Buffer without his voice is like a fighter with a torn rotator cuff.

★ ★ ★

Just prior to Gennady Golovkin's October 17, 2015, fight against David Lemieux at Madison Square Garden, Michael Buffer introduced the most notable celebrities at ringside.

Earlier in the evening, Donald Trump had entered the arena to a near-deafening chorus of boos. Now—prior to introducing Lennox

Lewis, Bernard Hopkins, and Oscar De La Hoya—Buffer bravely intoned, "He's an author, an entrepreneur, a TV star, and the number-one Republican contender, Donald Trump!"

There were more boos.

Buffer met Trump in the 1980s when the Trump Taj Mahal, Trump Plaza, and Atlantic City Convention Center hosted boxing's biggest fights on a regular basis. The Donald took a liking to The Michael and insisted on a clause in all boxing contracts requiring that Buffer be the ring announcer for any fight contested at a Trump property. Mark Etess (then president of the Taj Mahal) referred to it as "The Buffer Clause."

If Trump is elected president, one can imagine Buffer jump-starting the inaugural festivities with the proclamation. "Let's Get Ready to Rumble!" But there's no need for the imagination to stop there.

On October 26, 2015, Mike Tyson endorsed Trump's candidacy, saying, "He should be president of the United States. That's what he should be. Let's try something new."

Once Trump has the nomination, he could choose Tyson as his running mate. Iron Mike is a resident of Nevada, which is a swing state. It doesn't have as many electoral-college votes as Florida or Ohio. But in a tight election, every vote matters. Also, think of the media coverage that a Trump-Tyson ticket would engender.

If the current crop of presidential candidates falters, other boxing personalities could jump into the fray.

Lou DiBella would make an interesting president, although it's hard to imagine what life would be like with Lou's finger on the nuclear trigger.

If recent performance is any guide, an Al Haymon administration would run a significant financial deficit.

Al Bernstein would fail as a candidate because voters would think he's too nice to be tough on terrorists.

Michael Buffer by the way, would have a built-in campaign advantage if he ran on the pledge that he'd get our armed forces "ready to rumble."

Meanwhile, all of the candidates could learn something from Bob Arum. If attacked for flip-flopping on crucial issues, they could respond, "Yesterday I was lying. Today I'm telling the truth."

As for Hillary Clinton (the presumptive Democratic Party nominee), given the outsized role that a few large swing states will play in the election, she might be well-served by choosing Florida resident Roy Jones Jr as her running mate. Of course, now that Roy is a Russian citizen, that wouldn't play well with some voters. And Kelly Pavlik (from the great swing-state of Ohio) will only be thirty-four years old on election day, leaving him short of the constitutional age requirement.

Wait a minute! I just thought of something. Hillary can choose Don King as her running mate. Don is an Ohio-born Florida resident with homes in both states.

Curiosities

On May 2, 2015, at 8:45 p.m., Manny Pacquiao made his way to the ring in the MGM Grand Garden Arena. Sixty-four rotating spotlights shone down from above. The crowd roared. Pacquiao climbed four metal steps, maneuvered his body through the ring ropes, and went to the red corner. At 8:50, Floyd Mayweather followed.

Three days before Mayweather-Pacquiao, I climbed into the same ring at the MGM Grand with former WBO cruiserweight champion Johnny Nelson. The arena was empty. With Nelson's counsel, I imagined what it would be like for the fighters on Saturday night when they entered the ring. On Thursday, I repeated the exercise with Paulie Malignaggi. Their thoughts follow.

Before the Bell for Round One

You leave the sanctuary of your dressing room and walk down a brightly lit corridor; then through a short dark tunnel into the arena.

The worst part is the waiting. The waiting is over.

For every fighter, no matter how confident he is, there's a moment before a fight when he has to deal with fear. You should have dealt with it before now.

You make your way through the crowd.

The arena is packed to the rafters.

The roar of the crowd is like no other sound. It can energize and inspire. Or it can terrify like the full-throated roar of a lion in the jungle.

You feed on the crowd, or it will feed on you.

You tell yourself that you're ready. You remind yourself what's at stake.

The steps leading up to the ring are narrow. At the top, you can see everything clearly. You feel like you're on top of the world.

The killing field lies before you.

Four ropes are horizontally stretched on each side of the ring. From top to bottom; red, white, blue, white. The canvas is twenty feet square inside the ropes, stretched over plywood and foam mats. You can't walk around it in a circle like you want to because there are too many sanctioning body officials and other people who don't belong in the ring.

You were in the arena for satellite interviews earlier in the week. It feels bigger now that it's full. Row after row of spectators recede into darkness as far as the eye can see.

You look at the crowd. It's studded with icons who have shaped your life. Great fighters you admired over the years. Singers you've listened to, actors you've seen on screen.

These people mean nothing to you now. Nothing that happens outside of this ring matters. You block everything but the fight out of your mind.

You're at the center of the world. For the next hour, no place on earth will have more eyes focused on it.

"Let's get ready to rumble!!!"

It's easy to lose yourself in the fighter introductions. Don't!

Be in the moment.

The introductions are over. The sanctioning body officials and entourage members, even your trainer, have left the ring. There's no one standing behind you now, massaging your shoulders, shouting, "You da man!"

They're all gone. You're alone.

The ring looks smaller when there's a man trained in the art of hurting in the opposite corner. When you look across the ring, do you see predator or prey?

Do you want to get the fight started, or do you want get it over with?

You can fear failure. You cannot fear physical harm. If you do, you're done.

You wouldn't be where you are today if you hadn't mastered the mental part of the game.

The referee is standing in the center of the ring, holding you back with upraised palms, instructing you to wait.

You're stripped half naked before the eyes of the world. The crowd is watching your every move.

The referee steps back toward a neutral corner. Now there's nothing and no one in between you and your opponent.

You're bathed in light. Tens of millions of people around the planet are watching your every move. It's the loneliest place in the world.

One of the greatest highs or worst lows of your life lies ahead.

Embrace the moment. This means greatness for you.

The referee signals to the timekeeper . . .

DING!

This piece mixed fact and fiction on April Fools' Day.

A Look Ahead at Holyfield-Romney

On March 16, 2015, it was announced that Mitt Romney and Evander Holyfield will square off at a charity fundraiser to be held at the Rail Event Center in Salt Lake City on May 15. Sponsorships for the black-tie event will range in cost from $250,000 down to $25,000. Organizers say that "heavy hors d'oeuvres" will be served. There's a rumor afloat that anyone in attendance who can spell "hors d'oeuvres" will be given a "Stop Hillary" T-shirt.

The event is designed to raise funds for Charity Vision, an organization that donates medical equipment to doctors and medical facilities in impoverished countries.

Holyfield, age fifty-two, last fought on May 7, 2011, when he knocked out Brian Nielsen in round ten.

Romney, sixty-eight, last entered the ring on November 6, 2012, when he was stopped in the late rounds by Barack Obama. One month later, the defeated presidential candidate attended the December 8, 2012, fight between Manny Pacquiao and Juan Manuel Marquez at the MGM Grand in Las Vegas. After Pacquiao was knocked unconscious, Romney sat in the first row with a look of horror on his face as Manny's spit bucket was kicked over and the slop spilled onto Mitt's shoes.

Holyfield-Romney is being billed as a "sparring session." According to Josh Romney (one of Mitt's sons), it will share the card with two other bouts to be contested between "active professional fighters."

Like Romney's 2012 presidential campaign, Holyfield-Romney has been heavily scripted. However, the "Fan-Man" and Mike Tyson ear-bite incidents make it clear that Evander's fights don't always follow the script. Get ready for the following:

April 6—Posters trumpeting "Let's Get Ready to Rumble" herald Holyfield-Romney.

April 9—The WBC announces that Holyfield-Romney will be for its super-interim-silver-emeritus championship belt.

April 13—Mitt Romney signs with Al Haymon.

April 15—ESPN.com reports that USADA has contracted to test both fighters for PEDs. "I wanted VADA," Holyfield is quoted as saying. "But Mitt refused."

April 18—Shannon Briggs interrupts Romney and his wife while they're dining at Spago in Beverly Hills, grabs a hunk of Mitt's pâté de foie gras, and wolfs it down. "It tasted like chicken liver," Briggs says afterward. "And Mitt is a chicken because he won't fight me."

April 20—Romney receives a letter from an attorney representing Michael Buffer threatening to sue the promotion for infringement of Buffer's "let's get ready to rumble" trademark.

April 23—Al Haymon announces a time buy on Fox with Holyfield-Romney as the main event.

April 27—"I won't hurt Mitt," Holyfield tells reporters during a media teleconference call. "Just a couple of jabs to the face."

April 29—Mitt Romney begins asking people, "What does it feel like to get hit in the face by an Evander Holyfield jab?"

May 1—During an interview with Fox news, Romney praises Holyfield for the sincerity of his religious beliefs and Evander's "Mormon-sized family."

May 3—Backers of Jeb Bush grow concerned that Romney might use the Holyfield fight as a bridge to evangelical Christians and the launching pad for a 2016 presidential campaign.

May 7—George W. Bush meets with Holyfield and tells Evander, "We'll give you a million dollars if you knock him the fuck out."

May 7—"A million dollars is a lot of money," Evander says thoughtfully. "I could use a million dollars."

May 9—I'm taking this fight very seriously," Evander tells reporters. "A good showing here might get me a fight against Wladimir Klitschko."

May 11—Reports reach the Romney camp that Evander has been "punching pretty hard" in the gym.

May 12—Holyfield meets with Klitschko adviser Shelly Finkel and asks, "If I look good against Romney, that would put me back in the mix; right?" . . ."One thousand percent," Finkel answers.

May 15—Holyfield-Romney goes the full three-round distance. "I saw openings but I just couldn't pull the trigger," Evander admits afterward.

I met Don King in 1983. Thirty-two years later, we had dinner together for the first time.

Two Dinners with Don King

I had dinner with Don King last Thursday night (July 23, 2015) at RedFarm, a trendy Chinese restaurant on the upper west side of Manhattan.

King no longer stands astride boxing like a Colossus. In mid July, *Sports Illustrated* ran an article about him in its annual "where are they now" issue. He'll be eighty-four years old on August 20.

But King is still in the game. He promotes several fighters. He has rebounded nicely from recent health issues. His weight is down from 285 pounds to a healthier 220. And he remains an imposing physical presence with the vitality of a younger man.

Here's what happens when Don King walks into a restaurant. Heads turn. The host moves people around to seat his party of four by the front window. Diners entering the restaurant do a double take as they pass his table. The energy level in the room rises.

The other patrons are respectful. For the most part, they let him eat in peace. But more than a few stop to say hello on their way out. King has a smile and kind word for each of them. The staff is particularly attentive. He tips generously.

When King leaves the restaurant, a statuesque blonde asks if he'll take a smartphone photo with her. After the photo is taken, she wraps her arms around him in a long embrace.

There are a lot of celebrities today but very few icons. King is an icon and a larger-than-life legend. His style, his hair, his verbosity, his smile, his charisma, his bling; all of it is his own creation. He still stops a room when he enters. He may be old. He's no longer the force in boxing that he once was. But he's still Don King.

And Two Nights Later

Don King once observed, "Boxing is life personified. You get knocked down; you get back up. You dust yourself off and you get back into the fray. Your problem stands right before you. You cannot procrastinate and put it off. You can't run away from it. You've got to be able to deal with it. And that's what we have in life."

On the night of March 9, 2013, King and I were together in Tavoris Cloud's dressing room as Cloud readied to fight Bernard Hopkins, and Don uttered a variation on that theme.

King and I have had our differences over the years. I've written harshly about him in the past, and we've been on the opposing side in several legal proceedings. But I've always respected the extraordinary nature of his accomplishments. And like the rest of the world, I've been captivated by his persona.

Now, as Cloud hit the pads with trainer Abel Sanchez, King told me, "Boxing is like life. You knock each other down and then you hug each other. That's what you and me have done."

Fast forward to July 25, 2015. I was having dinner with Don (for the second time in three nights) at one of his favorite haunts, Palm Too in midtown Manhattan. There were five of us at the table. One of the guests—an attractive blonde with a winsome smile who was meeting King for the first time—asked what Don thought about Donald Trump's entry into the Republican presidential race.

That led to an extraordinary performance. For the next ninety minutes, King lectured without intermission on the history of civilization. He began with Hammurabi (who reigned over the Babylonian empire from 1792 to 1750 BC). Then he segued to classical Greek civilization, the Roman Empire, the Crusades, the Renaissance, the American Revolution, and myriad other historical landmarks. References to Robin Hood and numbers running in Cleveland were thrown into the mix as the narrative worked its way to the present.

Two years ago, a reader wrote to me and defined Don King as follows: "He is the criminal who becomes a revolutionary, rises to power, becomes a fabulously wealthy third-world dictator, and, after he is overthrown, lives the rest of his life in financially comfortable exile but still longing to return to power."

King would take issue with some of that characterization. But it's clear that, in recent years, his age, the decline of his empire, and the death of people he loves have brought a vulnerability to him.

For many years, I wanted to like Don King but couldn't.

I like him now.

Some thoughts on the light side of boxing.

Fistic Nuggets

Paulie Malignaggi is thirty-four years old and nearing the end of his ring career. But he's holding out hope for one last run on the theory that, in his words, he has "matured late physically" throughout his life.

"I grew up late," Paulie told me at the Boxing Writers Association of America dinner last month (April 2015). "I started puberty late. I didn't lose my last baby tooth until I was in high school."

High school?

"I was in ninth grade," Paulie elaborated. "The tooth had been loose. I wasn't sure if it was an adult tooth or a baby tooth. Then one day, I was eating lunch in the school cafeteria and I felt it come out. I spit it out, and a friend said, 'Bro! What's happening?' But everything was cool. After that, a new one grew in, so I knew it was a baby tooth that fell out."

"There's a peak age for everything," Paulie continued. "I'm thirty-four now. Since I matured late physically, I'm hoping that my peak as a fighter is still ahead."

"And one thing more," Paulie added. "In all the years I've been fighting, I've never lost a tooth. I'm proud of that."

★ ★ ★

A word of praise for Harold Lederman.

Sometimes we take the good in our midst for granted. So let's recognize the fact that boxing has a treasure in Harold. He loves going to the fights. He loves talking with people about boxing. His knowledge of the sweet science is encyclopedic.

HBO is the ideal platform for Harold. His role as the network's "unofficial ringside judge" gives him a ring's edge view of the action.

"I'm going to slip the usher ten dollars to see if I can get a better seat," Harold joked before one night's work.

And his commentating gig allows him to talk to millions of fans at once instead of one fan at a time.

Harold Lederman at the fights is a happy man. And his happiness is contagious.

★ ★ ★

After Amir Khan vs. Chris Algieri at Barclays Center in Brooklyn ended, I found myself sitting next to Lennard Jackson on the subway going home.

Jackson fought professionally in the 1990s, compiling a 14-and-1 record against non-threatening competition. He retired in 1995 and now teaches boxing, mostly to white-collar clients.

The subway ride passed quickly in animated conversation.

"I love body punching," Lennard told me. "I tell all my students, 'Hit Superman hard to the body, and he'll become Clark Kent.'"

★ ★ ★

There's a tale—no doubt apocryphal—that captures Don King's gift for charming virtually everyone he meets.

It seems that Don was in an airport one day and saw a little old lady crying. Being a gentleman, he went over and asked what the matter was.

The woman poured out her heart.

"Mr. King; my son and I are estranged. We're Jewish with a long family tradition in the faith. Nine months ago, my son married an American Indian woman. I said some things that I shouldn't have said about his marrying out of the faith. They just had a baby boy, and they won't speak to me."

King gallantly offered to call the woman's son on her behalf. She gave him the phone number. Don retired to the airport lounge, came back twenty minutes later, and told the woman, "You don't have to worry anymore. I've talked to your son and his wife. They have a healthy baby boy. I explained to them how important a mother's love is. And to prove their love for you, they've given the baby a nice Jewish name."

The woman hugged King and promised to remember him with gratitude forever.

"What did they name the baby?" she asked.

"Smoked Whitefish," Don told her.

★ ★ ★

Note to the World Sanctioning Organizations

Terry Malloy (the character made famous in Budd Schulberg's *On the Waterfront)* said, "I coulda been a contender," He did not say, "I coulda fought for an interim title."

★ ★ ★

Perhaps the most iconic Christmas image that relates to boxing is the cover of the December 1963 issue of *Esquire* magazine.

Sonny Liston was heavyweight champion of the world and the most feared fighter of his era. Liston had a long criminal rap sheet and the personality to match. *Esquire's* cover consisted of a headshot that featured a glowering Liston staring menacingly at the camera while wearing a red-and-white Santa Claus hat.

Photographer Carl Fischer, who took the picture, later recalled, "Everybody knew Liston was a nasty son of a bitch. Make him Santa Claus? It was just the wrong thing to do. But that was my assignment. There was no plan B. So I went out to Las Vegas, where Liston lived, and met him in a room at the Thunderbird Hotel. I explained what we wanted. He said, 'I'm not going to put on any goddamn Santa Claus hat.'"

Then Lady Luck smiled on Fischer.

"The manager of the hotel came into the room and brought his little girl, a six- or seven-year-old whom Liston took affection to. So we took a couple pictures of her. Then I said, 'Let's put the Santa Claus hat on her.' So we put the Santa Claus hat on her. And then, 'Let's take the pictures with the two of you together, and let's take the Santa Claus hat off her and put it on you.' We took a whole bunch of pictures of the two of them and then got rid of her."

★ ★ ★

Fifteen years ago, I wrote an article about George Foreman and Christmas.

"I'm low key about the holidays," George told me. "The buying and gift-giving never stops. The machinery of giving expensive things has gotten so well-established that nothing stops it. It's let's see how much we can buy, and a lot of people have forgotten about giving of themselves instead of giving things."

So what would Foreman have said if a young child asked him what Christmas is about?

"I wouldn't say anything," George answered. "I'd just hug him. Words can mess up anything, but a hug is always good. I'd hug him and spend the day with him. And the wonderful thing about a hug is, you don't have to wait for Christmas to give it. You can give hugs every day of the year."

Then I asked Foreman about some of his Christmas memories. They weren't all good.

"When I was growing up," George reminisced, "Christmas was the most dangerous time of the year for me. We didn't have a tree or anything like that. We were poor. Christmas trees cost money and, once you had a tree, you had to put something on it. So no tree at Christmas. But when I was young, I'd hear people saying, 'I'm giving my mother this; I'm giving my girlfriend that.' So I'd go out and prowl the streets, fourteen, fifteen years old, a mugger, to get money for presents."

Sugar Ray Leonard's most vibrant Christmas memory dates to when he was about ten years old.

"My father was the produce manager in a supermarket," Ray recalls. "His paycheck had just been garnished, so he didn't have money for Christmas presents. And what he did was, he brought home fruit for Christmas. I was looking for a toy. And to this day, I have a vivid picture in my mind of bananas, apples, and oranges in boxes and bags under the Christmas tree. But I was old enough to understand that my father was providing for us as best he could. And Christmas is about love, not gifts. Talking about it now, I still get a bit emotional."

Larry Holmes is as jolly as Santa Claus when discussing Christmas.

"All of my Christmases have been good," Holmes says. "I'm sixty-six years old now and the happiest guy in the world."

As for this year's festivities, Holmes reports, "My wife does all the work. I buy a present for her, and she buys the presents for everyone else. We just got a nine-foot tree and had to cut the top off. She decorated it. I don't do decoration. I just look at it. Except there were a few branches high up on the tree that she couldn't reach, so I reached up and put the decorations on them."

And Christmas Day?

"I'll sit home and relax," Holmes answers. "Eat, drink some wine, watch football on television, and talk with people who come by."

My own favorite Christmas memory as it relates to boxing dates to the time that Muhammad Ali telephoned to wish me a Merry Christmas.

"Think about it," I told Muhammad. "A Muslim calling a Jew to wish him well on a Christian holiday. There's a message in that for anyone who's listening."

Issues and Answers

A lie of omission is a lie.

The Big Lie

Sometime prior to fighting Floyd Mayweather on May 2, 2015, in Las Vegas, Manny Pacquiao suffered a torn right rotator cuff. In mid April, his condition was evaluated at the Kerlan Jobe Orthopedic Clinic in Los Angeles. Pacquiao later told Filipino journalist Ronnie Nathanielsz that he was advised to rest his shoulder for thirty to forty days.

At that point, Pacquiao considered postponing the fight. But he opted instead for a cocktail of pain-killing, anti-inflammatory, and healing drugs approved by the United States Anti-Doping Agency (USADA), which had contracted with Pacquiao and Mayweather to oversee drug testing in conjunction with the fight.

Thereafter, Pacquiao's preparation for the fight was significantly compromised. Among other things, he stopped sparring for at least a week in an effort to avoid exacerbating his shoulder injury.

At a pre-fight physical administered by the Nevada State Athletic Commission on May 1, Pacquiao (or advisor Michael Koncz; it's unclear which) filled out an NSAC medical questionnaire and listed the medications that Manny had been taking: lidocaine, bupivacaine, Celestone, PRP (platelet-rich plasma), and Toradol.

Koncz told the *New York Daily News* and BoxingScene.com that he was the one who filled out the questionnaire. Bob Bennett (executive director of the Nevada State Athletic Commission) told Fox Sports that Pacquiao did it.

The questionnaire specifically asked, "Have you had any injury to your shoulders, elbows, or hands that needed evaluation or examination? If yes, explain."

Pacquiao (or Koncz) answered "no."

At the bottom of the page, the questionnaire states, "I swear, under penalty of perjury, that the above information is true and correct to the best of my knowledge." Beneath that are lines for "contestant's signature" and "second's signature and name."

There are two signatures (presumably those of Pacquiao and Koncz).

In the dressing room before the fight, Team Pacquiao asked that a physician they had brought with them be allowed to inject Pacquiao with Toradol (a non-steroidal, pain-killing, anti-inflammatory drug). The NSAC denied the request.

A torn rotator cuff is extremely painful. The worse the tear, the more it hurts. At the post-fight press conference, Pacquiao told the media, "In the third round, I already feel the pain in my shoulder. It's hard to fight with one hand. What we wanted to do, I could not do because of my shoulder."

Four days after the fight, Pacquiao underwent surgery in Los Angeles to repair what Dr. Neal ElAttrache (who performed the ninety-minute operation) said was a "significant tear" in his right rotator cuff. Dr. ElAttrache estimates that Pacquiao will be to able resume training in six months and, if he chooses to do so, fight again three to six months after that.

Surgery was Pacquiao's only realistic option.

"Once you know he has a tear that's not going to heal on its own," Dr. ElAttrache told ESPN.com, "then the decision for an active person is you want to try to fix this before it gets bigger. This is a severe enough tear that it won't heal without being repaired."

The handling of Pacquiao's shoulder injury touches on a wide range of issues. Let's start with the role played by USADA.

USADA is an independent non-governmental sports drug-testing agency whose services are utilized by the United States Olympic and Paralympic movement. It receives approximately $10,000,000 annually in public funding; more in years when the Olympics are held.

At Mayweather's insistence, the bout contract that Mayweather and Pacquiao signed to fight each other provided that drug testing would be conducted by USADA. Manny's representatives asked USADA about the propriety of using the drugs in question and were advised that four of the five are not on the list of substances banned by WADA and the fifth (Celestone) is only prohibited "in competition" (within forty-eight hours of a fight).

Because the drugs are not banned, USADA did not need to know why they were being administered or have any legal obligation to report their use to the Nevada State Athletic Commission.

On May 4 (two days after Mayweather-Pacquiao), as questions regarding Pacquiao's injury resounded through the media, a "Joint Statement from Team Pacquiao and Top Rank" was released. In part, the statement read, "Manny continued to train and his shoulder improved, though not 100%. Again, in consultation with his doctors, promoter, and advisors, Manny decided to proceed with the fight, anticipating that he could receive his pre-fight treatment. That specific treatment had been approved by USADA in writing at least five days before the fight."

Pacquiao said one day after the bout that he did not disclose the fact of his injury to the public or to the Nevada State Athletic Commission because he feared Mayweather would use the knowledge to his competitive advantage in the fight.

That leaves open the issue of whether there should have been a fight.

Meeting with reporters in his hotel suite on May 3, Pacquiao acknowledged, "We talked about it [postponement]. But if it heals, if it recovers, it's okay. Let's just not use it in training. Then, on the night of the fight, it will be injected with the numbing agent. It's not a steroid, but it's legal here for numbing. The problem is we were sabotaged."

Some Pacquiao partisans have voiced conspiratorial theories. "It's not rocket science," says one Pacquiao advocate. "Everyone knew that, if Mayweather won, his next fight would most likely be in Las Vegas. If Manny won, his next fight could be in Macau or Cowboys Stadium or wherever. Who do you think the Las Vegas establishment was rooting for?"

Nevada State Athletic Commission officials take issue with that view.

Executive director Bob Bennett notes that the NSAC was unaware of Pacquiao's injury until fight night. "Imagine if you're Mr. Mayweather," Bennett told Geoffrey Gray of True.ink. "And you hear an hour before the fight the Commission granted a special request to have your opponent get an injection of medicine into his shoulder. The paperwork should have been filled out properly."

NSAC chairman Francisco Aguilar voiced similar sentiments, saying, "We get to the fight. A little after 6:00 p.m., we were made aware Pacquiao potentially had a shoulder injury. Then, after we were made aware about the injury, a request came to inject his shoulder with lidocaine and a couple of anti-inflammatories. We gathered our doctor, Dr. Trainor. We got with the two doctors that did his medical exam prior to weigh-in. And we started going through some of these questions as to what does this mean. I made the decision not to allow [the shot] because of the timing of the request and the fact that the fight was going to occur in the next ninety minutes. The medications he was taking were disclosed on his medical questionnaire, but not the actual injury. There is a process. And when you try to screw with the process, it's not going to work for you."

Mayweather-Pacquiao left a long line of aggrieved parties in its wake; people who spent thousands of dollars to journey to Las Vegas or a hundred dollars to buy the pay-per-view telecast. There were "little people" who bet their paychecks on Pacquiao.

The lawsuits have begun. Within a week of the fight, multiple class actions had been filed. Pacquiao, Top Rank, Mayweather Promotions, Showtime, and HBO have been named as defendants. Under Nevada law, the Nevada State Athletic Commission is immune to suit.

One of the problems that plaintiffs will face is, "Where do you draw the line?" Insofar as Mayweather-Pacquiao is concerned, there appears to have been a cover-up supplemented by affirmative misrepresentations over a period of several weeks. But what if, instead of a torn rotator cuff, Pacquiao had been suffering from a sprained ankle? A badly sprained ankle? What if a fighter has the flu before a fight and conceals that information? The NFL mandates pre-game injury reports. If Bill Belichick neglects to mention that Tom Brady has a "slight" rotator cuff tear in his right shoulder, are fans who bought tickets for the game entitled to get their money back? Mayweather-Pacquiao lasted the full twelve rounds. Suppose Manny had quit after round one because of his shoulder injury. Would that make a difference?

And there are more unanswered questions.

When the Nevada State Athletic Commission doctor who examined Pacquiao one day before the fight saw the medications listed on Manny's questionnaire, shouldn't standard procedure have led him to ask, "Why were you taking these medications?" And shouldn't that question have been followed by, "Is there an MRI?"

PRP (one of the medications listed) is a platelet-rich plasma injection commonly used to promote healing. Wasn't that a tip-off? Did the examining doctor ask when the Celestone was used? Unlikely. But Celestone use was illegal after nine o'clock on Thursday night.

The May 4 "Joint Statement from Team Pacquiao and Top Rank" reads in part, "The medication approved for fight night was a non-steroidal anti-inflammatory (Toradol) [parenthesis in original]."

Toradal increases the possibility of bleeding, both from cuts and in the brain. Was that really a wise choice?

And if the drugs were legal, which they are under the WADA Code and the rules of the Nevada State Athletic Commission (which incorporates the WADA Code by reference), why did Pacquiao need permission to use them on fight night?

There will be a lot of grandstanding in the weeks ahead. NSAC chairman Francisco Aguilar went so far as to suggest that Pacquiao could be indicted for perjury.

"It's something we're looking at, and an issue we'll be discussing with the Attorney General," Aguilar told True.ink. "It's a serious matter. We need to know the state of health of our boxers."

This from the chairman of a commission that, last September, accepted Floyd Mayweather's testimony that Showtime had defrauded the public by editing a sparring session to dishonestly portray it as a thirty-one-minute fight and used fake marijuana to help sell pay-per-view buys.

Let's get real! Does anyone on the planet think that the NSAC would have postponed the fight if Pacquiao had answered "yes" to the question of whether he'd suffered an injury to his shoulder?

Everyone—Pacquiao, Top Rank, Mayweather, Mayweather Promotions, the MGM Grand, Showtime, HBO, and the NSAC—wanted the fight to happen. Under the circumstances and given the parties involved, there was no way it was going to be pulled down.

That said; a fighter can't train seriously for a big fight if he isn't sparring. And the overwhelming likelihood is that Pacquiao's injury, however bad it was at the start, got worse if he put in any hard work in the gym. A small tear that would have healed on its own with rest became more pronounced and the muscle more inflamed in the weeks leading up to the fight and was further exacerbated in the fight itself.

Muhammad Ali vs. George Foreman was another "Fight of the Century." On September 17, 1974, eight days before the fight was scheduled to take place (and after hundreds of people associated with the promotion had traveled to Zaire), Foreman suffered a cut above his right eye in sparring. Nobody covered it up with "secret closed-door workouts."

Nobody said, "Let's stitch it up, cover the stitches with make-up, and take the stitches out on fight night." The fight was rescheduled for October 30 and is now a treasured part of boxing lore.

Floyd Mayweather was scheduled to fight Juan Manuel Marquez on July 18, 2009. In mid-June, he injured a rib in training and pulled out of the fight. The world didn't end. The fight was rescheduled for September 19, and Mayweather scored a lopsided unanimous decision triumph.

Mayweather-Pacquiao should have been postponed.

Jim Lampley, who handled blow-by-blow duties for the telecast, put the matter in perspective three days after the debacle when he told Rich Eisen of Fox Sports, "It was a cynical enterprise to begin with in certain ways and now seems even more so. To have gone ahead with the enterprise when one of the fighters turns out to be damaged goods, and for all of the advertising and promotion to have continued to base itself on the notion that this was the fight of the century and the best combat that boxing could offer; uninitiated fans who only know a little bit about boxing and buy in at the level at which they bought in are bound to feel cheated today. I think it's highly unfortunate for our sport. I think it's bad for Pacquiao's image and taints his great and noble career. I could go on and on about the ways in which this is unfortunate for boxing."

Floyd Mayweather has frequently complained that he doesn't get the respect he deserves from the media. But the relationship is more complicated that that.

Mayweather–Pacquiao and the Media

There's a famous seventeenth-century carving above the door of a temple in Nikko, Japan. In recent centuries, it has been popularized in the form of three monkeys who, respectively, are covering their eyes, ears, and mouth. The monkeys embody the concept of dealing with impropriety by looking the other way, refusing to acknowledge it, or feigning ignorance: "See no evil; hear no evil; speak no evil."

The carving would have been an appropriate logo for Mayweather-Pacquiao.

In the ring, Floyd Mayweather stands for excellence. Outside the ring, his conduct has been problematic. The media has chosen to glorify Mayweather's lifestyle, which is excessive at times to the point of being vulgar. More troubling, much of the media has glossed over his penchant for physically abusing women.

Mayweather has an anger-management problem. And it's particularly acute with regard to women. He has been criminally convicted five times for incidents involving violence against women. On the last of these occasions, he served sixty-three days in jail.

When asked about this abuse during the build-up to Mayweather-Pacquiao, Mayweather consistently answered, "Only God can judge me. "As ESPN.com senior writer Tim McKeown noted, that was "a meaningless and cynical dodge."

Mayweather is who he is and does what he does. As Greg Bishop of *Sports Illustrated* pointed out, one of the things he does is, "Mayweather makes everyone around him rich. That means he does and says exactly what he wants exactly when he wants. He doesn't apologize. He doesn't admit guilt. He doesn't surround himself with anyone who might, every once in a while, say, 'maybe that's a bad idea.'"

But Mayweather's circle of enablers extends far beyond his personal "Money Team" entourage. The media has played a role. It was widely reported when Floyd went to jail for physically abusing Josie Harris (the mother of three of his children). But few major media outlets pursued the story beyond that. Showtime (Mayweather's current network) and HBO (which televised the majority of Floyd's fights from 1997 through 2012) have largely soft pedaled his transgressions.

After Mayweather was criminally convicted in conjunction with the Harris incident, HBO aired a special in which Michael Eric Dyson (a professor at Georgetown University) interviewed Floyd and compared him with Muhammad Ali, Jim Brown, and Kareem Abdul-Jabbar as an oppressed black athlete that the system was trying to silence.

"Martin Luther King went to jail," Mayweather told Dyson. "Malcolm X went to jail. Am I guilty? Absolutely not."

Dyson then segued to the idea that there was a "racially-based resentment" against Mayweather and declared, "I think about Jay-Z on *Ninety-Nine Problems*, when he goes—the cop asks him a question, and he says—'Are you mad at me because I'm young, rich, and I'm famous and I'm black. Do you got a problem with that?'"

Dyson failed to mention Mayweather's previous convictions involving violence against women.

At another point in the interview, Mayweather told Dyson, "People want to know how much power Floyd Mayweather got. I can guarantee you this. I'll show you how much power I got. If I was to fight Manny Pacquiao, I'll let Barack Obama walk me to the ring, holding my belt. Can I make it happen? Absolutely."

Showtime (Mayweather's current network) has given him control over most of its Floyd Mayweather programming. More troubling, Showtime and HBO (two companies with a tradition of editorial integrity and excellence) agreed to a "non-disparagement" clause that discouraged commentary on either network regarding Mayweather's violence against women during the build-up to Mayweather-Pacquiao.

The rest of the media fell in line. As Mayweather-Pacquiao approached, there was an endless stream of content about "Money Mayweather" and "The Fight of the Century."

From TMZ, we learned that Mayweather wears a custom-made mouthpiece with gold flakes, diamond dust, and hundred-dollar bills sealed inside.

USA Today reported that Mayweather had bought more than one hundred cars (including sixteen Rolls Royces) from Towbin Motorcars in Las Vegas. "We never know when Floyd will get the bug to go car shopping," Jesika Towbin-Mansour told the newspaper in describing Mayweather's nocturnal shopping habits. "But it's worth the effort."

"A Rolls-Royce," *USA Today* informed its readers, "can run north of $400,000. A Bugatti passes $2 million like a speed bump. And Mayweather owns three of them. The champ pays in cash; sometimes duffel bags full of it. There's so much cash that the auto dealership had to buy a new cash-counting machine just to accommodate Mayweather."

Press releases from the promotion (dutifully quoted by the media) informed the public that (1) Twizzlers are one of Mayweather's favorite snacks; (2) when dining out, Floyd always orders a glass of hot water and lets his silverware soak in the glass before using it; and (3) Mayweather's morning routine includes brushing his teeth for ten straight minutes.

It was all aimed at engendering pay-per-view buys. Writer Bart Barry summed up the sales pitch as follows: "Television tells me the best today is the best of all time, and my athlete is much richer than yesterday's best athlete, who, regardless of what readily available video may suggest, could never beat my favorite athlete because he didn't have swagger."

There was some blowback to the glorification of Mayweather. Rasheda Ali (one of Muhammad Ali's daughters) took exception to comparisons between Floyd and her father.

"My dad stood for things," Rasheda told TMZ. "Mayweather; I don't think there's a comparison."

Freddie Roach (Pacquiao's trainer) spoke with Brin-Jonathan Butler of SB Nation and observed, "A lot of people like to hit girls. He's not the only one I ever heard of that likes to do that. I don't know why they get off doing that. Who can't beat up a girl?"

Following that, on *The Jim Rome Show*, Roach said of Mayweather, "He's not a good guy. He's not a good person. He's a bad role model for kids. That's why I get a little pissed off at him for what he does. It's just crazy, and you got these young kids looking up to him."

Then, on April 24, ESPN televised an episode of *Outside the Lines* that focused on Mayweather's physical abuse of women in a way that could not be glossed over or ignored.

Producer Simon Baumgart, reporter John Barr, and host Bob Ley put together a devastating indictment of Mayweather's conduct. At the end of the show, ESPN columnist Jemele Hill declared, "For me, the difference between Floyd Mayweather and Ray Rice is that Ray Rice, since his incident on a number of different platforms, has tried to own responsibility for what he has done. He has apologized for it in many different forums. We don't get that from Floyd Mayweather. That's why he has created more of a maelstrom of hate as opposed to other athletes who have been in that situation. For me, as a woman beyond being a journalist, that's the part that sickens me about watching him. What he has done to his victims post serving time is just as shameful as what he has done to them physically."

Excerpts from the *Outside the Lines* episode aired on *SportsCenter*, and it was rerun in its entirety on April 26. Meanwhile, Keith Olbermann (who hosts a show on ESPN2) was calling on potential viewers to boycott the pay-per-view telecast.

"The week ahead is going to be bad," Olbermann told his audience. "You and I are going to have to be adults and make some serious choices. The choices are about where we as human beings draw the line on domestic violence in this country."

Olbermann dealt first with Florida State quarterback Jameis Winston and the NFL draft. Then he turned to Mayweather-Pacquiao: "The juries have already ruled on Floyd Mayweather, five times. In a report this afternoon on *Outside the Lines*, John Barr told of Floyd Mayweather's record of criminal violence against women, which cascades down upon you like an avalanche. You will support this excuse for a man? You will help him continue to behave as if his conduct is acceptable in the 21st century? I won't. I will not give Floyd Mayweather a dime."

The boycott had no traction. Meanwhile, in Las Vegas, a media circus was unfolding.

There had been seven hundred credentialed media in Los Angeles at the March 11 kick-off press conference for Mayweather-Pacquiao with hundreds more denied entry. During fight week, thousands of media personnel descended on Las Vegas.

By contract, Mayweather Promotions controlled the credentials process. Top Rank (Pacquiao's promoter) was a largely powerless bystander.

It's difficult to coordinate a response to requests for media credentials for a mega-event. The MGM Grand has a good infrastructure in terms of physical layout and personnel. But thousands of men and women from around the world were converging on site. They all wanted food, lodging, a place to work, power lines, and access.

The credentials team for Mayweather-Pacquiao had to balance applications from longtime boxing writers who work for small media outlets and have helped keep the sport afloat for years against applications from major publications that hadn't staffed a fight since Lennox Lewis vs. Mike Tyson and were sending writers who'd never been to a fight before and might never go again.

Within that framework, there were two issues of concern.

First, many members of the media—particularly those who don't work for major media outlets—felt disrespected.

Mayweather advisor Al Haymon has made it clear over the years that he has limited use for boxing writers. Much of the boxing media has been frozen out of his Premier Boxing Champions press conferences (such as the press event announcing PBC's groundbreaking time buy with NBC).

At Mayweather-Pacquiao, many longtime boxing writers who've covered the sport for years and helped built Mayweather and Pacquiao were pushed aside.

For most big fights at the MGM Grand, the ringside press section consists of twenty rows of tables with twenty-two chairs in each row and three rows of chairs in back. That's roughly five hundred seats. There's also usually an auxiliary press section in the upper reaches of the arena.

For Mayweather-Pacquiao, although the demand for credentials was at an all-time high, the ringside press section was considerably smaller and there was no in-arena auxiliary area.

Initially, most media personnel who were credentialed for the fight were told they'd be advised by April 23 whether they'd actually be in the arena on fight night. April 23 became April 27, which then became "sometime during fight week." In the end, many journalists were advised on the morning of the fight that they would not be allowed in the arena and would have to watch the proceedings on a video screen in the media tent or broadcast center.

Later that day, many media members had to stand in line in ninety-degree heat for an hour and a half to pick up their credential.

Joe Santoliquito (president of the Boxing Writers Association of America) said afterward, "I understand the need to have as many high-level people as possible at ringside. But don't forget who helped Mayweather and Pacquiao get to where they are. The little guys—the ones who write for Internet websites and boxing magazines—helped make these guys. When Mayweather was coming up, we were the ones who wrote about him. We were the ones who wrote about Manny Pacquiao when no one else in America knew who he was. And then you have another group of people who wrote about boxing for major newspapers and left their jobs but still write about boxing from time to time. Too many writers who deserved to be at ringside were pushed out the door because the people in charge felt they didn't need them anymore."

And there was a second, more troubling issue. The Mayweather camp (which controlled the credentials process) seemed to have an us-against-them mentality toward anyone in the media who didn't toe the party line.

Journalists like Steve Kim (one of the founders of MaxBoxing and Undisputed Champions Network), Martin Rogers (*USA Today*), Hamilton Nolan (Gawker), and Daniel Roberts (Deadspin) were denied credentials of any kind, not just an arena credential. Each of them had written important articles in the past that were critical of Mayweather's mistreatment of women.

That sent a message and had a "chilling effect" on some writers who were in Las Vegas but wouldn't know until fight day whether they'd be credentialed for arena access.

Here, the treatment of CNN correspondent Rachel Nichols is instructive.

During a satellite interview conducted on September 11, 2014 (two days before Mayweather's second fight against Marcos Maidana), Nichols confronted Mayweather regarding his history of physical violence against women. Mayweather tried to deflect the issue, saying, "Everything has been allegations. Nothing has been proven." But Nichols persevered, noting, "In the incident you went to jail for, the mother of your three children did show some bruising [and] a concussion when she went to the hospital. It was your own kids who called the police, gave them a detailed description of the abuse. There has been documentation."

"Umm," Floyd responded. "Once again . . . Ahh . . . No pictures; just hearsay and allegations, and I signed a plea bargain. So once again, not true."

Nichols pressed forward.

"But the website *Deadspin* recently detailed seven separate physical assaults on five different women that resulted in arrest or citation. Are we really supposed to believe all these women are lying, including the incidents when there were witnesses like your own kids?"

"Everybody actually . . . Ummm . . . Everybody is entitled to their own opinion. You know, when it's all said and done, only God can judge me."

Rachel Nichols was in the broadcast center at the MGM Grand for Mayweather-Pacquiao during fight week. On the night before the fight, she left Las Vegas, having been given the very clear impression that she'd been denied an arena credential because of her work regarding Mayweather's history of violence against women. HBO's Michele Beadle (who has also been critical of Mayweather) left Las Vegas under the same impression.

Mayweather's publicity team later said that this was the result of a "misunderstanding" and that Nichols and Beadle would have received in-arena fight night credentials. I don't have first-hand knowledge of their situation. I do have first-hand knowledge of what happened to me.

On March 18, I submitted a credential request for Mayweather-Pacquiao in conjunction with a series of articles that I planned to write about the fight. Like many writers, I received periodic updates telling me that my credential had been approved but that I could not be guaranteed a seat in the arena on fight night.

Meanwhile, HBO submitted my name on its own credentials list in conjunction with work that I was doing on its behalf. On April 23, it was confirmed in writing to me that HBO had been advised I'd have arena access on fight night. More specifically, I was told that I'd receive "a green colored credential with the letters M, P, T printed on it . . . Green gives you access to the arena and grants you access to a permanent position on the main floor."

The following day (April 24), the *Outside the Lines* episode dealing with Mayweather's violence against women aired on ESPN. I appeared on the show and was critical of Mayweather's conduct.

On the afternoon of Thursday, April 30, when I was in Las Vegas, I was told that the Mayweather camp was unhappy with things I'd said regarding Mayweather's physical abuse of women, and that I should be careful regarding what I said in the future if I didn't want to further alienate them.

On Friday afternoon, one day before the fight, Rachel Nichols asked if I would sit with her in the broadcast center for an interview on CNN regarding Mayweather's physical abuse of women. I agreed.

On Saturday morning, I was advised that, without prior notice to me or to HBO, my arena credential had been revoked.

HBO gave me a ticket, so I was in the arena for the fight.

The issue here isn't Thomas Hauser. It's the overall interaction between Floyd Mayweather, Mayweather Promotions, and the media.

The Al Haymon Era officially began when Haymon Boxing, armed with a reported $400 million war chest in venture-capital funding, put the finishing touches on its first time buy.

On January 14, 2015, NBC Sports announced that it had entered into an agreement providing for twenty fight telecasts in 2015 (five on NBC on Saturday nights, six on NBC on Saturday afternoons, and nine in prime time on NBC Sports Network). The reaction of competing promoters and television executives left out in the cold ranged from denial to panic. Some in between these extremes noted that Haymon now had the burden of selling advertising for programming that advertisers have resisted for decades.

Haymon is trying to create a sense of inevitability. And he's spending a lot of his investors' money to do it. One of many unanswered questions is whether or not the investors will get their money back.

Haymon Boxing on NBC

Almost always, the place to be for a big fight card is in the arena. On the night of Saturday, March 7, 2015, the place to be was at home, watching on television.

Keith Thurman vs. Robert Guerrero and Adrien Broner vs. John Molina were credible, not remarkable, match-ups. But they highlighted what, in some respects, was the most significant televised fight card in decades: the rollout of Al Haymon's plan to "take over" boxing.

Writing about Don King in the September 15, 1975, issue of *Sports Illustrated*, Mark Kram declared, "Don King is boxing, the man with the show, the man with the fistful of dollars and the imagination to match."

Haymon, like King, is from Cleveland. Unlike King (who graduated from the Marion Correctional Institute after serving four years in prison for manslaughter), Haymon graduated from Harvard Business School. Right now, Haymon is the man with the show, the man with the fistful of dollars and the imagination to match. If he has his way, he might soon be boxing.

HBO was Haymon's first bank. Then it was Showtime. Now he has venture capital support that's believed to exceed $400 million. He no longer has to cajole network television executives into giving him dates. He simply buys them.

During the past few months, Haymon has orchestrated a heavy schedule of time buys on NBC, NBC Sports Network, CBS, CBS Sports Network, Spike, Bounce TV, and Telemundo. A time buy on ESPN2 is expected to be announced shortly. Haymon Boxing will also have dates on Showtime on a more traditional license-fee basis.

The time buys will allow Haymon to bypass normal media filters in delivering his boxing programming to the public. In a sense, they're similar to the paid infomercials that run on television at odd hours asking consumers to buy a five-CD set of "Golden Oldies." Only here, Haymon's investors hope to recoup their investment through the sale of advertising, pay-per-view fights, and (possibly) a subscription package and/or public stock offering.

March 7 marked the first fight card televised on NBC in prime time since Larry Holmes defended his heavyweight championship with a fifteen-round decision over Carl Williams on May 20, 1985. The match-ups weren't great. But they were as good as a lot of what boxing fans have seen lately on premium cable and far superior to the standard "free" fare.

Broner (who weighed in one pound over the 140-pound contract weight) entered the fight with a 29-and-1 record and 1 no contest. There was a time when Adrien was considered a potential superstar. Now, after being beaten down by a one-dimensional Marcos Maidana and looking lethargic in two subsequent outings, he's known in some circles primarily for X-rated videos of himself that he posts on the Internet.

Molina, who'd lost four of his last seven outings, had been brought in to make Broner look good. John's last victory was in 2013 against Jorge Pimentel (who has been on the short end in seven of his last eight fights). Molina has trouble against speed and movement. That didn't augur well for his chances against Broner.

Broner-Molina was an inauspicious way for Haymon's *Premier Boxing Champions* on NBC to start. Broner is a safety-first fighter who doesn't take chances. He's good at blowing out overmatched little guys and dancing rings around plodding opponents. But the latter has limited entertainment value, as evidenced by the fact that the crowd booed for much of the fight and also during Adrien's post-fight interview.

Broner outlanded Molina 219 to 54 according to CompuBox and outpointed him on the judges' scorecards 120–108, 120–108, 118–110. At the end of the bout, Sugar Ray Leonard (who'd been kind to Adrien in his earlier commentary) noted disapprovingly, "You have to close the show." Broner didn't.

Keith Thurman is an entertaining fighter who came into his contest against Robert Guerrero with 24 wins and 21 knockouts in 24 fights. Thurman's power hasn't had the same effect against credible opponents that it had against the men he fought earlier in his career.

Guerrero began his career as a featherweight and has worked his way up to 147 pounds. Both men can be hit. Thurman hits harder.

The most damaging blow landed by Guerrero during the fight was an accidental head butt in round three that raised an ugly bump on the left side of Thurman's forehead. Thurman avenged that affront in round nine with a right uppercut that put Guerrero on the canvas and opened an ugly gash over Robert's left eye.

Guerrero fought back with the heart of a champion. He survived and, needing a knockout to win in round twelve, he went for a knockout. But there were few moments during the course of twelve rounds when the outcome of the bout was in doubt. Thurman outlanded Guerrero 211 to 104, and outscored him 120–107, 118–108, 118–109.

But the fights were only part of the show. Virtually every aspect of *Premier Boxing Champions* on NBC was publicized and subjected to scrutiny.

Three iconic sports personalities formed the core of the announcing team.

Al Michaels implanted himself in the consciousness of sports fans at the 1976 Winter Olympics with his call of the United States men's hockey team victory over the Soviet Union ("Do you believe in miracles!"). He's one of the best in the business at calling sports, most notably Major League Baseball and NFL football. But that wasn't his role here. Instead, he hosted the telecast from a glitzy in-arena set, following a script that didn't do justice to his considerable acumen and persona.

Marv Albert handled the blow-by-blow chores. Like Michaels, Albert is sportscasting royalty. His resume begins with the NBA and covers every major sport, including boxing. Marv seemed a bit rusty on Saturday night, not having fully updated his encyclopedic knowledge with regard to the minutiae of boxing.

Ray Leonard, in addition to being one of the greatest fighters ever, is articulate and smooth behind a microphone. But he and Albert haven't fully jelled yet.

And additional personages supplemented the telecast.

B. J. Flores is engaging but was one voice too many in the booth.

Kenny Rice did little but repeat official pre-scripted story lines.

Laila Ali was there to provide a female presence and a bit of Ali magic. But for the most part, she did little more than state the obvious. After the first round of Broner-Molina (in which Molina landed one punch), Laila informed viewers that Molina's corner was "not happy with his connectivity in that round."

Referee Steve Smoger provided an occasional useful rules interpretation.

It would have been appropriate to have some editorial reference— perhaps by Al Michaels—regarding Al Haymon's master plan. That was an obvious and calculated omission.

Haymon Boxing poured an enormous amount of money into production of the telecast. There was a huge floor set augmented by giant video screens. Twenty-seven cameras caught the action from every possible angle under enhanced lighting.

The telecast tried for a UFC-WWE feel. Academy Award–winner Hans Zimmer wrote the signature music. *The Lion King, Gladiator,* and *The Dark Night Trilogy* are among Zimmer's screen-score credits. If the *Premier Boxing Champions* music sounded evocative of *The Contender,* it's because he wrote that music too.

One of the production innovations was not effective. NBC had trumpeted the use of a 360-degree over-the-ring video rig with thirty-six still cameras to offer a moving panoramic view of the action. But when pieced together, the photos had the feel of a not-very-good video game from the 1980s.

In a nod to *The Contender,* the fighters walked to the ring alone. That seemed unnecessarily contrived. A fighter's corner men should take that walk with him.

There were no round-card girls and no visible ring announcer. If *Premier Boxing Champions* is going to continue using a disembodied voice to impart information to fans, the voice should be more authoritative than the one heard on Saturday night.

I love the fact that Haymon Boxing eliminated the mob that pours into the ring before and after fights. There were no people in the ring shouting, "You da man." No sanctioning body officials shamelessly draping T-shirts and phony belts over the combatants. No promoters, managers, commissioners, or mistresses jockeying for position in front of the camera.

Thank you, Al Haymon. I hope every network that televises boxing follows your lead on that one.

Now let's return to numbers; only this time, the numbers revolve around dollars, not punches.

Haymon Boxing isn't doing business as usual, but it is a business. The idea is to make money.

It was expected that advertising sales would be weak for the first NBC fight card, and they were. The promotion had difficulty selling ad time.

There were a handful of commercials for Nissan, Mazda, Lincoln, McDonald's, and Verizon-Fios, as well as some Corona spots. But the Corona commercials were part of a broader sponsorship deal that included logo placement on the ring canvas. Many of the commercials that aired in New York (where this writer watched the telecast) were local rather than national and were for fringe enterprises. In other slots where ideally there would have been commercials, viewers saw dozens of promos for NBC programming, *PBC* fighters, and future *PBC* shows.

Ad sales are dictated in large measure by ratings. There were full-page ads for the March 7 telecast in the *New York Times*, *Sports Illustrated*, and other publications. NBC ran promotional spots in advance of the show.

Interim ratings released on Monday indicate that the NBC telecast averaged 3,400,000 viewers. That trailed two *CSI* reruns and an episode of *48 Hours* on CBS as well as a rerun of *20/20* and *In An Instant* on ABC. For purposes of further comparison, NBC as a network averaged 4,800,000 viewers on Saturday nights in 2014.

Haymon Boxing expects to lose money on many of its early fight cards. March 7 was considered a loss leader, and it lost. Factoring in undercard costs, the fighters' purses totaled roughly $4 million. There were large production and promotional expenses.

Haymon is said to be looking at an initial term of three-to-four years before evaluating the overall success of his effort. He knows that hardcore boxing fans will watch *Premier Boxing Champions* in each of its incarnations. But his target audience isn't boxing junkies. It's the general sports fan that he needs and covets. That's why Al Michaels and Marv Albert are part of the NBC package.

There will be more bells and whistles as *Premier Boxing Champions* unfolds. Viewers have been told to expect that, in some jurisdictions, referees will wear a tiny camera mounted on a headband. There's also talk of a dubious technology that might accurately estimate the speed of punches but is less likely to accurately estimate their force.

All of that is window dressing. At the end of the day, it's about the fights. It would have been nice if the fights on March 7 had been more entertaining. Neither Thurman nor Broner did much to implant himself in the consciousness of the general sports public. Next time out, it would be great to see Thurman vs. Broner; not Thurman and Broner vs. two more "B-side" opponents.

Boxing fans and Haymon's investors have different priorities. Haymon's investors want to make money. Boxing fans want to see good fights. These goals aren't necessarily irreconcilable. Ideally, they will coincide.

If Haymon succeeds in pushing boxing back into the consciousness of mainstream sports fans, it will be good for Haymon and good for boxing. Beyond that, one has to ask, will he use the power of his purse to honor the essence and best traditions of the sport? Will he make quality fights available to the public free of charge on a regular basis? Will he make a sincere effort to eliminate the use of illegal performance-enhancing drugs from boxing? Or will he promote mismatches, find creative new ways to separate fans from their dollars, corrupt the sport's already-inadequate drug-testing protocols, play an illegal shell game with dollars, and substitute one group of bogus belt holders for another?

Al Haymon interviews are scarcer than hen's teeth. But twenty years ago, he sat for a Q&A with *Ebony Men* (an offshoot of *Ebony* magazine).

In that interview, Haymon spoke of his role as a music promoter and declared, "Promoters are viewed as shady characters. I had the opportunity to represent something fresh and new to the artists. I don't imagine a lot of information is being provided about this industry because it's not a conventional industry for people of higher education to pursue. Black people, if they knew how much money was in it and how much opportunity there was and how fertile the ground was and how successful and influential one could become by being in it, then perhaps more would be in it. The entertainment industry, and professional sports particularly, represent an area where we are basically the natural resource. When you have an industry that offers high returns, you're going to have high risk. We have to be willing to take those risks because, believe me, the opportunities are there. I saw the potential. I saw, if done right, one could make a lot of money and control a good deal of commerce and have a business."

Sound familiar?

Six days after Haymon Boxing launched Premier Boxing Champions *on NBC, its time-buy telecasts on Spike began.*

Haymon Boxing on Spike

The rollout of *Premier Boxing Champions* continued on March 13, 2015, with Haymon Boxing's inaugural show on Spike.

Let's look first at the fights, which were contested at Citizens Business Bank Arena in Ontario, California.

Shawn Porter (24-1-1, 15 KOs) was coming off a majority-decision loss to Kell Brook, but had impressive victories over Paulie Malignaggi and Devon Alexander in his two fights immediately preceding that defeat. Roberto Garcia was the intended "B-side" opponent. But Garcia failed to appear at the weigh-in and was replaced by Erick Bone of Ecuador. To make Bone's task more difficult, he was called upon to take a long flight to California one day before the bout. Porter stopped him at 2:30 of round five in a lackluster fight.

Then, despite the fact that it was Friday the 13th, *Premier Boxing Champions* had a stroke of luck. Because Porter-Bone ended early, Chris Arreola vs. Curtis Harper was inserted in the telecast as a swing bout.

Arreola entered the ring weighing 262 pounds, 23 more than for his last fight. Harper was a blubbery 265. The assumption was that Curtis would get whacked out early. He's a club fighter who was taken the distance by Jamal Woods (5 wins in 21 fights) in his last outing, a six-round bout in Arkansas. That assumption was further bolstered in round one when Harper was decked by a right hand and rose on wobbly legs, looking like 265 pounds of Jell-O.

But Arreola was woefully out of shape. And Harper had the mindset, if not the skills, of a good fighter. The bout devolved into two huge guys staggering each other back and forth in what resembled a barroom brawl, highlighted by a POP-CRASH-POW seventh round. Arreola won a 76–75, 77–74, 78–73 decision, the latter score being too kind to Chris. It did not speak well for his showing that he was pushed to the limit by a nomadic club fighter. But it was highly entertaining television.

Then came the main event: Andre Berto (29-3, 22 KOs) vs. Josesito Lopez (33-6, 19 KOs).

Berto is Exhibit A for how Al Haymon was allowed to distort the decision-making process at HBO in an earlier era. Andre was a two-time national Golden Gloves champion, a bronze medalist at the 2003 World Amateur Championships, and a 2004 Olympian (representing Haiti as a consequence of his father's dual citizenship). He turned pro in 2004, and was ESPN's 2006 "prospect of the year." Thereafter, Berto was on HBO too many times against soft opponents for inflated license fees with less-than-enthusiastic viewer response. No longer a "star of the future," he entered the ring on March 13 having won just two fights since 2010.

Lopez is a game fighter who has trouble getting by world-class opposition. He beats the guys he should beat and loses to the fighters that he's expected to lose to. His marketability was built on a 2012 outing against Victor Ortiz in which Ortiz (ahead on points) retired after nine rounds because of a broken jaw. In Josesito's next two fights, he was knocked out by Canelo Alvarez and Marcos Maidana.

Berto-Lopez was a fast-paced spirited fight. Lopez was ahead on the scorecards in round six, when Andre landed a sharp right hand that staggered Josesito. Then Berto hit him again, and Lopez went down. He rose, was knocked down for the second time, and referee Raul Caiz Jr stopped the fight.

Insofar as the production of *Premier Boxing Champions* on Spike is concerned, the most readily apparent difference from *PBC*'s fights on NBC is the announcing team.

Dana Jacobson, a former ESPN Sports Center anchor who has hosted a variety of sports radio and television shows, opened the Spike telecast. Later in the evening, she was paired with Thomas Hearns. Hearns was a great fighter. He's not a great commentator.

Scott Hanson, known primarily for his work as an NFL Network host, was the blow-by-blow announcer. Jimmy Smith (a veteran of Spike's Bellator MMA telecasts) and Antonio Tarver (an expert analyst for Showtime Boxing before he tested positive for illegal performance-enhancing drugs) served as analysts. Nigel Collins had an off-camera role, unofficially scoring the fights.

Smith made the most credible commentating contributions to the telecast. When Hanson told viewers that Bone was in shape to fight

Porter because he'd been working in the gym, Smith correctly noted, "There's no such thing as fighting shape if you're not getting ready for a fight." Smith also picked up nicely on an apparent ankle injury suffered by Bone just before he was stopped by Porter. There should have been a follow-up on Bone's medical condition later in the telecast but wasn't.

Overall, the announcing team devoted too much energy trying to sell the concept of Premier Boxing Champions. Phrases like "a new era in boxing" and "a new day for boxing" were repeated more than necessary. If the fights are good, viewers will figure it out. If the fights are bad, viewers will figure that out too.

And a few more observations . . .

The fighters' ring walk music written by Hans Zimmer isn't effective. I know it's branding for PBC. But it takes away from the individuality of the fighters and has the homogeneous feel of a television game show. Ditto for the staged visuals of the combatants walking to the ring. That kind of entrance works for Wladimir Klitschko because he's Wladimir Klitschko. None of the fighters we've seen so far on *Premier Boxing Champions* has a legitimate claim to being King of the World.

As with the March 7 NBC telecast, the ring announcer and round-card girls were out of sight on Spike. Once again, there was no mob in the ring before and after each fight. The 360-degree overhead ring camera was used less often on Spike than on the NBC telecast. In this instance, less is better. As was the case on March 7, the ring ropes were black instead of red, white, and blue. That effectively highlighted the fighters.

PBC also introduced a new toy on the Spike telecast: a miniature camera installed on a headband worn by referee Jack Reiss during the first fight of the night. But contrary to its billing, the "ref cam" didn't show viewers "what the referee sees" because it follows the referee's forehead, not the referee's eyes.

Where broader business issues are concerned; the past week has seen a flurry of press releases and comments by interested parties on all sides regarding PBC's March 7 NBC telecast. Many of these statements have been evocative of the spin doctoring that follows a presidential debate.

The key talking points regarding the NBC telecast have revolved around ratings (which will dictate how much advertising is sold in the future—which, in turn, will be crucial to the success or failure of Haymon Boxing).

Team Haymon sent out a press release that declared, "The PBC on NBC telecast averaged 3.4 million viewers, ranking as the most-watched professional boxing broadcast in 17 years ('Oscar De La Hoya's Fight Night' on FOX, 5.9 million, March 23, 1998)."

This implied to the uninitiated that De La Hoya fought on March 23, 1998. He didn't. It was a Top Rank show, and the main event was Yory Boy Campas versus Anthony Stephens. Oscar (who was then with Top Rank) lent his name to the promotion.

Also, on October 15, 2005, NBC televised a live fight card headlined by Sergio Mora vs. Peter Manfredo that drew 8 million viewers. But Team Haymon and NBC say that doesn't count because the telecast was the finale of a TV reality show.

Let's put these numbers in perspective.

On May 11, 1977, Ken Norton fought Duane Bobick on NBC on a Wednesday evening in prime time. That fight earned a 42 percent audience share and was watched by 48,000,000 people.

Obviously, those were different times. So let's leave it at this for the moment. The advertisers will sort out the ratings. Either the audience for *PBC* will grow or it won't. Boxing fans should hope that it does. But significant growth won't be easy to accomplish.

The Haymon Boxing juggernaut continued with an April 4, 2015, time buy on CBS.

Haymon Boxing on CBS

The unveiling of Al Haymon's *Premier Boxing Champions* continued on Saturday afternoon, April 4, 2015, with a two-hour presentation on CBS.

Haymon has pursued ring hegemony so aggressively as of late that one half-expects to go online and read that he has signed Joe Louis and Rocky Marciano. On Saturday, boxing fans settled for Adonis Stevenson and Artur Bieterbiev.

Beterbiev is a two-time Olympian and 2009 World Amateur champion from Russia, who lives and fights out of Montreal. He turned pro in 2013, was placed on a fast track, and had compiled a 7-and-0 record with 7 knockouts. His opponent—36-year-old Gabriel Campillo (25-6, 12 KOs, 3 KOs by)—had four wins in his last eight bouts and was regarded as a measuring stick for a potential star.

From the opening bell, Campillo had all the earmarks of a shot fighter (which is why he was chosen as Bieterbiev's opponent). His balance was poor. His timing was off. His reflexes were slow. He offered virtually no resistance. Bieterbiev decked him in the opening minute of round one (the tenth time in Gabriel's career that he'd been on the canvas) and ended matters convincingly at the 2:22 mark of round four (the eleventh time in Gabriel's career that he'd been on the canvas).

Stevenson, age thirty-seven, came into ring with a 25-and-1 record and 21 knockouts. Two years ago, he made a splash with a first-round knockout of Chad Dawson to claim the WBC 175-pound crown. That looks less impressive now than it did then, given the fact that Dawson has 1 win, 3 losses, and 2 "KO's by" over the past three years. Stevenson also looked good in stopping Tavoris Cloud in seven rounds. But Cloud is 0-and-3 over the same time period.

Sakio Bika (Stevenson's opponent) entered the ring with 32-6-3 (21 KOs) record. Bika, who is winless since 2013, had never fought above

168 pounds, and has never beaten a world-class fighter. Worse, Sakio
initially weighed in for the Stevenson fight eight-tenths of a pound over
the 175-pound limit. Given the fact that he'd never fought above 168
pounds before, that suggested his training regimen had been less than
diligent.

Stevenson-Bika was wasn't much of a fight. Adonis dropped his
opponent twice en route to a unanimous twelve round decision.

Some observations on the telecast . . .

The CBS commentating team consisted of Brent Stover, Kevin
Harlan, Paulie Malignaggi, and Virgil Hunter.

Stover, who's best known as a studio host for CBS Sports Network,
was the host and also handled post-fight interviews. During the intro, he
told viewers that Bika "is annoying to fight because he won't go away
quietly." After Stevenson-Bika, Brent declared, "It was an absolutely epic
fight" (which was an absolutely silly overstatement).

Harlan (a play-by-play veteran, who has been behind the microphone for NFL, NBA, and NCAA basketball telecasts) was a disappointment. During the fights, he offered a lot of stats and pre-scripted lines.
But his blow-by-blow call was shaky, and he didn't seem to understand
the difference between orthodox and southpaw fighters (for example,
telling the world "another shot with the left hook" when Stevenson
landed straight lefts).

Eventually, Harlan was reduced to commentary like, "Oh! He got hit
with a left!" After a while, that simply became "Oh!"

Malignaggi is a solid commentator, who has proven his value in the
past.

Hunter was excellent. His insights were solid and he communicated
them well, although he needed to be miked differently. That was part of
a larger audio problem. The sound kept cutting in and out during the
telecast.

Stevenson and Bika both wore gold trunks in the main event, which
can be confusing to viewers when a telecast changes camera angles.

Also, Stevenson was referred to as *the* light-heavyweight champion
of the world throughout the telecast. That was a disservice to Sergey
Kovalev.

The lack of paid advertising was a more troubling issue in terms of
the overall landscape. In the New York market (where I watched the

telecast), there was roughly two minutes (almost all of which was local) over the course of two hours. That was supplemented by twenty-two *Premier Boxing Champions* promotional spots and ten CBS promos. The *PBC* spots were repeated again and again to the point of being ineffective because of boredom.

After the inaugural *Premier Boxing Champions* telecasts on NBC and Spike, there was a lot of spin-doctoring by pro- and anti-Haymon forces with regard to the ratings. The fact that virtually no advertisers were onboard for the CBS telecast is a sign that advertisers didn't think the NBC and Spike ratings were particularly good.

Equally important, Al Haymon has a well-deserved reputation for putting his favored fighters in soft. To be entertaining over the long haul, boxing needs competitive fights.

Stevenson was a 12-to-1 betting favorite over Bika. Beterbiev was favored over Campillo by 25-to-1. The favorites are now 7 and 0 on Haymon's NBC, Spike, and CBS telecasts. That got old on premium cable a long time ago. And it will get old here fast.

The May 2, 2015, fight between Floyd Mayweather and Manny Pacquiao was an important piece of the Al Haymon puzzle.

Mayweather–Pacquiao:
How Big a Winner Was Al Haymon?

By the start of 2015, it appeared that Al Haymon, not HBO or Showtime, was the industry leader in boxing. A recent article by Bill King in *Sports Business Journal* confirmed that Haymon Boxing will have hundreds of millions of dollars in investment capitol to support an audacious takeover plan.

Mayweather–Pacquiao brought boxing front and center in the public consciousness. Haymon stayed largely behind the scenes during fight week, surfacing most notably as an active participant at a Friday rules meeting when the fighters' gloves were discussed with representatives of the Nevada State Athletic Commission. But his presence was felt throughout the promotion.

Mayweather–Pacquiao happened because Mayweather and Haymon wanted it to happen; not because Mayweather and Pacquiao crossed paths at a Miami Heat basketball game. CBS Corporation CEO Les Moonves might have thought he was calling the shots, but he wasn't. Haymon was.

Haymon has leveraged Mayweather brilliantly. But the success of Haymon Boxing is not inextricably tied to Mayweather. Haymon is building for a future after Floyd and has kept his company free of obligations to him. There was no Premier Boxing Champions branding during Mayweather–Pacquiao fight week. But Haymon was counting on the fight to give his vision a boost.

Mayweather could win or lose to Pacquiao. Haymon, it was thought, could only win. The key question was how Haymon would leverage the fight to increase his power. In that regard, he appears to have been successful in several ways:

(1) Some powerful people and institutions made a lot of money off Mayweather–Pacquiao and feel beholden to Haymon. The MGM Grand

is already the venue of choice for *Premier Boxing Champions* fights that are contested in Las Vegas. It's possible that the good feelings the MGM Grand has for Haymon as a consequence of Mayweather-Pacquiao will spill over into contract negotiations for PBC fights (if they haven't already). Showtime is also likely to look kindly upon Haymon when buying future fights.

(2) Haymon was entitled by contract to thousands of tickets for Mayweather-Pacquiao. Presumably, he made a lot of money selling tickets at a significant mark-up; money that he might not have been required to share with Haymon Boxing investors.

(3) Haymon had both tickets and rooms at the MGM Grand that he could give to Haymon Boxing investors, *Premier Boxing Champions* sponsors, executives at networks he's doing business with, his fighters, and other allies. That sort of generosity strengthens relationships.

And perhaps most important—

(4) Haymon can tell his investors, "We're losing millions of dollars now. But stay the course and there will be paydays amounting to hundreds of millions of dollars for us in the future."

Mayweather-Pacquiao will gross close to $500 million. That will be divided among many parties, including roughly $150 million to DIRECTV and the cable-system operators that distributed the fight to the public. But after the pie is carved up and everyone else takes their share, a staggering amount of money will be left for the fighters and their respective teams.

Putting numbers in perspective; in 2011, NBC Sports negotiated a ten-year contract with the National Hockey League to televise NHL regular season and playoff games. The price-tag was $2 billion. Mayweather-Pacquiao, in one night, grossed almost 25 percent of that amount.

But there was a potential downside for Haymon in the way Mayweather-Pacquiao played out. The fight soured a lot of people on boxing—fans who felt suckered after buying the pay-per-view telecast and people who became aware that boxing's poster boy has a penchant for physically abusing women. That might make it more difficult for Haymon to attract advertisers for his *Premier Boxing Champions* offerings.

One of the things that drove boxing off broadcast television in the 1980s was the fact that advertisers didn't want to be associated in the public mind with Don King and Mike Tyson. How many advertisers will want their product to be identified with price-gouging for an inferior product and a leading man with a long police record for violence against women?

Haymon is well endowed to face the future. He has a huge financial war chest, the largest stable of professional boxers assembled in boxing's modern era, and contracts for time buys with multiple television networks. But a counter-assault against him is underway.

On April 28, 2015, the Association of Boxing Commissions sent a letter to the United States Department of Justice asking that the attorney general investigate Haymon's conduct and enforce the Muhammad Ali Boxing Reform Act, which, the ABC says, Haymon is violating.

It's also possible that one or more state athletic commissions will demand that Haymon or one of the companies he controls be licensed as a promoter.

And on May 5, Golden Boy and Bernard Hopkins filed suit in the United States District Court for the Central District of California against Haymon, various companies that Haymon controls, Waddell & Reed (Haymon's primary source of funding), and Ryan Caldwell (a Waddell & Reed fund manager). The lawsuit alleges violations of the Muhammad Ali Boxing Reform Act, the Sherman [Anti-Trust] Act, and other causes of action.

More government inquiries and more litigation may follow. Haymon will have a unified defense and the best lawyers that money can buy. He has been planning for this eventuality for a long time. He might be most vulnerable legally for predicate acts committed long ago when he was building the foundation for his current empire. A faulty foundation stone at the base of a building is more potentially damaging than a faulty brick near the top.

There's also an issue as to whether the plethora of fights currently on television will build interest in boxing among casual sports fans. Haymon's business plan seems to rest on the hope that this will be the case. But with multiple fight cards on television week after week, fans are likely to become more discerning about what they watch. Oversaturation of the market could lead to a decline in ratings that would make it even harder to sell advertising in the future than it is now.

After all; boxing isn't like football, where there seems to be an inexhaustible demand for content.

Haymon has been enormously successful in the music business. But in boxing, it doesn't matter what a person has done before. He has to prove himself all over again. Don King did it. The people behind *The Contender* couldn't. Shawn Carter (aka Jay Z) and Curtis Jackson (aka 50 Cent) haven't been able to so far.

So a cautionary tale . . .

According to the Bible, there was once a wicked man named Haman (pronounced "Haymon") who "set his seat above all the princes that were with him. And all the king's servants bowed and reverenced Haman" (Esther 3:1-2).

But let's not forget what eventually happened. In the end, "Haman was hung on a gallows that were fifty cubits [74 feet] high" (Esther 7:9-10). And now, each year at Purim, people eat pastries called hamantasch to commemorate the occasion.

In 2008, I wrote in opposition to West Point's alternative service option that
allowed graduating cadets to play professional ball rather than fulfilling their
military commitment in the same manner as their classmates. In 2015, I stood
with West Point on the issue of its compulsory boxing program.

The Service Academies and Boxing

The United States Military Academy at West Point, the United States Naval Academy at Annapolis, and the United States Air Force Academy in Colorado Springs have boxing courses that are required for the young men who attend the academies. At Annapolis, women are required to participate in boxing classes too.

On September 30, 2015, the *New York Times* ran a front-page article that focused on the concussions suffered in West Point's boxing program. The thrust of the article was that these programs constitute a barbaric tradition that should end.

Boxing was installed as a required course at the United States Military Academy in 1905 at the suggestion of President Theodore Roosevelt. At West Point today, all plebes (first-year cadets) take a boxing class consisting of nineteen 45-minute "lessons" that prepare them for three "test" bouts.

Owing largely to similar requirements at Annapolis and Colorado Springs, the three service academies have won twenty-eight of the past thirty-three National Collegiate Boxing Association championships.

Boxing is not required for students who enroll in the Reserve Officer Training Core at other colleges, nor is it part of the basic training for regular military enlistees.

In its article, the *Times* noted that there have been ninety-seven documented concussions from boxing at West Point during the past three academic years. That equates to roughly 3 percent of all male plebes. The Air Force Academy has reported seventy-two concussions during that time frame and the Naval Academy twenty-nine.

The *Times* article further stated, "Minor concussions become major disruptions to cadets' lives because West Point medical protocols require any cadet with a concussion to rest for at least two days, skipping all academic work, sports, and military training."

And it quoted Brenda Sue Fulton (a West Point graduate who is chairwoman of West Point's civilian advisory committee), who said, "There is an argument that whatever benefit a cadet gains from boxing, the cost of missing studies, of missing training, of becoming more vulnerable to injury down range, are detrimental to military readiness. It's possible, by trying to prepare our cadets, we are making them less ready."

Plebes who are forced to drop out of the cadet boxing course due to a concussion are required to complete the course the following year.

Are the required boxing courses a good idea?

Let's start with the understanding that service-academy training is rigorous in other ways as well. The *Times* acknowledged that boxing is the cause of only 20 percent of the concussions suffered by West Point cadets and a quarter of the concussions suffered at Annapolis and Colorado Springs.

Moreover, the ultimate purpose of the boxing classes isn't to teach boxing skills. It's to instill mental toughness and teach disciplined aggression, to show young men how to face their fears and prepare cadets for that moment down the road in military combat when they have only themselves to rely on.

Cadets graduate from the United States Military Academy as second lieutenants. Many of them are soon in the field, leading other soldiers in combat. The curriculum at West Point is designed to put them under pressure. Each student is tested in and out of class in multiple ways every day.

Boyd Melson graduated from West Point in 2003. After fulfilling his service commitment, he turned to professional boxing and has compiled a 15-1-1 record as of this writing.

"When you're in combat," Melson told me last year, "it's not about American freedom at that particular moment in time. It's about you and your buddies surviving. In boxing, you're trying to hurt someone to win, and that person is trying to hurt you. You learn to think and make decisions under stress. You train your mind to not give up before your body does. Military combat is far more serious than boxing, but some of the demands are the same."

Then Melson talked about a fight he had against Donald Ward on February 12, 2014, at Roseland Ballroom in New York. In round three, Boyd injured his brachial plexus (a network of nerve fibers running from the spine through his neck into his right arm).

"The pain was excruciating," Melson recalled. "I couldn't control my arm. I couldn't feel my fingers in my glove. I thought I was having a stroke. My first thought was, 'I don't know what's happening to my body. I'm scared. I have to quit.' I started to turn to take a knee. Then I thought about my training at West Point. To survive in combat and in the ring, you slow time down around you when, in reality, real time is taking place. You gut it out and do whatever you have to do to survive. That's what I did that night."

From that point on, Melson was a wounded soldier. But he survived and won a majority decision.

"Of all my fights, that's the one that's the most meaningful to me," Melson concluded. "It confirmed what I've always believed about myself; that I can overcome the worst kind of adversity and do what I have to do to prevail. The idea of quitting kept trying to creep into my head. But I was able to block out worrying about my injury and stay in the moment when I couldn't move my arm and didn't know what had happened to me and suppress the fear and do what I had to do to win. Boxing is the ultimate experience for testing physical ability and intelligence under threat of the greatest adverse consequences possible short of death."

Mike Tyson once said, "Everyone has a plan until they get hit."

In combat, every commanding officer has a plan until his troops are attacked. Then things can change.

West Point isn't Princeton. The military isn't Wall Street. The service academies have a mission. They're training young men and women to be elite soldiers. Combat isn't a video game. It's real.

The idea of being punched in the face is frightening. And if it has happened before with adverse consequences, the idea of it happening again is even more frightening. But a bloody nose can prepare a soldier for far more serious battlefield wounds. And having learned how to face the fear of physical harm, soldiers are better equipped to face whatever else might come their way.

Three days after this article was posted online, the New York State Athletic Commission advised its inspectors that they would no longer be allowed to judge fights regardless of the site.

Inspectors Shouldn't Judge

On Saturday, October 17, 2015, Lamont Peterson fought Felix Diaz in the main event of a *Premier Boxing Champions* card televised by NBC. The fight was closely contested. Peterson was widely regarded as the "house fighter."

Jake Donovan summed up the proceedings as follows for Boxing Scene.com: "Lamont Peterson managed a disputed majority decision win over previously unbeaten Felix Diaz in their welterweight headliner Saturday afternoon in Fairfax, Virginia. An even score of 114–114 was overruled by cards of 117–111 and 116–112 in favor of Peterson, scores that reeked of hometown favoritism for the former ex-champion fighting less than 45 minutes from his Washington D.C. backyard."

The NBC commentating team that called the fight openly questioned how a judge could arrive at a 117–111 scorecard.

The judge with the 117–111 scorecard in favor of Peterson was Dorothea Perry. What makes this particularly problematic is that Ms. Perry is also an inspector for the New York State Athletic Commission.

Inspectors are the eyes and ears of the governing state athletic commission in the dressing room and at ringside on fight night. The job involves direct contact with fighters and the members of each fighter's team.

Inspectors make mistakes from time to time. But their impartiality is rarely, if ever, questioned. The assumption is that they are scrupulously evenhanded. They don't make judgments. They simply follow the rules, observe what's going on, and report any possible irregularity to the chief inspector and commissioners.

By contrast, the impartiality of judges is often questioned. Indeed, in many states, there's a process in place by which a fighter's camp can object to the assignment of a particular judge.

There's no normal procedure in place to object to the assignment of a given inspector to a fighter's dressing room. In many jurisdictions, inspectors aren't even matched with fighters until an hour or two before the fight.

Also, inspectors are paid a set fee by the governing state athletic commission. Technically, in many jurisdictions, judges are also paid by the commission. But in reality, the money to pay judges comes from the promoter and the amount that judges are paid varies widely depending on the magnitude of the fight.

Several years ago, trainer and TV commentator Teddy Atlas told Robert Ecksel of Boxing.com, "You go into a certain place the night before a big fight. You go into a restaurant. The head of the organization and all the officials, all the judges, all the referees; they're all having a five-thousand-dollar dinner. Guess who's paying for it? The promoter. Would the Steinbrenners have a deal like that with the head of the umpiring organization before the World Series? They couldn't because there's someone there to make sure that doesn't happen. But it happens in my sport. And what else do you think happens besides picking up the tab and having wine and lobster and caviar and steak and all the best of everything? You don't think those judges know who has to win? And you don't think some of those guys come over and say, 'Can I get my room upgraded to a suite?' 'Yeah, sure. Sure, Mr. Referee. Sure, Mr. Judge. Yes, okay, no problem.' 'Oh, by the way, can I also get my room extended for an extra two days? My girlfriend is coming in and she wants to stay for an extra two days.' 'Yeah, no problem.' 'Oh, by the way, my wife decided she's going to fly in. Can I get two plane tickets instead of one?' 'Sure.' You don't think that's happening? I'll think for you. It is. That is corruption. I don't even think I'm going to call them bad decisions anymore. I think I'm just going to call them what they are: fixed fights. I'm going to say 'fixed fight, fixed fight,' because that's what they are."

What Atlas neglected to mention is that judges have been paid as much as $20,000 to judge a single fight.

That brings us to the matter of Dorothea Perry.

According to Boxrec.com, Ms. Perry has judged twenty-eight professional fights. The first twenty-two were in Delaware. The last six have been in Virginia.

Peterson-Diaz was Ms. Perry's first high-profile judging assignment. She was also a judge in the other featured TV fight that afternoon: Prichard Colon vs. Terrel Williams. The scoring of that fight has been largely ignored in the aftermath of the tragic injury suffered by Colon. But it's worth noting that, like Peterson, Colon was perceived as the "house fighter." When the bout was stopped at the end of nine rounds, the other two judges had Williams ahead. Ms. Perry's scorecard favored Colon.

It's not necessary for purposes of this discussion to decide that Ms. Perry's scorecard in Peterson-Diaz was off base (although that seems to have been the case). Nor should one impute any inappropriate intent. The issue here is whether or not an inspector should judge fights.

The New York State Athletic Commission (which oversees Ms. Perry's performance as an inspector) has a conflicts of interest policy that prohibits its inspectors from judging fights in New York. Indeed, if an NYSAC inspector wants to be a ring judge in New York, the inspector must resign his or her position and wait two years before applying to become a judge.

Some NYSAC inspectors have followed this ethical code to the letter. Former boxer Tyrone Jackson gave up his position as an inspector and is now waiting out the two-year period. Similarly, Ernie Rodriguez left inspecting and is hoping to referee professional fights in the future.

Ms. Perry is exploiting what appears to be a loophole in the NYSAC policy. While continuing to work as a New York State Athletic Commission inspector, she is judging fights out of state.

When Melvina Lathan was first named a commissioner in New York, she had hoped to continue judging in other jurisdictions. She was told by the powers that be in New York that she could not.

Inspectors in New York aren't allowed to work directly for sanctioning organizations. An NYSAC inspector was recently dismissed because he accepted a T-shirt from a fighter in the dressing room on fight night.

A commission inspector shouldn't be allowed to judge fights.

Giving an inspector the perks of a judging assignment (including the possibility of a large paycheck and travel to a desirable out-of-town location) has the potential to influence that inspector's performance in the dressing room. An inspector might be reluctant to stand up to a fighter's camp and might accede to their wishes in the hope of getting a lucrative future judging assignment. An inspector with visions of a judge's seat at a big fight is less likely to tell a fighter, "We've already tested your urine. You can't drink that vitamin shake."

This conflict of interest is the same whether the inspector hopes to judge fights in New York or elsewhere.

And it's an inadequate response for the New York State Athletic Commission to say, "We won't assign Ms. Perry to work fights where an advisor, manager, or promoter from a fight she judged out of state is involved." In boxing today, most promoters, managers, networks, and fighters are at least tangentially connected by common interest or antipathy.

Greg Sirb is executive director of the Pennsylvania State Athletic Commission and one of the most knowledgeable boxing regulators in the country. Recently, Sirb was asked about the propriety of an inspector in one jurisdiction serving as a ring judge in another.

"To me, it's a no brainer," Sirb answered. "There's no way it should be allowed. It's a conflict of interest, plain and simple. Suppose a fighter or manager or promoter feels that a bad decision has gone against them. And the next month, they're stuck with the same inspector. Or an inspector does, or doesn't, order a fighter to rewrap in the dressing room. And sometime in the future, that inspector gets a high-profile judging assignment where the same promoter is involved. I don't care how capable or honest the inspector is. It's just plain wrong."

What doesn't the New York State Athletic Commission understand about that?

If Dorothea Perry wants to continue working as a ring judge, she should resign as an NYSAC inspector now and work as a judge in Virginia, Delaware, and any other jurisdiction that licenses her services. Then, after two years, she can apply for a judge's license in New York, and the NYSAC can decide if her judging meets its standards.

Meanwhile, the New York State Athletic Commission should rethink its policy of allowing its inspectors to judge fights. As things stand now, the commission is looking for trouble.

Despite the timeless nature of the competition, boxing remains a work in progress.

The Drawbreaker Round

Ties might play well in fashion circles. But for the most part, they're unwelcome in sports. Hence, the oft repeated maxim: "A tie is like kissing your sister."

Virtually all sports have a tie-breaker formula. An extra period, a play-off, whatever. Boxing has traditionally accepted draws on a fighter's record, but that might be changing.

The recent Boxcino tournament on ESPN2 called for a "drawbreaker" round in the event that a bout would otherwise have been declared a draw on the judges' scorecards. The first two fights in the heavyweight Boxcino tournament that aired on February 20, 2015, went to overtime.

The "drawbreaker" round isn't new in boxing. On April 15, 1977, Don Elbaum promoted a fight at Dickinson High School in Jersey City between Bruce Curry and Rafael Rodriguez. The contracts provided that, if the judges' scorecards were even after ten rounds, there would be an eleventh stanza. That's what happened, and Curry won it.

Russell Peltz promoted two championship fights for vacant titles in the 1980s that ended with a drawbreaker round. On November 6, 1987, Doug DeWitt outpointed Tony Thornton over thirteen rounds in a USBA title bout. On October 18, 1988, Sanderline Williams won a thirteenth-round drawbreaker against Ronnie Essett in a NABF title contest.

Top Rank also employed an extra-round drawbreaker for several tournament fights during the early years of *Top Rank Boxing* on ESPN.

"I love it," says Elbaum. "I think it should be done for all title fights, all tournament fights, and all main events."

Should it?

It's important to start with the understanding that rules in sports aren't religious scriptures. They're revised all the time to make action more exiting, accommodate television, and improve safety standards. Once, there was no shot clock in basketball and no designated hitter in baseball. Championship fights were fifteen rounds.

Two issues head the list of concerns where drawbreaker rounds in boxing are concerned. The first is whether they endanger the health and safety of fighters.

Michael Schwartz is chief ringside physician and chairman of the medical advisory board for Foxwoods Resort Casino, Mohegan Sun Casino, and the Connecticut State Athletic Commission.

"I don't have a problem with a drawbreaker round," Dr. Schwartz says, "I think it's important that the doctors look at each fighter after the final regulation round and that the scores are tabulated quickly after the final regulation round. That way, in terms of the break in the action and the fighters cooling off, it's similar to the five-minute recovery period that a fighter is allowed after a low blow."

Margaret Goodman (former chief ringside physician and chairperson of the medical advisory board for the Nevada State Athletic Commission) takes a contrary view.

"Boxing isn't like other sports," Dr. Goodman posits. "You train a fighter to fight for a certain number of rounds and tell him to give it everything he has in the final round. And then, when he's exhausted and thinks the fight is over, you tell him he has to fight another round. I'm not aware of hard medical evidence one way or the other as to whether a fighter is more susceptible to injury in a tiebreaker round. But I have an uneasy feeling about it."

There are also conflicting opinions with regard to how a drawbreaker round effects the essence of the competition.

"I love it," promoter Lou DiBella declares. "A round when both fighters know with certainty that everything is on the line is as compelling as anything you can get in sports."

But Teddy Atlas isn't sold on the drawbreaker round.

"I'd rather that they get to the conclusion of a fight without it," Atlas says. "Fighters prepare physically and mentally to fight for a certain number of rounds. A fighter thinks the fight is over after six or eight rounds or whatever it is. There's a psychological release no matter what you've told him before about a tiebreaker round. And in something as difficult as boxing, once you have that release, it's hard to get the right mindset back. That means you're likely to see competition that's a little less pure. Either the fighter is holding something back in what's most likely the final round or he's spent when he goes out for the extra round. Neither one is good."

Also, there's a significant flaw in the "drawbreaker" formula. The fighter who wins the extra round on the judges' scorecards is declared the winner. But under that formula, it's possible for a fighter to end the night trailing on two of the three judges' scorecards and still win the fight.

Here's how that could happen.

At the end of six rounds, Judge A scores the fight 58–56 for Red Corner. Judge B scores the fight 58–56 for Blue Corner. Judge C has the fight even. Then Judges A and B score the drawbreaker round for red corner, so Red Corner wins the fight. That means, overall, Judge A has Red Corner ahead by three points. But Judges B and C each had Blue Corner (the loser of the extra round) ahead by one point after seven rounds.

So . . . How should draws be eliminated if one feels the need to eliminate draws?

A coin flip is too arbitrary.

Relying on a social media poll (which was Boxcino's fallback position in the event a drawbreaker round was judged even) would open the door to ballot-box stuffing.

It would also be inadvisable to add the three judges' scorecards together to arrive at a total points tally because that would give too much influence to one judge.

A fourth alternative would be to call upon the referee to score the fight in the event that the judges' scorecards are even. Referees scored fights for more than a century. Indeed, there were many jurisdictions in which the referee cast the only vote.

Finally, one might apply a supplemental points system to a judge's scorecard that's even after the scheduled number of rounds. Some rounds are easy to score. They're clearly 10–9 in favor of a given fighter. Other rounds are hard to call. When a judge fills out his or her card for a fight where a drawbreaker might be necessary, the "10" could be circled for each round where the winner is clear. Add up the number of circled 10–9 rounds on that judge's card, and you're likely to have a winner.

State athletic commissions should think this issue through rather than simply rubber stamping a solution.

*In 2015, continuing a tradition, I asked a panel of industry experts to predict
the results of a fantasy middleweight tournament.*

Sugar Ray Robinson Is Still #1

Ranking great fighters from different eras, when done seriously, is a
daunting task. It's easy to sit down and put together a shoot-from-the-hip
list. But that doesn't do justice to the fighters.

In recent years, I've sought to quantify ring greatness in a credible
way. I've compiled lists of great champions who reigned at 135 and 147
pounds and matched them against each other in round-robin tourna-
ments with the results of each fight being predicted by a panel of boxing
industry experts. This time, it's modern 160-pound greats.

The middleweight champions chosen for the tournament, in alpha-
betical order, are Nino Benvenuti, Gennady Golovkin, Marvin Hagler,
Bernard Hopkins, Roy Jones, Jake LaMotta, Carlos Monzon, Sugar Ray
Robinson, and James Toney.

The list is limited to middleweights from the post World War II era.
It does not include fighters like Stanley Ketchel, Harry Greb, and Mickey
Walker because not enough film footage is available to properly evaluate
them. Golovkin is the wild card in the tournament. His fans have complained that none of today's elite fighters will fight him. This is his chance
to be matched against the best.

The panelists were asked to assume for each hypothetical fight that
both fighters were at the point in their respective careers when they were
still able to make 160 pounds and were capable of duplicating their best
160-pound performance.

One can look to side issues such as same-day weigh-ins versus
day-before weigh-ins. And there's a difference between going twelve
rounds as opposed to fifteen. But at the end of the day, either a fighter is
very good, great, or the greatest.

Twenty-four experts participated in the rankings process. Listed
alphabetically, the panelists are:

Trainers: Teddy Atlas, Pat Burns, and Don Turner.

Media: Jerry Izenberg, Harold Lederman, Paulie Malignaggi, Larry Merchant, and Michael Rosenthal.

Matchmakers: Eric Bottjer, Don Elbaum, Bobby Goodman, Brad Goodman, Ron Katz, Mike Marchionte, Chris Middendorf, Russell Peltz, and Bruce Trampler.

Historians: Craig Hamilton, Don McRae, Bob Mee, Clay Moyle, Adam Pollack, Randy Roberts, and Mike Tyson.

If each of the nine fighters listed above had fought the other eight, there would have been thirty-six fights. And there were twenty-four panelists. Thus, 864 fight predictions were entered into the database. Fighters were awarded one point for each predicted win and a half point for each predicted draw (too close to call). A perfect score would have been 192 points.

In two instances, an elector chose not to make a prediction on certain fights. One matchmaker said that he never saw Robinson, LaMotta, or Benvenuti fight and didn't feel comfortable predicting outcomes for their matches. One historian felt the same way regarding Golovkin. A weighted average from the other electors was used to fill in the fights at issue in those two tournament grids.

In some instances, the fighters actually fought each other at middleweight. For example, Roy Jones conclusively decisioned Bernard Hopkins when they fought at 160 pounds. But Hopkins's prime middleweight years came after that. Thus, two electors gave Bernard the nod over Roy at 160 pounds and two called their match-up a draw.

Sugar Ray Robinson was the clear choice for #1.

Two years ago, Robinson finished first in a similar 147-pound fantasy tournament with a projected record of 186 wins, 3 losses, and 7 draws. Now the experts have rated Robinson #1 at 160 pounds. Fourteen of the twenty-four electors predicted that he would win all eight of his tournament fights. But Robinson is considered beatable at middleweight, where his projected tournament record is 173 wins, 17 losses, and 2 draws.

Here, it should be noted that we're talking about the Sugar Ray Robinson of 1951, who put a brutal beating on Jake LaMotta; not the

Robinson who lost desire and saw his physical skills diminish as he got older.

Marvin Hagler, Roy Jones, and Carlos Monzon are grouped behind Robinson in that order.

"Picking against Robinson has become almost a sacrilege," one matchmaker said. "But I think Hagler at his best beats him."

Another Hagler backer noted, "I'll go with Hagler over Robinson. But if Marvin comes out in an orthodox stance and gives away the first four rounds like he did against Sugar Ray Leonard, I'm changing my vote."

Roy Jones finished close behind Hagler, eliciting kudos such as, "People forget how good Roy was when he was young . . . Jones was so athletically gifted at that time in his life—far beyond anything normal— that I can seen him beating any of these guys . . . Roy at middleweight was special with his amazing speed and power. He did things I never saw anyone else do. He could have stolen this tournament."

Three of the electors thought that Jones would win all eight of his fights. One elector gave Hagler (who finished second to Robinson in the voting) a perfect 8-and-0 record.

Three voters predicted that Monzon (who finished fourth) would win all eight of his fights. "The downside to Monzon," one matchmaker said, "is that he fought a lot of elite fighters, but he didn't fight them at their peak."

Jake LaMotta, Gennady Golovkin, and Bernard Hopkins were also closely grouped.

"To be fair to LaMotta," one historian said, "he was slipping when he fought Robinson the last time, which was the only time they fought at middleweight. Was he as great as Robinson? No. But he beat Robinson once, and he was good enough to test him every time."

Golovkin was 12-10-2 in head-to-head competition against Hopkins and edged Bernard out in the rankings by a half point. A repeated theme with regard to Gennady was, "He's good, but I don't know how good because the best fighters in his weight range are avoiding him . . . We just don't know about Golovkin. I've seen fighters who looked great be great. And I've seen fighters who looked great fall short . . . Golovkin is hittable, and these guys could hit. It's one thing to knock out Daniel Geale after he punches you in the face. It's very different if you're punched in the face by Carlos Monzon."

As for Hopkins; one trainer predicted that Bernard would beat Roy Jones at 160 pounds and fight Sugar Ray Robinson even. "Hopkins got better after he lost to Jones," the trainer noted. "I think that Bernard at his best would have smothered Roy, roughed him up, and made Roy fight ugly."

James Toney and Nino Benvenuti rounded out the field.

The final rankings and point totals are:

Sugar Ray Robinson	174 points
Marvin Hagler	134
Roy Jones	131
Carlos Monzon	126
Jake LaMotta	71.5
Gennady Golovkin	67.5
Bernard Hopkins	67
James Toney	54
Nino Benvenuti	39

Charts #1 and #2 contain underlying statistical data from the tournament. Chart #1 shows that the matchmakers, trainers, media representatives, and historians all ranked Robinson in the #1 slot. There was a divergence of opinion after that. Chart #2 shows how the panelists thought each fighter would fare against the other eight.

CHART 1

Name Points	Overall Rank	Matchmaker Rank	Trainer Rank	Media Rank	Historian Rank
Robinson 174	1	1	1	1	1
Hagler 134	2	3	5	2 (tie)	2
Jones 131	3	2	3	2 (tie)	3
Monzon 126	4	4	2	2 (tie)	4
LaMotta 71.5	5	5	4	7 (tie)	7
Golovkin 67.5	6	8	9	5	5
Hopkins 67	7	6	8	7 (tie)	6
Toney 54	8	7	7	6	8
Benvenuti 39	9	9	6	9	9

CHART 2

—	Robinson	Hagler	Jones	Monzon	LaMotta	Golovkin	Hopkins	Toney	Benvenuti
Robinson 173-17-2	—	18.5	19	20	24	23	22.5	23	24
Hagler 129-53-10	5.5	—	13	13	20	20	20	20.5	22
Jones 130-60-2	5	11	—	12	18	19	21	23	22
Monzon 123-63-6	4	11	12	—	19	19	17.5	20.5	23
LaMotta 66-115-11	0	4	6	5	—	12	13	15.5	16
Golovkin 64-121-7	1	4	5	5	12	—	13	12	15.5
Hopkins 61-119-12	1.5	4	3	6.5	11	11	—	13.5	16.5
Toney 52-136-4	1	3.5	1	3.5	8.5	12	10.5	—	14
Benvenuti 37-151-4	0	2	2	1	8	8.5	7.7	10	—

As a contrast to "Fistic Nuggets," these "Notes" were on the serious side.

Fistic Notes

There has been heated controversy recently regarding an article I wrote entitled "Can Boxing Trust USADA?" Wherever readers stand on this issue, I would urge them to remember that the people who criticize what's happening in boxing today the most vehemently are often the people who care the most about boxing.

If one made a short list of the greatest sports heroes in history, the most meaningful names on that list would be belong to boxers. There have been times when the sweet science sent what seemed like a karmic wave around the world. Jack Johnson's destruction of James Jeffries, Joe Louis's annihilation of Max Schmeling, Muhammad Ali's fall at the hands of Joe Frazier and his resurrection against George Foreman. Each of these happenings reached far beyond sports.

A quarter century ago, Tom Callahan wrote in *Time* magazine, "Regional vainglories like the World Cup or World Series only aspire to the global importance of the heavyweight championship. John L. Sullivan, Jack Dempsey, Joe Louis, and Muhammad Ali truly possessed the world."

Jack Johnson, Joe Louis, and Muhammad Ali redefined what it meant to be black in America. Even today, the loss of a beloved fighter is a small death for those who love him. Not only has he been defeated in the ring; he has been physically beaten down in front of the multitude that loves him.

Boxing is a public trust. Shame on those who despoil it.

★ ★ ★

The sad story of Jermain Taylor got sadder on January 19, 2015, with his arrest on charges of aggravated assault, endangering the welfare of a minor, and possession of marijuana after he fired a gun during a parade in Little Rock honoring Martin Luther King Jr.

Taylor was out on bail at the time, pending trial on charges of first-degree battery stemming from an incident last August, when he shot his cousin in the leg. His bail was revoked after the parade incident.

There was a time when Jermain was considered a model citizen, and rightly so. Those days are gone.

"It's possible that brain trauma from boxing is contributing to this," Dr. Margaret Goodman (one of the most knowledgeable advocates for fighter safety in the United States) posits. "With CTE [chronic traumatic encephalopathy], you see extreme personality and mood changes. But you wouldn't know whether that's the case here without a lot of tests."

Drug abuse is also believed to be a factor. After Taylor defeated Bernard Hopkins twice in 2005, he left his longtime trainer, Pat Burns, to work with Emanuel Steward, who was assisted by Ozell Nelson. Thereafter, Jermain was introduced to some not-so-healthy aspects of street life.

Taylor reunited with Burns in 2011. Last year, he won a watered-down 160-pound "championship" belt.

"If I sound perturbed," Burns told this writer last week, "it's because I am. Jermain was completely against drugs when I first knew him. And now, it's not just marijuana. It can't be. Marijuana doesn't make you crazy like this. I'm told there's stuff on the streets now that's marijuana processed in a certain way that's very dangerous. Maybe it's that; I don't know. But he's out of control. That's the scary part. The drugs are kicking Jermain's ass."

★ ★ ★

Bill Littlefield once declaimed on National Public Radio, "About the only excuse for boxing—and I'm not sure it's sufficient—is that the sport has generated some good writing."

British doctoral student Andrew Douglas opined, "Boxing is little more than organized crime behind a smokescreen of professional sport."

Littlefield and Douglas are outsiders. But over the years, numerous insiders have also voiced reservations about the sweet science. A sampler follows:

★ John Schulian (past winner of the Nat Fleischer Award for Career Excellence in Boxing Journalism): "Life isn't always fair. The fight racket never is."

★ Hall of Fame trainer Ray Arcel: "I don't think boxing should be abolished. But the way boxing is today, it wouldn't make any difference. It's not boxing anymore. It's exploitation."

★ Bill Slayton (honored by the Boxing Writers Association of America as its 1977 "Manager of the Year"): "Boxing has some of the most rotten people you'll ever meet. Not all of them. But ninety percent of the people in boxing are rotten."

★ Randy Neumann (referee and former heavyweight contender): "They don't dig graves in boxing. They screw people into the ground."

★ Hall of Fame trainer Angelo Dundee: "Boxing is a dog-eat-dog sport. You have to be ready to use every trick in the book. It's not a sport for priests and rabbis. You park your conscience and do what has to be done."

★ Former HBO commentator Larry Merchant: "In boxing, you can't keep a bad man down."

★ Roy Jones (pound-for-pound king in the 1990s): "One thing I learned from the '88 Olympics; it's not a question of if they can screw you over. It's a question of if they will."

★ And last but not least, promoter Lou DiBella: "It's a miserable fucking business."

★ ★ ★

On June 4, 2011, forty-three-year-old Christy Martin, who was nearing the end of her trailblazing ring career, suffered a broken hand in a scheduled six-round fight against Dakota Stone at the Staples Center in Los Angeles. The bout was stopped and Stone was declared the winner.

What happened next was frightening.

"When they put me to sleep to fix my hand," Martin (who now uses her maiden name, Christy Salters) recently told writer Tom Gerbasi, "I had a stroke. When I finally come to, I can't walk; I can't talk; I can't feed myself; I can't see clearly. I just tried not to deal with any of it. Finally, I get back on my feet. I get my balance somewhat back. I can walk. I can feed myself."

So Martin's boxing career was over. Right?

Wrong.

"I said I'm gonna fight again," Christy continued. "I'm just not gonna tell anybody I had the stroke."

And that's what happened. On August 14, 2012, Martin fought Mia St. John at the Table Mountain Casino in California for the "vacant WBC world female super-welterweight title." Ten years earlier, Martin had beaten St. John with ease. In the aftermath of her stroke, she lost to Mia and then, finally, retired from boxing.

This is another example of why boxing needs more comprehensive medical oversight, regulatory authorities that know what they're doing, and sanctioning bodies that care more about the health and safety of fighters than gobbling up sanctioning fees.

★ ★ ★

Words of Wisdom from the Always Quotable Freddie Roach

"The biggest regret I have in boxing is not training hard for Greg Haugen [in a 1985 bout near the end of Roach's career]. Haugen is the only person I disliked going into a fight. He was cocky and arrogant, and I took him lightly. I didn't train right. I went into the fight unprepared and got knocked out. Sometimes I think I'd trade all my wins to have that fight back."

"You might not believe this, but my favorite sport to watch on television is golf. I tried playing, and I was terrible at it. These guys are amazing, the way they hit that little ball three hundred yards and the way they put it on the green with backspin on it. I couldn't do that except by accident."

"When I was fighting, I fought angry. I always wanted to hurt my opponent. I don't have that anger in me anymore. If I get mad now, I get sued."

"What motivates me as a trainer? I like the money. But more than anything else, I want to be the best in the world at what I do."

"The most painful loss that I experienced as a trainer was Manny [Pacquiao] getting knocked out by [Juan Manuel] Marquez. I thought he was dead. That one scared me. And the Mayweather fight disappointed me a lot. I wanted that fight called off because of Manny's shoulder. It interfered with Manny's training, and a bad shoulder is a bad shoulder. But Manny was getting better, and fighters go into fights with injuries all the time. In fact, when I was warming Manny up in the dressing room, I was pleased. There was some pop to his punches. He looked good. Then, in the fight, the shoulder started bothering him and he couldn't do what either of us wanted him to do. Losing to Mayweather sucked."

★ ★ ★

Boxing fans are often collectors, and fight programs catch their eye.

Craig Hamilton is the foremost boxing memorabilia dealer in the United States. The most valuable fight program that he's aware of was for three championship fights that took place at the Olympic Club in New Orleans over the course of three days in September 1892. Jack McAuliffe knocked out Billy Myer. George Dixon stopped Jack Skelly. And in the big one, James J. Corbett dethroned John L. Sullivan to claim the heavyweight crown.

"Collectors hadn't even known that a program for those fights existed," Hamilton says. "Then, sometime around 1990, I was contacted by a woman who was a descendant of a man who'd been a boxing instructor at the Olympic Club. She had eight programs for the event. They were in good condition with a beautiful ornate color cover on each one. The family kept several of the programs, and I helped her sell the others. Depending on their condition today, I'd say that each of them is worth between $15,000 and $20,000."

The magnitude of a fight is important to the value of a program. There are particular fighters who are more in demand than others. The condition of the program is important too. But rarity is the key factor.

"The most valuable Muhammad Ali program," Hamilton continues, "is for Cassius Clay versus Tunney Hunsaker. It's just a one-page bout sheet. But it was Clay's debut fight and only seven or eight are known to exist, all of them from the collection of [Clay's first trainer] Joe Martin.

I'd say they're worth $8,000 to $10,000 each. There are no known programs for Clay versus Lamar Clark or Clay versus Alex Miteff. So if a bout sheet for one of those fights surfaced, it would be a big deal. Guys who collect Ali programs would be bidding against each other, and it could go for $10,000."

Where Ali's most notable fights are concerned, the most valuable on-site program is for Ali-Foreman. "Rarity and demand," Hamilton explains. "In excellent condition, it can bring as much as $7,500."

Ali-Frazier III ("another rare one") goes for up to $3,000. Ali-Frazier I ($300 to $400) and Ali-Frazier II ($100 to $200) are less valuable because there are so many of them.

Clay-Liston I is also rare and, in excellent condition, is in the $1,500-to-$2,000 range. There were two different on-site programs for Ali-Liston II, now worth about $400 each.

But Hamilton adds a word of caution, noting, "The thing about paper is, there's always the danger that people will find more, a lot more. Clay-Liston II in Lewiston, Maine, was a scarce ticket that sold for $1,500 to $2,000. Then, about twenty years ago, someone in Maine made a big find. Now they're worth $200 to $300."

★ ★ ★

I've often said that the primary reasons for boxing's decline in popularity among mainstream sports fans are (1) there are so many phony belts that the sweet science no longer has recognizable champions; and (2) the sport has an economic model that minimizes viewership of its flagship events.

But there's a third reason: the best no longer fight the best. Too many elite fighters avoid challenges because they're afraid of losing.

Here, the thoughts of manager Cameron Dunkin are instructive.

"They've just ruined the business with this no-loss policy," Dunkin says. "Back in the old days, guys defended their titles fifteen times in one year, twice in one month, and they lost fights. I'll never forget when Shane Mosley, who was a great great fighter, year after year winning and winning and winning, beating everyone. Then all of a sudden he loses to Vernon Forrest. My phone lit up. People saying, 'See, I told you he can't fight; I told you he was nothing.' And when Roy Jones lost, everybody was, 'See, I always knew he wasn't that good,' What is wrong with people? Baseball, you hit the ball three times out of ten, you're an All-Star. Golf, people lose. Tennis, people lose. Stock car racing, people lose. It happens."

And to that, ESPN commentator Teddy Atlas has added a word about former amateur standouts who opt for a long string of mismatches after turning pro.

"It's kind of like they go to a great university like Harvard," Atlas observed. "Then they get out of Harvard and go to kindergarten and start playing with crayons. Throw the crayons away, please. Go forward now."

★ ★ ★

The World Boxing Council recently released its all-time "Top Ten" list of WBC heavyweight champions.

Muhammad Ali is #1. That's well and good.

Lennox Lewis, Larry Holmes, Mike Tyson, George Foreman, Joe Frazier, and Evander Holyfield hold down the #2 through #7 spots in that order. Some knowledgeable observers would quarrel with that progression. But it's within the realm of reason.

Except . . .

Oops! What about Sonny Liston?

That's where things get crazy.

The WBC ranks Liston (who was its first heavyweight champion) in ninth place. Behind Frank Bruno.

★ ★ ★

Mike Stafford, who trains Adrien Broner and assists Barry Hunter in training Lamont Peterson, had some thoughts to share at the final prefight press conference for the April 11, 2015, *Premier Boxing Champions* card.

Referencing recent studies that document the brain damage suffered by football players at all levels of competition, Stafford observed, "In a way, it's helping boxing. There were parents who wouldn't let their children box because they didn't want them getting hit in the head, but they'd let them play football. Now they see that football is just as dangerous. In fact, in football, you got guys 310 pounds smashing little guys around. In boxing, the weights are even."

★ ★ ★

Recently, I was leafing through Joseph Heller's classic World War II novel, *Catch 22*, and came across an interesting passage.

A character named Major Major asks bombardier John Yossarian why he won't fly any more missions, and Yossarian answers, "I'm afraid."

"That's nothing to be ashamed of," Major Major counsels. "We're all afraid."

"I'm not ashamed," Yossarian answers. "I'm just afraid."

Those sentiments could be applied to boxing. All fighters feel fear. How they deal with it is one of the factors that spells the difference between winning and losing.

★ ★ ★

A word on Sergio Martinez, who announced his retirement from boxing on June 13 at age forty.

Martinez walked into a boxing gym for the first time at age twenty. He turned pro three years later and compiled a ring record of 51 wins, 3 losses, and 2 draws. On April 17, 2010, he decisioned Kelly Pavlik to claim the world middleweight crown. Six successful championship defenses followed. But as Sergio grew older, his body betrayed him. Plagued by a bad knee that limited his training and ring movement, he was dethroned last year by Miguel Cotto.

I was privileged to spend the hours before and after a fight in Martinez's dressing room on six occasions. The first of these came on November 20, 2010, when Sergio rendered Paul Williams unconscious with a crushing overhand left in the second round.

Williams and his trainer, George Peterson, later spoke of a "lucky punch."

"It definitely wasn't a lucky punch," Sergio countered. "Anybody who has seen the tape—it's not too long—sees me throwing the same punch six times and landing five, and then I knock him out. It was a premeditated punch, not lucky."

David Greisman's analysis supported Sergio's view.

"Can we please put this to rest, already," Greisman wrote. "Martinez landed the same timed overhand left as the knockout punch numerous times in both his first fight with Williams and in their rematch. By my tally, Martinez landed it fifteen times in their first bout, including nine times in the final three rounds of the bout, as he realized it was another weapon that would work on Williams. And in the rematch, Martinez landed it half a dozen times in four minutes. Seven times, if you count the final blow."

Outside the ring, Martinez has been an advocate for women who have been subjected to domestic violence and for children who've been the target of bullying in school.

"A world-class fighter doesn't have to act like a thug," he says. "As a professional athlete who is in the public eye, I have a duty to speak out on behalf of people who need help and are not heard."

Sergio Martinez has always conducted himself with dignity and grace. Boxing will miss him.

★ ★ ★

A Parable for Roy Jones Jr

There a story about an old man who lives in an area that's being evacuated because of rising flood waters. The local authorities send a police car to bring the man out. But he refuses to leave, saying, "God will save me."

The waters rise higher and flood all of the surrounding roads. The authorities send a boat to bring the old man to safety. But again, he refuses to leave, saying, "God will save me."

The flooding continues, and the old man is forced to seek sanctuary on the roof of his house. This time, a military rescue helicopter hovers overhead. But the old man refuses to climb onboard, saying, "God will save me."

The inevitable happens. The flood waters rise above the roof of the house. The old man drowns and, with his final breath, cries out, "Lord; I trusted in you. Why did you not save me?"

And God answers, "I tried to. I sent a car, a boat, and a helicopter."

Why is that story relevant today?

Brin-Jonathan Butler recently wrote an excellent article about Roy Jones for Bleacher Report. When Butler raised subject of retirement, Jones told him, "If God truly wanted me to stop, all He'd have to do is have one doctor at the Mayo Clinic find something wrong with my brain. Just one little CAT scan showing any sign of trauma or damage and I'd be done. I'm right where God wants me to be. To stop now would be to spite God with everything he gave me and everything he has planned. That's why I'm here, and nobody can tell me different."

Roy . . . You'll be forty-seven years old next month. God has sent Antonio Tarver, Glen Johnson, Danny Green, Denis Lebedev, and Enzo Maccarinelli. Each of them knocked you woozy. Three of them knocked you unconscious. What more do you need?

★ ★ ★

HBO announced on November 30, 2015, that Peter Nelson would be the new head of HBO Sports.

My role as a consultant for HBO Sports is inconsistent with in-depth analysis of the events that led to this decision. But I would like to say a few words about Peter Nelson.

I met Nelson eight years ago when he was a freelance writer. I've followed his career closely since he joined HBO in 2011.

Nelson is uniquely suited for his new role. I can't think of anyone better qualified to lead HBO Sports through the years ahead. He's smart, hard working, and honest. He appreciates what's best about the HBO culture and brand.

Boxing is still at the core of what HBO Sports does. Nelson is grounded in the sport and business of boxing. During his time at HBO, he has reached out to people at all levels of the boxing community to listen to what they have to say and learn. He's popular within the boxing industry and also within HBO. Because he knows both boxing and the HBO Sports personnel, he can hit the ground running.

Nelson's task isn't to rebuild what HBO Sports once was. It's to reshape and revitalize HBO Sports and lead it to new heights. That will take time. Most of the sports department budget for 2016 has already been committed to specific fighters and projects. There will be complaints as hard choices that encroach upon vested interests are made. It's impossible to make everybody happy in boxing or in television. But with the support of senior management, Nelson has the potential to be an effective, bold, visionary leader, who will be good for HBO and good for boxing.

Gloves are part of a fighter's arsenal. Shouldn't that part of each fighter's arsenal be equal?

What's With the Gloves?

Boxing gloves protect fighters' hands and allow them to punch harder.

Professional fighters who weigh 150 pounds or less are generally required to wear eight-ounce gloves. Above 150 pounds, it's ten ounces. Apart from these numbers, there's relatively little standardization. That's a problem.

As a general rule, the promoter provides the gloves used in fights, and gives them to the governing state athletic commission in advance for inspection, approval, and safe-keeping.

However, in recent years, an increasing number of fighters have requested that they be allowed to wear their own gloves. Most commissions now adhere to the view that a fighter can use any gloves he wants as long as the gloves meet certain specifications.

Taking New York as an example; the gloves used in a professional fight must be on an "approved" list compiled by the New York State Athletic Commission. At present, that list includes four different Everlast models, two models manufactured by Rival, and single models from Ediroc, Fuel, Grant, Reebok, Reyes, and Ringside.

Boxers must request NYSAC approval no later than the weigh-in to use gloves other than those provided by the promoter. The gloves provided by the boxer must be new and in the manufacturer's original sealed packaging. It is in the commission's sole discretion to determine whether or not to allow the use of the gloves.

That all sounds good. But in truth, there are gaps in quality control from state to state. And even "approved" models have problems.

Greg Sirb is executive director of the Pennsylvania State Athletic Commission.

"The first thing we do is weigh the gloves," Sirb says. "Let's be honest about this. With all manufacturers, there can be variations in weight. The gloves don't always weigh exactly eight ounces or exactly ten ounces. We allow for a variation of a tenth of an ounce either way. More than that can be a problem."

Other issues include poor stitching and raised seams, both of which can cause cuts. The issue of padding is more complicated.

Traditionally, the padding in boxing gloves was horsehair. In recent decades, synthetic materials have become more popular. Some gloves, such as Reyes and the Everlast MX, have foam over horsehair. Others have multiple layers of padding with each layer being a different type of foam.

One of the most significant differences among gloves is how the padding is distributed. Gloves can weigh the same and be very different because the padding is distributed differently. The less padding there is in the punching part of a glove (as opposed to the wrist area), the harder the punch is likely to be (although that also increases the risk of damage to the puncher's hand).

By way of example, in most Everlast gloves (but not the Everlast MX), the padding is equally distributed. Reyes gloves have some of that padding shifted toward the wrist, which has earned them the reputation of being a "puncher's glove."

Here, Sirb notes, "Before we approve a glove in Pennsylvania, we take a sample from the manufacturer and cut it in two at the wrist. Then we weigh the wrist and punching parts of the glove separately. In an eight-ounce glove, I don't like to see much more than two ounces in the wrist. But one of the problems we have is that you can get three gloves from the same manufacturer. And they look good; but even with the same model, there are variations from glove to glove."

There are no specific standards anywhere in the United States that govern the hardness and resilience of gloves. Also, as Sirb notes, "Some of the heavyweights today have huge hands. They need specially manu-factured gloves, but the gloves still only weigh ten ounces. So right there, you're redistributing the padding over a larger surface and there's less of a cushion."

A ten-ounce pillow and a ten-ounce rock weigh the same. But most people would rather get hit in the head by the pillow.

The color of boxing gloves is another area that hasn't been fully explored.

In days of old, fighters wore brown gloves. Then black became the fashion. With the advent of color television, red came into vogue. Now most state athletic commissions allow fighters to choose their own color with no clear guidelines to follow.

When Bernard Hopkins fought Sergey Kovalev in Atlantic City on November 8, 2014, "The Alien" wore electric blue gloves with neon pink and yellow thumbs.

That raises an intriguing issue. Does the color of a fighter's gloves make a difference in a fight? Are some colors more difficult for a fighter to see and react to as a punch hurtles toward him? Are judges more likely to see a scoring blow if the glove that lands is a certain color?

No one has conducted a serious scientific study to answer these questions.

Also, when fighters who are about to participate in a major fight select the gloves that they intend to wear, they choose an "A" pair and a back-up pair (the latter to be used if a glove replacement is necessary during the fight). On occasion, the "A" pair and back-up pair are different colors.

That's the height of stupidity. What happens under those circumstances if a glove needs to be replaced? Is the action halted to replace both gloves rather than one? Or would the fight proceed with the fighter wearing different color gloves?

The Association of Boxing Commissions needs to set standards for gloves. The concept of a level playing field for fighters is at stake.

"I have striven in my life," Charles Dickens wrote. "I strove to climb. Only an inch gained brought me nearer to the height."

Richmond Unchained

Telling the story of Bill Richmond's life is like trying to complete a jigsaw puzzle with some of the pieces missing.

Richmond rose to prominence as a prizefighter in England and was the first black sportsman to achieve national fame. *Richmond Unchained* by Luke G. Williams (Amberley Publishing) is a worthy effort that does him justice.

The best available evidence indicates that Richmond was born a slave on Staten Island (now one of New York City's five boroughs) in 1763. Quite possibly, his biological father was the Reverend Charlton, who owned Richmond's mother.

In 1777, British brigadier general Hugh Percy (who was in the colonies to suppress the revolution) took a liking to Richmond and persuaded Charlton to release him. Then Percy brought Richmond to England.

British merchants and seamen were deeply involved in the slave trade at that time, although slavery was illegal in England. People of color were looked down upon and not particularly welcome on Shakespeare's sceptered isle. Percy arranged for Richmond to receive a rudimentary education and be apprenticed to a cabinetmaker. In the early 1790s, Richmond married a white woman named Mary and is believed to have had five children with her. The fragmentary evidence that exists suggests that their marriage was a stable one.

Richmond turned to prizefighting late in life. His first bout of consequence (which he lost to a man named George Maddox) took place on January 23, 1804, when he was forty years old. Other than an October 8, 1808, defeat at the hands of future English champion Tom Cribb, he did not lose again.

Boxing in the late-eighteenth and early-nineteenth centuries was very different from what it is today. Throwing an opponent to the ground, hitting and holding, and other roughhouse tactics were allowed. A combatant who was knocked down had thirty seconds to recover and return to the battle. The fighters were ungloved.

Richmond was adept at defense—"milling on the retreat" as it was known. He also developed a well-earned reputation as a knowledgeable strategist and trainer whose services were much in demand. In 1810, he assumed ownership of a well-established pub called The Horse and Dolphin, evidence that prizefighting and training were profitable for him. That same year, he met Tom Molineaux.

Little reliable biographical information about Molineaux exists today. Williams debunks many of the myths about him but is unable to fill in the blanks in the narrative created by their absence.

What is known is that Molineaux was born in 1784 and, like Richmond, was a former slave from America. Unlike Richmond, he had a loud boastful personality, was a profligate womanizer, could neither read nor write, and was lacking in social graces. But he was larger than Richmond, interested in prizefighting, blessed with intimidating natural power, and had youth on his side.

Meanwhile, as Williams writes, "By the summer of 1810, Richmond had few options to advance his own career, and the prospect of becoming a full-time trainer of other fighters looked increasingly attractive. Molineaux's arrival was a piece of fortuitous timing. Richmond was a man who possessed a streak of cold commercialism which had enabled him to survive and thrive as a black man in Georgian England. His motives in befriending Molineaux cannot be solely attributed to altruism. He was intrigued and excited by Molineaux's earning potential. Richmond saw in Molineaux a delicious business opportunity; namely the chance to introduce, promote, and parade a new black sensation in front of the fancy. From the moment he first met Molineaux, the notion seems to have crystalized in Richmond's brain that the young American was ideally suited for the purpose of ultimately defeating the champion [Tom Cribb]. Richmond realized, though, that, before Molineaux could be matched with Cribb, he would need to dramatically improve his technique."

Richmond soon became trainer, manager, promoter, and mentor to Molineaux. On December 18, 1810, Molineaux challenged Cribb for the crown. Their encounter was arguably the first sporting contest of international significance and the most significant sporting event ever up until that time. A black man trained by another black man was on the verge of becoming England's boxing champion.

Ten thousand spectators gathered in the rain on Copthall Common, Sussex, to watch Cribb defend his championship. The fight lasted fifty-five minutes with the crowd becoming a mob and, to Molineaux's detriment, a participant in the flow of the action.

Molineaux was allowed to fight. But he was not allowed to win. Ultimately, under dubious circumstance, Cribb prevailed. Pierce Egan later wrote, "It will not be forgotten, if justice holds the scales, that [Molineaux's] colour alone prevented him from becoming the hero of that fight."

In the aftermath of Cribb-Molineaux, Williams recounts, "The Horse and Dolphin became the unofficial headquarters of black pugilism, Richmond's reputation now being so elevated that his public house was the first port of call for any black man who fancied trying his hand in the prize ring."

Equally important, Richmond skillfully martialed public opinion in support of a rematch. Nine months later, Cribb and Molineaux met again before twenty thousand spectators on the outskirts of London. This time, Cribb had trained more diligently and Molineaux was more poorly prepared. Cribb brutalized Molineaux and, after nineteen minutes, emerged victorious.

"There is little in Richmond's remarkable life for which he should be reprimanded," Williams writes. "But dragging Molineaux back to scratch [again and again in the rematch] was arguably the most callous act he ever performed. Such was Molineaux's debilitated state that Richmond and Gibbons [Molineaux's other second] had to lift him up as they would a lump of lead before leading him back to the center of the ring for the tenth round." By the eleventh and final round, Williams recounts, the fight "more resembled a public execution than a sporting contest."

Richmond and Molineaux had a bitter falling out after the second Cribb-Molineaux fight. "From Richmond's point of view," Williams notes, "the way Molineaux was now behaving was an example of rank ingratitude. Molineaux had been an unknown penniless novice when Richmond first met him and was now a national celebrity."

Moreover, in brokering the second Cribb-Molineaux fight, Richmond had lost most of what he owned. In 1812, he was forced to sell The Horse and Dolphin to pay his debts and moved with his family to new lodging. He even entered the ring again, fighting for the last time on November 12, 1818, when he was fifty-five years old.

Molineaux died in 1818 at age thirty-four. Richmond continued to give boxing lessons and remained a respected figure in the boxing community until his death in 1830. But none of his charges excelled as had Molineaux.

Richmond Unchained brings a long-ago time and the people in it to life. Williams re-creates London well and succeeds in describing the role of prizefighting in England at the start of the nineteenth century. The two Cribb-Molineaux fights are the dramatic high points of the narrative. But the portrait of Richmond that Williams crafts outshines them.

It's a difficult task to accurately portray a man who's enshrouded in myth and lived two centuries ago and then place that man in the historical context of his times. That Williams succeeds is a tribute to his painstaking research.

"Richmond is a historical figure of vital importance," Williams observes in closing, "not because of what he achieved in terms of sporting excellence, for as worthy and admirable as those achievements are, they are not in isolation truly 'historic.' Rather, Richmond is important because he achieved these things during an era when racism was so ingrained within society that for a black person to attain the levels of success that Richmond did required formidable powers of determination and enterprise. A black celebrity in Georgian England was seen as an oddity, a freak, or an accident; not as a harbinger of the fundamental social change and revolution to come."

It's also worth quoting from a letter that Williams sent to this writer in which he described researching *Richmond Unchained*: "I soon discovered that many 'facts' about Richmond in boxing history books and online sources were inaccurate, had been misinterpreted, or were invented. I realized that relying on any accounts written later than his lifetime was a waste of time. Instead, I would have to access sources such as birth, marriage, and tax records, as well as contemporary newspapers from the Georgian era in order to assemble the most complete and factually correct account of his life and times as possible. *Richmond Unchained* is the result of this work, which ended up taking twelve long years. Although there are still some things we do not know about Richmond, I am satisfied that his life story has now been told."

And told well.

Boxing's literary tradition continued to grow in 2015

Literary Notes

In 2001, Tris Dixon (an aspiring amateur boxer in England) came to the United States with an eye toward improving his ring skills. Then he changed course.

Armed with a Greyhound bus pass and extremely limited funds, Dixon traveled around the United States for several months, interviewing former fighters. Many of them weren't doing well. In addition to hard economic circumstances, boxing had taken a physical toll upon them. Dixon learned a great deal about boxing and also about himself. By the time he left America, he was a writer.

In the years that followed, Dixon wrote for numerous publications and served as editor of *Boxing News*. Now he has recounted his American journey in book form.

The Road to Nowhere (Pitch Publishing Ltd.) has the feel of Roger Kahn's baseball classic, *The Boys of Summer*. Kahn tracked down members of the 1955 Brooklyn Dodgers sixteen years after their World Series triumph over the New York Yankees and used their circumstances to tell the story of their lives and baseball.

Dixon's work is similar in tone. He writes well. He understands boxing. And he puts things in context.

There are a lot of thoughts in *The Road to Nowhere* that are worth repeating. Among my favorites are:

★ Harold Johnson: "Of course, I got nervous before a fight. Going into the ring is like walking in a cemetery at night."

★ Jeff Chandler [on winning the WBA bantamweight crown]: "I remember the night like yesterday. When I won, I threw my arms up and I thought they were going to stretch forever. I felt I could jump straight up and never come down."

★ George Chuvalo: "If I told you how much I made clear for fighting Ali [in 1966], you would say, 'What happened?' After taxes and everything else, I made seven hundred dollars per round. People ask, 'How much did you make for fighting Ali? Half a million bucks?' . . . A little lower . . . 'Quarter of a million?' . . . No, a little lower than that."

★ Dwight Qawi [on the powers that be in boxing]: "They make money off us, but their attitude is that we owe them."

★ Marvin Frazier [on being knocked out in the first round by Larry Holmes]: "I felt like a maggot or a worm. I felt I had embarrassed my whole family in front of the entire world."

★ Micky Ward: "People lose and they fall apart like it's the end of the world. But if you take a loss like a win and learn from it, you come back stronger. It makes you a better fighter and person. I should know. I've had eleven of them."

★ Arturo Gatti [on his three fights against Micky Ward]: "I'd always said, 'The day I fight somebody who has the same mentality that I have, I'm going to have problems.' Then Micky Ward came along with that mentality. People were cheering us for the way we fought. Not cheering either one of us but both of us. We showed you don't have to hate someone to give it your best."

★ Buster Douglas [on fighting Mike Tyson]: "Before the fight, I didn't have nobody bothering me because nobody gave me a chance. We had a press conference in Japan, and there were like four people there. When Tyson had one, it was packed. He's a monster; he's a beast. But he's short to me. He's one-dimensional. I never thought he was shit. I thought he was going to get up [after I knocked him down]. But when I saw him reaching for his mouthpiece, I thought, 'It's over. It's over, baby.'"

Reflecting on the fighters that he met on his journey across America, Dixon writes, "They all had once bounced off the colorful pages of magazines and books in my childhood like superheroes. They were strong, muscular, and powerful. Now, after every sorrowful encounter with a faded champion, I felt more worldly-wise. I felt myself hardening. They were helping me grow and mature."

It's a pleasure to read good writing. *The Road to Nowhere* is good writing.

★ ★ ★

Mark Kram was a gifted writer. *Great Men Die Twice* (St. Martin Griffin) is a collection of his best articles as selected by his son, Mark Kram Jr.

Kram started writing for *Sports Illustrated* in 1964, when the magazine was ten years old. Managing editor Andre Laguerre oversaw what was known as a "writers' magazine."

Kram took his writing seriously. "When he read his own work," his son writes in the foreword to *Great Men Die Twice*, "his eye always fell to a line that could have been worded better, a paragraph that wandered astray, a beginning or ending that was not as acutely observed as it should have been."

Unfortunately, Kram was also a heavy drinker. In his son's words, "It would be accurate to say that he did not do himself any favors by the way he comported himself. He had a foul temper. In keeping with the unsavory heritage of the Kram men, not one of whom has lived beyond the age of seventy because of alcohol addiction, Dad became aggressive when he overindulged."

Rumor has it that, on assignment in Manila for the historic third encounter between Muhammad Ali and Joe Frazier, Kram missed the fight because he was bedridden that morning with a severe hangover. What we know with certainty is that he spent some time with both fighters the evening after the bout and wrote one of the best articles ever written about a fight ("Lawdy, Lawdy, He's Great," October 13, 1975, *Sports Illustrated*).

More troubling—and also acknowledged by his son—were allegations that Kram took money from Don King to ease his financial problems. An investigation by *Sports Illustrated* uncovered what the powers that be believed were ethical breaches amounting to "gross misconduct." More specifically, Kram admitted to accepting payment from King for "screenplay proposals." He was fired by *Sports Illustrated*.

Late in life, Kram cut down on his drinking. *Ghosts of Manila* (HarperCollins)—his pro-Frazier (and sometimes mean-spirited) reflections on what he called "the fateful blood feud" between Ali and Frazier—was published in 2001. He then signed a contract to write a book about Mike Tyson. It was never written. One week after journeying to Memphis to witness Tyson's June 8, 2002, destruction at the hands of Lennox Lewis, Kram died of a heart attack at age sixty-nine.

Great Men Die Twice contains twenty articles, ten of which are about boxing. There's one notable omission. Kram's seminal September 2, 1974, *Sports Illustrated* article about Don King, which introduced King to mainstream sports fans, is not included. Still, King, Ali, Frazier, and other denizens of the sweet science are well represented.

In Kram's words, Ali's jab was "a straight left of jolting electricity." Don King "dresses like an MC in a cheap nightclub" and has hair that "looks like a bale of cotton candy just retrieved from a coal bin." Brain damage is "the common cold" in a fighter's life.

Read and enjoy Kram's work. At his best, he wrote about boxing as well as anyone.

★ ★ ★

Few fights are as enshrined in boxing lore as the September 14, 1923, confrontation between Jack Dempsey and Luis Firpo. The bout took place at the Polo Grounds in New York before more than 80,000 fans, who paid $1,188,603 to witness history in the making. It was boxing's second largest gate up until that time.

Dempsey and The Wild Bull by John Jarrett (Pitch Publishing) tells the story of the fight. The material on Dempsey is familiar. The material on Firpo is not.

Firpo was born in Argentina in 1894. He had huge hands, stood a shade over 6-feet-2-inches tall, and weighed 216 pounds. Dempsey, eight months younger, was an inch shorter and weighed 192 pounds when they entered the ring.

Firpo came to the United States in 1922 after five years as a professional boxer. Legends about him abounded. Some newspaper reports maintained that he was the son of a wealthy railroad builder and a Cantalonean noblewoman. The fighter himself rebutted that notion with the declaration, "My father is a railroad builder, but he builds with a pick and shovel."

About the only thing the newspapers agreed on was that Firpo spoke no English. Damon Runyon affixed the label "The Wild Bull of the Pampas" to him. In truth, Firpo was not from the pampas (a vast plains region). He'd grown up in Buenos Aires and worked as a stevedore, boot black, and bottle washer in a drugstore before turning to boxing.

The Argentinean was a raw crude fighter with strength and endurance, monumental defensive deficiencies, and a virtually useless left hand. "His left hand," Runyon wrote, "seems of no use whatever to him in a fight. He holds it out in front of him, but knows nothing of jabbing or hooking with it."

Firpo's right hand could render an opponent unconscious with one blow. His most notable victory prior to challenging Dempsey was an eighth-round stoppage of Jess Willard at Boyle's Thirty Acres in New Jersey on July 12, 1923. That led Willard (who'd been knocked out four years earlier by the Manassa Mauler) to declare, "They talk about the wallop in Dempsey's punches, but I will tell you that Firpo hits the hardest. I know."

Former welterweight champion Jack Britton said of Firpo, "Why teach him to be clever. It would spoil him. He's a natural fighter and a dangerous one."

Dempsey-Firpo was attended by the rich and powerful. Vanderbilt, Whitney, Biddle, Gould, Rothschild, and Morgan were some of the names at ringside. They were joined by Florenz Ziegfeld, James Corbett, Babe Ruth, and Al Capone.

Dempsey floored Firpo seven times in the first round and was knocked down twice himself. One of those knockdowns saw the champion blasted through the ropes onto the laps of reporters; a moment immortalized on canvas by George Bellows's famous painting, *Dempsey and Firpo.*

In round two, Dempsey knocked Firpo down twice more. Fifty-seven seconds into the second stanza, the Argentinean was counted out.

Ford Frick, then a reporter for the *New York Evening Journal*, wrote afterward, "Eighty-five thousand persons rose to their feet as one man when the bell called the two fighters for the opening, and eighty five thousand persons were still standing at the finish."

Frank G. Menke followed suit, writing in *The Sporting News*, "From the moment the first gong banged, there was action so rapid, so cyclonic, that the eye could not follow nor the brain record the exact details."

Jarrett's writing is a bit dry at times, but he has done his homework well. *Dempsey and The Wild Bull* is a strong factual recounting of events. Anticipation for the climactic fight builds nicely.

And one final note: In the Bellows painting, Firpo's body is twisted in a way that, in reality, would have robbed him of his punching power.

Worse, as Jarrett notes, Firpo is depicted as knocking Dempsey through the ropes with a left hand, not his right.

* * *

British writer Jonathan Rendall taped ten interviews for a book that he was planning to write about Mike Tyson. Then he fell victim to lifestyle issues and died in 2013 at the much-too-young age of forty-eight. Richard Williams has edited Rendall's unfinished manuscript. The result is an intriguing oral history entitled *Scream: The Tyson Tapes* (Short Books).

Scream is divided into four parts: "The House," "The Coronation," "The Fall," and "The End." The last three parts are sketchy and superficial. "The House" (in Catskill, where Tyson lived with Cus D'Amato) is well constructed and informative.

Rendell's interviews are woven together to re-create the atmosphere in the house where Tyson spent his formative years as a boxer and young man. The most interesting of these interviews are with Kevin Rooney and Teddy Atlas, who disrespect and dislike each other to the point where the tension between them all but curls the pages of *Scream*.

Rooney told Rendall, "Anything Teddy Atlas tells you is bullshit."

Atlas responded in kind, saying, "I consider myself above Rooney. If I'm on an anthill, I'm on Mount Everest compared to him."

The tangle of emotions between Tyson, Atlas, Rooney, and Cus D'Amato is at the heart of *Scream*. Sage commentary from boxing maven Don Majeski adds to the book. And Rendall recorded some interesting insights from Nadia Hujtyn, a young woman who was in the gym in Catskill during the Tyson years.

Hujtyn recalls D'Amato being enthralled by Tyson's potential as a fighter. But at the same time, she remembers Cus prophetically noting, "If he loses desire, it doesn't matter about the rest."

* * *

She's a Knockout by L. A. Jennings (Rowman & Littlefield) has an unfortunate title that obscures a serious book.

Jennings is a former mixed martial artist, who researched the history of women in combat sports as part of her studies at Florida State University. The book's emphasis is on women who engaged in competition in England and the United States, rather than those who trained for the purpose of conditioning, self-defense, or simply to learn a new art.

The writing is a bit dry at times. But Jennings has conducted serious research and compiled excellent source material on her subject. Although the book covers all combat sports, boxing is well represented.

How much have attitudes toward the involvement of women in combat sports changed over the years?

I have a collection of uncut boxing tickets from historically significant fights. As I write these words, I'm looking at a "working press" ticket for the September 23, 1952, fight in which Rocky Marciano dethroned Jersey Joe Walcott to claim the heavyweight championship of the world.

The ticket is stamped in capital letters in red ink, "LADIES NOT ADMITTED TO PRESS SECTION."

★ ★ ★

Adam Pollack is an Iowa attorney who loves boxing. In 2006, McFarland & Company published his first book, a biography of John L. Sullivan.

Like all first-time authors, Pollack was happy to be published. But McFarland controlled the editorial and business side of the process in ways that made him unhappy. So for his next book, he started his own publishing company.

Win By KO Publications now has twelve books in print with more on the way. Six of the twelve are biographies of early gloved champions written by Pollack himself. There's one novel in the mix, a book by Margaret Goodman entitled *Death in Vegas*. Authors contribute to the start-up cost of publication. But if their book sells even modestly well, they make it up on the back end.

Like all good publishers, Pollack rejects books that fall short of his standards for readability and scholarship. "I want to establish a brand name," he says. "It would bother me if a reader felt betrayed after buying one of our books."

Win By KO Publications has tapped into a niche market and is making a significant contribution to the preservation of boxing history. Its most recent offering is *Tony Zale: Man of Steel*, written by boxing historian Clay Moyle in collaboration with Thad Zale (Tony's nephew).

Zale was a good fighter and, by all accounts, a good guy. His three brutal middleweight championship fights against Rocky Graziano (Zale won two of the three) are part of boxing lore.

"Rocky wasn't the toughest guy I fought," Zale told his nephew years later. "But he got the best press."

Tony Zale: Man of Steel has strengths and weaknesses similar to Moyle's earlier biographies of Sam Langford and Billy Miske. There's a treasure trove of information, but the book reads at times like a 365-page Wikipedia article. On balance, it's worth the read for a look at an important fighter and a bygone era.

★ ★ ★

For more than a century, the heavyweight championship was the most coveted title in sports. But there was a strange interregnum between Gene Tunney and Joe Louis when five men played musical chairs with the throne and its luster dimmed.

Four of these men have taglines that identify them. Max Schmeling became a symbol of Nazi Germany. Prima Carnera was the mob-controlled giant. Max Baer was a hard-hitting playboy. James Braddock was the impoverished dockworker struggling to survive during the Great Depression.

Jack Sharkey is virtually unknown.

Jack Sharkey by James Curl (Win By KO Publications) is the antidote to that malady.

Joseph Zukauskas learned to box in the United States Navy. He changed his name before his first pro fight in 1924 as a tribute to Jack Dempsey and Tom Sharkey.

"Sharkey," Curl writes, "was a fighter who ran hot and cold and gave erratic performances throughout his career." His final ring record was 37 wins (13 KOs), 13 losses, and 3 draws. The most notable opponents he faced were Harry Wills (WDQ 13), Jack Dempsey (KO by 6), Tommy

Loughran (KO 3, L 15), Max Schmeling (LDQ 4, W 15), Mickey Walker (D 12), Primo Carnera (W 15, KO by 6), and Joe Louis (KO by 3).

Curl blends extensive newspaper fight reports with other sources. One of his best accounts is of Dempsey-Sharkey (contested before eighty-thousand fans at Yankee Stadium in 1927). Dempsey went flagrantly low often and hard. Finally, Sharkey turned to the referee to complain, and the Manassa Mauler knocked him out with a picture-perfect left hook to the jaw.

Years later, Sharkey recalled, "When Dempsey hit me, it was like someone dumped a load of concrete over my head. I never thought a man could hit so hard. I've felt that punch for thirteen years." At age eighty-five, he said of that night, "Dempsey broke every rule of the prize ring. He hit me in the nuts all night long." Asked if he was still bitter about it, Sharkey answered, "Nah, he saw an opening and he took it."

Sharkey's first fight against Max Schmeling (in 1930, when Schmeling won the vacant heavyweight title in front of eighty-five thousands fans at Yankee Stadium on a questionable disqualification) is well told. There's curiously little material in Curl's book on Schmeling-Sharkey II, when Sharkey captured the crown on a fifteen-round split decision two years later.

Then came Sharkey's first title defense: a one-punch sixth-round knockout loss at the hands of Primo Carnera in a bout that many observers thought was fixed. Curl presents both sides of the "fix" debate, giving the last word to Sharkey who, nearing the end of his life, declared, "I'd never have done anything like that. I was raised Catholic. I was raised to be honest. I was on top of the world. Why would I purposefully lose?"

Asked what it felt like to lose, Sharkey responded, "It's a terrible feeling. You devalue yourself. You don't want to see anyone. You just want to hide."

The last fight of Sharkey's career was a third-round knockout loss to a young Joe Louis.

"Youth was served tonight," Sharkey said afterward. "Good luck to him. He's a good fighter, better than I am. Whether he'll be as good as I was tonight [when he's] thirty-four remains to be seen."

★ ★ ★

William Detloff calls Ezzard Charles "one of the best prizefighters who ever lived." *Ezzard Charles: A Boxing Life* (McFarland & Company) supports that thesis.

Charles was born in Georgia in 1921, raised in Cincinnati by his maternal grandmother, and turned pro for a five-dollar purse on March 12, 1940. Over the course of nineteen years, he amassed a ring record of 95 wins, 25 losses, 1 draw, 52 KOs, and 7 KOs by. He was diagnosed with amyotrophic lateral sclerosis (also known as Lou Gehrig's Disease) in 1966, suffered through the inevitable physical horrors that followed, and died at age fifty-three.

How good was Charles?

He began his career as a middleweight and fought his way to the heavyweight championship of the world. He was undefeated against Archie Moore (3-0), Joey Maxim (5-0), and Charley Burley (2-0); had winning records against Jimmy Bivins (4-1) and Lloyd Marshall (2-1); and won three of seven bouts against Joe Louis (1-0), Jersey Joe Walcott (2-2), and Rocky Marciano (0-2). In his last 29 fights, he suffered 17 losses and was knocked out five times. Remove those fights from his record and Charles's ledger is more in keeping with the fighter he was.

Charles fought in an era when baseball and boxing were America's two national sports. "Joe Louis and Sugar Ray Robinson," Detloff writes, "were as famous as any movie stars. Every fighter who held a world title was a household name."

But Charles never achieved the acclaim that his more heralded contemporaries enjoyed.

"Some guys had the gift of gab or a thunderous punch or a great back story," Detloff recounts. "Some had unusual charisma or presence. Charles had none of these. He wasn't a palooka. He didn't talk in broken or mangled English. He didn't get a big push from the mob. He'd never done any jail time. He didn't get into fistfights outside the ring or get caught in pictures with lily-white prostitutes. [But] Charles was never anyone's hero. Not the way he should have been. American sports fans were looking for a hero who was as good as [Joe] Louis in the same exact way. It never occurred to them that there was more than one way to be great."

Charles's problem—or one of them, anyway—was that he succeeded Joe Louis as heavyweight champion of the world.

Louis had been Charles's boyhood idol. He'd listened to the Brown Bomber's fights on the radio and kept a scrapbook with newspaper clippings that detailed Louis's ring conquests.

In 1949, after Louis temporarily retired, Charles decisioned Jersey Joe Walcott to claim the vacant heavyweight throne. The following year, he successfully defended his championship against Louis. That left him with a predicament similar to the one that Larry Holmes faced when he followed Muhammad Ali.

"I'm a little disappointed," Charles said of his situation. "I thought that, after I whipped Joe Louis, the fans would accept me as a true heavyweight champion. But now I know they want a bigger different type champ. Joe made those quick knockouts popular. It's a bit tough on the guy that follows him."

In a similar vein, Rocky Marciano observed, "I was at ringside the night Ezzard defeated Joe Louis. It was a real good fight. But as I was leaving, all the people seemed to be talking about Joe. In the papers the next day, the same thing. Everybody seemed to be crying for the loser. Nobody gave any credit to Ezzard. People just didn't want to see Louis lose. It wasn't Ezzard's fault. He has simply come along in a time in history when a blood-hungry public couldn't appreciate him."

Detloff's book has strengths and flaws. Clearly, he thoroughly researched his subject. But there are some nagging factual errors, such as saying that Charles died in 1973 (the actual date of death was May 28, 1975).

Also, there are times when Detloff writes extremely well about what it meant to be a fighter in Charles's day: "Poor boys from the worst ghettos could turn themselves into something in the fight game. If they were any good, they'd hear a crowd cheer for them; they'd get a few dames that were hotter and looser than what they'd get otherwise; and maybe they'd get their name in the paper once or twice. Plus they'd get to know the singular joy of cracking a man on the jaw with a perfect left hook. They'd find out how it felt to dominate another man, to make him quit. It could make a poor nothing from the neighborhood a god for a few minutes."

Similarly, in one of the book's better passages, Detloff describes "that strange world that all fighters come to know eventually. Where you can see the ringsiders cheering but can't hear them; when you can see the referee's face up close to yours, but it's behind a blanket of fog, and you can tell he's saying something but don't understand the language."

But *Ezzard Charles: A Boxing Life* doesn't have the nuanced texture of Russell Sullivan's masterful biography of Rocky Marciano or Michael Isenberg's seminal work on John L. Sullivan. After a while, the fight reports become repetitive. And with some notable exceptions (such as Charles vs. Joe Louis and the two Marciano-Charles encounters), Detloff is prone to recounting major bouts with no more drama than less important ones.

That said; *Ezzard Charles: A Boxing Life* makes a compelling case for its subject's ring greatness. Although never given the opportunity to fight for the 175-pound world title, Charles was unquestionably one of the greatest light-heavyweights of all time.

"The heavyweight version of Charles," Detloff sums up, "would get a lot of good work done. But on the best day of his life, he was no more a heavyweight than Ray Robinson. He never would be as good there as he was at light-heavy and below."

★ ★ ★

Journeymen by Mark Turley (Pitch Publishing) recounts the story of ten British fighters who are professional losers. They might bridle at that label. But losing fights is essential to what they do. Turley calls them "journeymen" (which, on this side of the Atlantic, would connote a more respectable ring record). These fighters have records like 0 wins, 67 losses, 2 draws (Bheki Moyo); 1 win, 51 losses (Robin Deakin); 9 wins, 180 losses, 7 draws (Kristian Laight); and 5 wins, 91 losses, 5 draws (Matthew Seawright).

They are often hopelessly outclassed. And when they might be able to put up a competitive fight, they don't. The referee, who's usually the sole judge, is in on the arrangement. Should one of these opponents get the better of the house fighter, the referee frequently ignores what happened in the ring and raises the hand of the favorite in victory. The regulatory authorities are negligent and shameless.

"The stories here," Turley writes, "come from the wrong end of the fight game. It is the elephant in the room of professional pugilism. Most fights at this level have a predetermined outcome. Officially, there is nothing stopping a journeyman from going all out for a win and knocking out the home fighter. But if he wants regular work and the paychecks that come with it, he needs to play the game. Keeping busy and avoiding injury are the keys. They fight while holding themselves in check to preserve the status quo."

"This is how it works," says James Nesbitt (one of Turley's subjects, who had a 10-173-4 record at the time of publication). "Before we go out there, I get a quiet word in my ear. 'Jase, you've got to take it easy. This lad's sold six grand worth of tickets, so we can't have him losing. If you go out there and knock him out, I promise you, you're not getting any fights.' The taking it easy bit happens with most of my fights. I'm not actually trying to win because I'm told not to. And that's basically what I do to earn my money in boxing. It's my weekly wage, so I'm going to do what I need to do to keep it coming. I'm not there to win. I'm there to make the fight and give the lad a workout. Any more than that and people get upset."

Johnny Greaves (4 wins and 96 losses) has similar thoughts. "For me," Greaves says, "being a paid opponent was the obvious choice to make. I knew I was never going to be a world champion. Going down the journeyman route gave me a way to make a living. The thing is, I don't go in there to lose, not exactly. But if you upset the ticket sellers, then the promoters won't use you. So if you want to get rebooked, you have to do enough to make the fight interesting without causing a problem. I could open up, bash him about, maybe catch a couple myself, and I'm still not going to get the decision. So what's the point? I might as well make things easy."

Turley's work is thoughtful and honest. There are times when his recitation of each journeyman's story is repetitive. And readers have to remind themselves from time to time that there's nothing noble about a fighter pulling his punches to lose a fight. It's like a basketball player shaving points.

In the end, Turley acknowledges as much, writing, "In the final analysis, the stories here have not been about heroes. They have been about reality. Losing on purpose for money is not what sport is meant to be about." But he adds in closing, "Journeymen didn't create the system. They just operate within it."

★ ★ ★

Slats: The Legend and Life of Jimmy Slattery by Rich Blake (NFB/ Amelia Press) is about a fighter and an era when local fighters were heroes, the good-looking ones were matinee idols, and boxing mattered.

Slattery was born in Buffalo in 1904. He turned pro at age seventeen, won his first thirty-eight fights, lost a six-round decision, and reeled off ten more wins before manager Red Carr inadvisedly matched him against world middleweight champion Harry Greb, who beat him badly. Slattery was twenty years old at the time.

"Slats," Blake writes, "was a comet, the rage of the nation. Never was anyone so assuredly fated for ring supremacy. Slats more resembled a silent movie star than a pugilist. He fought in a fast fluid unique manner—arms dangling loose at his sides, dancing on his toes, avoiding punches with a deft tilt of his head before snapping his right like a cobra. Considered so far above everyone else in the game, Slattery drew comparisons to Man O'War. When he fought at Yankee Stadium, Babe Ruth sat ringside."

But by 1927, Slattery was an alcoholic. He partied before fights and, once he lost, after them.

"He sold his boxing birthright for a mess of good times," Ed Hughes of the *New York Telegraph* wrote.

"He was washed up at 24," Blake acknowledges.

In the last major fight of his career, Slattery fought Maxie Rosenbloom for the seventh time (a fifteen-round-decision loss at Ebbet's Field in Brooklyn). The action, or lack thereof, was so abysmal that Westbrook Pegler wrote in the *Chicago Tribune*, "Rosenbloom won and Slattery lost, but the patrons took the punishment." The *Police Gazette* added, "The 5,000 fans would probably have gotten more thrills had they gone instead to the Brooklyn Botanical Garden across the street."

Slattery retired at age twenty-nine with a ring record of 111 wins, 13 losses, 49 KOs and 4 KOs by. Asked to put his career in perspective, boxing historian Craig Hamilton told this writer, "He was a good fighter and a hot prospect when he was young. But he was poorly matched and never developed into a championship-caliber fighter. He fought a lot of tough guys: Harry Greb, Young Stribling, Jack Delaney, Dave Shade, Paul Berlenbach, Maxie Rosenbloom, Tommy Loughran, James Braddock,

King Levinsky. And for the most part, he fought them at the wrong time. What he really needed was a guy like Bruce Trampler to matchmake for him."

On a personal level, Slattery married, had a son, walked away from the marriage (which ended in divorce), and saw his son roughly twenty times during the course of his life. After boxing, he was arrested countless times for public intoxication, driving while intoxicated, and other alcohol-related offenses in addition to at least one robbery. He lived in flophouses and was homeless for a time. He never stopped drinking.

Slats is thoroughly researched and well-written with an eye for detail. It's a bit hyperbolic at times, as evidenced by the book's opening sentence that maintains "no boxer [in the mid-1920s] transfixed fans like Jimmy Slattery" and a later chapter that calls him "the most talked about boxer on the planet." Outside of Buffalo, those who were familiar with Jack Dempsey might have disputed that notion.

Dempsey himself makes several appearances in the book, including an anecdote that dates to 1925 when the Manassa Mauler (still heavyweight champion) appeared on the vaudeville circuit in Buffalo.

Ike O'Neil, a Buffalo-born trainer, came by the theater to say hello.

"Remember this fellow?" Dempsey was asked.

"Aren't you the fellow who worked in Willard's corner that day?" Dempsey answered, harkening back to July 4, 1919, when he beat Jess Willard to a bloody pulp and claimed the heavyweight throne.

"Yeah, that's me," O'Neil told the champ. "I'm the guy who threw in the towel."

"Jess stayed in the game too long," Dempsey responded, a reference to the knockout loss that Willard suffered at the hands of Luis Firpo four years later. "When I lose the title, I'm done. They're not going to make a punching bag out of Jack Dempsey."

And there's an entertaining bit of boxing lore in Blake's recounting of a 1956 television appearance in which Maxie Rosenbloom told an interviewer, "I fought Jimmy Slattery [three times] in Buffalo and beat him every time, but I was robbed on hometown decisions. I saw it was hopeless trying to beat him in Buffalo and I decided to make some money out of losing. So [in our 1930 fight] I bet $5,000 on Slats. Along about the fourth round with neither of us doing anything, I said to Jimmy, 'Come on, Slats, do something. I bet on you to win.' And Slats said, 'I bet on you.'"

Claiming that he'd been falsely defamed, Slattery sued Rosenbloom, CBS, and Gillette (which had sponsored the telecast) for $500,000. The case was settled for five hundred dollars.

★ ★ ★

Brin-Jonathan Butler's new book, *The Domino Diaries* (Picador Publishers), opens with a chapter entitled "How Did This White Mother-fucker Get Inside My House?"

That's the way Mike Tyson introduced himself on Easter Sunday 2010, when, speaking through "a thick cloud of marijuana smoke," he descended the staircase in his Henderson, Nevada, home for an interview with Butler.

The Tyson-Butler encounter is only a small part of *The Domino Diaries*. But it sets the tone and gives readers a feel for both Tyson and Butler.

One of the next thoughts Tyson uttered was, "I'm guessing you being here in my home, sitting across from me right now—I'm guessing this is pretty intense for you, huh?"

The Domino Diaries is a personal memoir with boxing ever-present in the background. The opening portions are devoted largely to Butler's fragile early family life and torturous adolescence. "Getting beat up [at age eleven by a mob of classmates]," he writes, "changed my life forever."

There was a brief stint as an amateur boxer.

"You can't learn to take a punch," Butler observes. "Whether you have a glass chin or you don't, the only way of finding out is having it land." That observation is joined with reminiscences like, "I knew I was going to get hurt. And any time you got hurt, there was a chance you could spend the rest of your life picking up the pieces."

Ultimately, Butler's life adventure led him to Cuba. Much of his time there was devoted to experiences culminating in a film documentary that explored the reasons why Cubans remain on the island or flee, as examined through the prism of its most celebrated boxers.

Butler writes lyrically and well.

Re-creating a fight card in Havana, he recalls, "They were watching sports in a way that the rest of the world could only dream about. While the fights lasted, it was pure. No interviews. No cameras. No advertising. No commercial breaks. No merchandise. No thanking of sponsors. No luxury boxes. No Tecate or Corona ring girls. No VIP seating. No scalpers outside. No venue named after a corporation or corporately owned anything anywhere. No air conditioning. No amenities of any kind. Instead, you had a full auditorium of intensely proud people who didn't require cues to cheer. Without the incentive of money, I watched people fight harder in the ring than anywhere else I'd ever seen. And they fought this way before an audience who cheered louder than anywhere I'd ever heard."

Butler crafts a particularly poignant portrait of Teofilo Stevenson; the intensely handsome, 6-foot-5-inch giant, who won Olympic gold medals in the heavyweight division at the 1972 Munich, 1976 Montreal, and 1980 Moscow Olympics. He was favored to win a fourth gold medal in 1984, but the Communist bloc boycotted the Los Angeles games.

In 1976, Stevenson was offered five million dollars to leave Cuba and fight Muhammad Ali. He declined.

Butler interviewed Stevenson in his modest Havana home in May 2011.

"By now," Butler writes, "Stevenson was a full-blown alcoholic without enough money to replace a flat tire on his car. Yet while his life remained an open wound, I saw no evidence of regret."

The price that Butler paid for the interview was $130 and a bottle of vodka.

Stevenson died thirteen months later at age sixty. His conversation with Butler was his last known filmed interview.

★ ★ ★

Wiped Out, written with Mark Turley, (Pitch Publishing) is Jerome Wilson's first-person account of a boxing horror story.

On September 24, 2014, Wilson (8-2, 2 KOs) entered the ring in Sheffield to fight a rematch against 3-and-0 Serge Ambomo, who'd defeated him on points three months earlier.

Wilson wasn't a ticket-seller. As a rule, he performed more ably in the gym than on fight night. As Turley notes in an introduction to the book, Jerome's story is made extraordinary only through great misfortune. The bulk of his ring career was unremarkable.

In his rematch against Ambomo, Wilson was knocked out at 2:15 of the sixth and final round.

"The life he had known for so long, the fighter's life, was finished in an instant by a right hand," Turley writes. "His momentum moved him on to the punch. Immediately unconscious, Jerome toppled like a chainsawed tree. As he made his descent, neck loose, he was caught again with a left. The back of his head bounced off the boards. There was an almost imperceptible twitch in his legs. Then stillness, complete stillness. After frantic attempts to revive him, Jerome had to be stretchered away. He did not open his eyes to start his new life for ten days."

Wilson had suffered an acute subdural hematoma. Five months later, Turley met with him to discuss the possibility of writing a book.

"I'd never met anyone with such a terrible injury before," Turley recalls. "It was like a movie special effect. His head literally had a slice cleaved out of it. As we introduced ourselves, I found it difficult not to stare at the area where surgeons had removed a bone flap, a quarter of his skull from above and behind his right ear, leaving a mango sized indentation. The skin there sagged down like a parachute caught between two trees. An angry scar circled the crater. While he made affable small-talk making light of his situation, you could actually see his brain undulate below the skin. It was unsettling and fascinating at the same time."

The most dramatic parts of *Wiped Out* deal with Wilson's injury and recovery to date.

"Emerging from a coma is a bit like being born," Wilson recounts. "People have the wrong idea. They think it's like being asleep, then waking up. I wouldn't describe it that way at all. I opened my eyes, but it was as if I hadn't. Darkness became whiteness, but there was nothing there. I closed them again, and it all faded away. At the beginning, that's how it was. In and out, out and in. There was little difference between unconsciousness and alertness, between death and near-death. I understood nothing. After a while, my vision gained more definition but everything was split. I'd look at a person, and it was like they had four heads. Another period of time passed, and a nurse told me that I had to have an X-ray. I still didn't know what was wrong."

Wilson was in the hospital for seven weeks. Extended rehabilitation therapy followed. He had to learn to eat, walk, read, and perform simple personal hygiene functions all over again.

"The passage of days, weeks, and years doesn't seem that important to me anymore," Jerome says. *Wiped Out* is sketchy on the details of exactly what he can and can't do today.

There's some good writing in *Wiped Out*, but the book also has flaws. The format that Wilson and Turley decided upon is intended to show Wilson's mental confusion in the aftermath of his injury. Unfortunately, it's poorly executed in places with the result that the narrative is often muddled. Characters and events that the reader is led to believe are important turn out to be illusory. The addition of a bit more order to Wilson's chaotic thoughts would have been welcome.

That said; at the beginning of the book, Turley writes: "It is not and never will be my aim to attack boxing. I have been connected to it in one way or another all of my life and always will be. But I also strongly believe that we should discuss its dangers with openness."

Wiped Out is true to that end.

The ritual "ten count" was a sad part of boxing in 2015.

In Memoriam

Cedric Kushner was a strange man.

He had few active family ties. Love seemed beyond his reach. He spoke openly, even proudly, of his involvement with prostitutes. His greatest pleasure derived from being in boxing and spending time with boxing people.

"Boxing," he once said, "is a business in which I sue you on Tuesday and buy you lunch on Wednesday. I like that."

Kushner was born in South Africa in 1948. A self-described "disobedient youngster who had no interest in school," he abandoned academia after failing the American equivalent of seventh grade and worked at a series of jobs, including a stint as a tally clerk on the docks of Capetown. He left South Africa in 1970 as a deckhand onboard a freighter and came to the United States.

Kushner worked as a laborer in a Boston warehouse; in Florida, cleaning swimming pools and handing out towels at the Fontainebleau Hotel; and as a Ferris-wheel operator at an amusement park in New Jersey. In 1974, he formed Cedric Kushner Promotions with the aim of promoting rock concerts. Eight years later, he began promoting fights.

There was a time when Kushner promoted fifty fight cards a year, many of them in Europe. He was a tireless worker with a good eye for talent. His "Heavyweight Explosion" franchise developed marketable fighters. For one glorious moment, he was on top of the world.

On April 22, 2001, Hasim Rahman knocked out Lennox Lewis to claim the heavyweight throne. At the same time, Shane Mosley was ranked second on most pound-for-pound lists. Kushner promoted both men.

Then came the fall.

Don King lured Rahman away with a duffel bag filled with cash. Mosley fulfilled his contractual obligations and left Cedric for greener pastures.

Meanwhile, Kushner was overreaching. A series of unprofitable fight cards at the Hammerstein Ballroom in New York incurred hundreds of thousands of dollars in losses. An ill-advised venture called "ThunderBox" led to an even greater cash drain.

And Cedric's health was failing. For much of his life, he'd abused his body, becoming morbidly obese. After undergoing a gastric bypass operation in 2003, he failed to follow the required vitamin regimen, which led to more health problems.

In the final years of his life, Kushner suffered from acute physical issues and the onset of dementia. He died on January 29, 2015, after suffering a massive heart attack at age sixty-six.

Kushner had a variety of nicknames over the years. But the one that stuck among his friends was "Uncle Ced."

I understood that sentiment. When I began writing about boxing on a regular basis, I was regarded as a fringe Internet writer. As such, I was accustomed to slights. Often, I found myself in conversation with a promoter or other insider who was looking over my shoulder for someone better to talk with.

That never happened with Cedric. In those early days, he treated me the same way he treated everyone else in boxing. With respect. I was grateful for that.

Cedric Kushner wanted to be liked.

He was.

★ ★ ★

I would be remiss if I didn't note the passing of Joe Dwyer, who died on February 8, 2015, after a period of declining health.

Joe was born and raised in the Bay Ridge section of Brooklyn. His father was a New York City police detective who fought professionally in the late 1920s but gave up boxing when he married Joe's mother.

"My parents separated when I was young," Dwyer told me years ago. "My mother raised us. My father was my idol, and he was a great guy in many ways. But he never took responsibility and, because of that, my mother had a rough life."

Dwyer dropped out of high school on his sixteenth birthday, and worked as a mail clerk for American Express. One year later, he joined the United States Navy Reserves. At age eighteen, he went on active duty. He earned a high-school graduation equivalency degree in the Navy and served as a mechanic onboard the USS *Franklin D. Roosevelt.*

After being discharged from the Navy, Dwyer worked for two years as a cargo checker on the Brooklyn waterfront. He joined the New York City Police Department in 1961, and served for thirty-four years, rising to the rank of detective.

Joe was also a boxing guy. In 59 amateur fights, he had 56 wins, 2 losses, and 1 no contest. Fighting as a middleweight, he won the New York City Metropolitan AAU, New York State AAU, and US Navy 6th Fleet championships. In 1983, while still a cop, he became an inspector for the New York State Athletic Commission. One year later, he was elevated to chief inspector. In 1995, ring judging became part of his duties. He left the NYSAC in 2000 to become chairman of the IBF championship committee and later served two terms as president of the NABF.

Through it all, he had a strong sense of loyalty to whatever organization he was affiliated with.

Joe and I talked on the phone two or three times a month. The conversations were usually issue oriented. Often, we were on opposite sides of an issue. But the exchanges were cordial.

I didn't always agree with Joe's convictions. But he lived up to them.

★ ★ ★

Gene Fullmer, who died on April 27, 2015, at age eighty-three, will be best remembered for one of the less auspicious moments in his ring career.

Fullmer was a rough tough brawler from Utah, who compiled a 55-6-3 ring record over the course of twelve years. He lacked a big punch, but was blessed with a granite chin and wore opponents down through attrition.

On January 2, 1957, Fullmer challenged an aging Sugar Ray Robinson for the middleweight crown. "There's nothing I can say," Robinson acknowledged after the unanimous decision against him was announced. "The better man won tonight."

Four months later, on May 1, 1957, they fought again. Fullmer was a 3-to-1 favorite. After four rounds, he was in control. Robinson seemed to be tiring, and the assumption was that he'd wilt further as the fight wore on.

"Up to that time, it wasn't a tough fight," Fullmer later recalled. "I was winning on everybody's card. I was working on his body a lot, and he was hurting. Never seen the punch coming. I don't know anything about the punch except I've watched it on movies a number of times. I didn't know anything about being hit. I didn't know anything about being down. The first thing I knew, I was standing up. Robinson was in the other corner. I thought he was in great condition, doing exercises between rounds. My manager crawled in the ring. I said, 'What happened?' He said, 'They counted ten.' Up to then, I didn't know."

Sugar Ray Robinson, two days shy of his thirty-sixth birthday, had landed the ultimate highlight-reel punch of all time: a short compact left hook that exploded on Fullmer's jaw. It might have been Robinson's greatest single moment as a fighter and was his last moment of true ring greatness. Later, he called it "the most perfect punch of my career."

Fullmer regained the title in 1959 with a twelfth-round knockout of Carmen Basilio. He then fought Robinson twice more. Their third encounter was a draw. Fullmer won by decision in the finale.

So don't feel sorry for Gene Fullmer. Yes, his being knocked unconscious is an enduring part of boxing lore. But it was his granite chin that made Robinson's punch so remarkable. And Fullmer would be among the first to recognize that it's an honor to be remembered in history in tandem with Sugar Ray Robinson.

★ ★ ★

Bob Foster, who died on November 21, 2015, at age seventy-seven, was one of the greatest, hardest-hitting light-heavyweight champions ever. He won the title with a one-punch, fourth-round knockout of Dick Tiger in 1968, and held it until announcing his retirement six years later. During his reign, he challenged Joe Frazier and Muhammad Ali but was knocked out both times. He couldn't take a heavyweight punch.

But he had one.

Ali-Foster was particularly memorable. The bout took place in Stateline, Nevada, on November 21, 1972. Outweighed by forty-one pounds, Foster was knocked down seven times before being counted out in the eighth round. But in the fifth round, he did something that no one had been able to do before. He cut Ali—a gash on the left eyelid that required five stitches to close.

"The fight was in a nightclub," Foster reminisced when we talked years ago. "You go up in the ring, and there are people sitting there, eating dinner, having drinks all around you. But once the fight started, it was him and me and the referee. It didn't feel that different. My strategy going in was to hit him with jabs, because I had a stiff jab that would bust anybody up. That's all I wanted to do. Jab, jab, jab, until I could drop the bomb. But Ali never stood in one place. The first round, I couldn't catch him. I couldn't see his hands at all. They say he slowed down after the layoff, but the guy was still just too fast. At the end of the round, I went back to my corner. My trainer, Billy Edwards, asked, 'Bobby, what do you see?' And I said, 'I can't catch this guy.' So Billy told me to counterpunch, and that's what I did. When Ali jabbed, I jabbed, and after a while I began to connect."

"Busting him up is what I remember most about the fight," Foster continued. "It wasn't one punch. It was a lot of jabs that got the skin raw and finally cut him. I like to think that back then I had the hardest jab in boxing. I stopped a lot of guys with it by ripping them open in three or four rounds. I figured I could beat Ali. But what happened was, his weight wore me down."

In 1986, Foster was in Las Vegas for the rematch between Larry Holmes and Michael Spinks. Ali was there too.

"I walked over to Ali and said, 'How are you, champ?'" Foster recalled. "But he didn't recognize me."

Muhammad Ali fought fifty different opponents in his sixty-one professional fights. Twenty-nine of them have now predeceased him.

★ ★ ★

Everybody who knew Howard Davis liked him. He had a warm way about him and was a nice guy.

Davis won four national Golden Gloves titles and an amateur world crown. He vaulted into the public consciousness at the 1976 Olympics in Montreal. Five American boxers won Olympic gold medals that year.

Davis (who reigned supreme at 132 pounds), was awarded the Val Barker Trophy as the outstanding fighter of the 1976 games.

Putting that achievement in perspective, the other American gold-medal winners were Ray Leonard, Leon and Michael Spinks, and Leo Randolph.

"Winning the gold medal was a moment of mixed emotions," Davis later recalled. "It meant I'd won the greatest prize in amateur sports. But three days before the Olympics, my mother had died. So even now, the Olympics are a memory tinged with sadness. I was never able to complete the feel-good process about them."

Two of Davis's teammates—Ray Leonard and Michael Spinks—rose to superstardom. Leon Spinks embarked on a roller-coaster ride that included a 1978 upset of Muhammad Ali for the heavyweight championship of the world. Leo Randolph fought professionally for only two years, but captured the WBA junior-featherweight title. Of the five gold-medal winners, only Davis failed to win a world crown.

He came close twice.

In 1980, in Glasgow, Davis challenged Scotland's James Watt for the WBC lightweight title. Watt won a hard-fought unanimous decision by scores of 145–144, 147–144, and 149–142.

Responding to the first loss of his professional career, Davis ran off thirteen consecutive victories. In 1984, he challenged again for the WBC title. This time, the opponent was Edwin Rosario, with the bout in Rosario's backyard, San Juan.

Rosario started fast, dominating the first three minutes and flooring Davis in the second stanza. But in round three, an overhand right caught Rosario flush on the cheekbone and turned the tide. After eleven rounds, one judge had Rosario ahead by two points and a second favored Davis by three. The third judge, Sid Nathan of Great Britain, had the bout dead even. The twelfth round would decide.

For two minutes and fifty seconds of the last round, Davis dominated. Then, with ten seconds left, a flash knockdown sent him to the canvas again. That was the difference. By a margin of one point, Rosario retained his title on a 115–114, 117–113, 113–114 split decision.

Four years later, Davis had one more title opportunity, this one an IBF bout at 140 pounds. But he was past his prime and was stopped by Buddy McGirt in the first round.

Let it be noted that each of Davis's three championship-bout losses was to an elite fighter on the champion's home turf.

I was friendly with Davis. He was in my home several times. One of those occasions stands out in my mind.

I collect books. Over the years, I've amassed a library with more than four thousand volumes. Howard was looking at them one day, and his eye was drawn to a seven-book set entitled *The World and Its People* published in 1925. He took Volume One—*The Ancient World and Ancient Lands*—off the shelf and turned to a chapter entitled "Mesopotamia: The Land of the Beginning."

"When I think about history like this," Howard told me, "it makes me feel spiritual."

Howard Davis was a welcome spirit and a breath of fresh air in the sometimes-putrid atmosphere of boxing. He died from lung cancer on December 30 at age fifty-nine. It's sad that he's gone.

Sam Simon wasn't a religious person. He once told me that the Bible was "a hate-filled collection of fairy tales that, if taken literally, would require true Christians to stone anyone who works on Sunday to death." But he was a caring man in harmony with nature and the world.

Sam Simon: A Remembrance

The first time I met Sam Simon, I didn't particularly like him. I was at the Sovereign Center in Reading, Pennsylvania, for the February 2, 2002, fight between Bernard Hopkins and Carl Daniels. Sam was managing Lamon Brewster, who was fighting Nate Jones on the undercard.

Sam came over, introduced himself, and told me he liked my writing. There are some people you just don't take to. Several months later, I saw Sam at another fight. We talked again, and I said to myself, "Hauser, you were wrong. This is a really good guy."

A friendship followed.

Sam died on March 8, 2015, at age fifty-nine. I'd like to share some memories of him.

Sam was born and raised in southern California. One of his earliest memories, dating to age four he told me, was of finding his mother in pari delicto with Groucho Marx.

"I was a child of Hollywood," he said. "If not literally, then certainly in a figurative sense."

Sam had a privileged upbringing. He went to Beverly Hills High School and was an undergraduate at Stanford, where he worked as a cartoonist for the school newspaper. That led to assignments from the *San Francisco Chronicle* and *San Francisco Examiner*. Next, he was hired as a story-board artist at Filmation Studios, where he worked on a number of projects including *Fat Albert*.

"Then I wrote a script on spec for *Taxi* and sent it in," Sam reminisced when I wrote a profile about him in 2004. "They liked it; they made it; and all of a sudden, at age twenty-three, I was producing *Taxi*."

The entries on Sam's resume after that were the stuff of dreams. He was a writer, director, producer, and creative consultant for *Cheers,*

The Drew Carey Show, The George Carlin Show, It's Garry Shandling's Show, Barney Miller, Best of the West, Bless This House, Men Behaving Badly, Norm, and *The Tracey Ullman Show.*

The latter venture led to Sam's greatest creative and commercial triumph. Each segment of Tracey Ullman contained a one-minute animated segment. Sam and co-producer James L. Brooks thought that the animated characters were strong enough to support a half-hour series. In 1989, they launched *The Simpsons,* which became the longest-running animated series in the history of prime-time network television.

"I'm delighted with all the success *The Simpsons* had," Sam told me. "But it bothers me that I helped to build FOX."

When *The Simpsons* was sold into syndication, Sam received tens of millions of dollars. He was a dedicated animal-rights activist, and put most of that money into the Sam Simon Foundation. Through it, he funded a program that rescues dogs from shelters and trains them as companions for the deaf. He donated so generously to the Sea Shepherd Conservation Society (a global marine conservation group) that the organization named one of its four ships the MY *Sam Simon.* PETA's headquarters in Norfolk, Virginia, are in The Sam Simon Center.

Sam's bounty from *The Simpsons* also led to his involvement with boxing.

"I was a fan of two sports: football and boxing," he told me years ago. "I knew I couldn't own an NFL franchise, but I thought I might be able to manage a heavyweight champion. I knew Lamon Brewster from the Wild Card Gym in Los Angeles. I'd seen him fight. The word around Southern California was that he was a prospect. Then Freddie Roach told me that Lamon was having managerial problems, so I put my lawyer on the case and became his manager."

Brewster's first fight under Sam's guidance was a second-round knockout of Mario Cawley on June 22, 1999. Sam took a modest 10 percent of Lamon's purses, and Lamon lived rent-free in a house that Sam owned. On April 19, 2004, Brewster knocked out Wladimir Klitschko to claim the WBO heavyweight crown. Then Lamon dumped Sam for Al Haymon. That hurt Sam terribly. It wasn't about the money. He had more than enough money to live in comfort for a dozen lifetimes. He felt betrayed by a friend.

Meanwhile, my own friendship with Sam blossomed. I wasn't in his inner circle. But I enjoyed our time together and think he did too.

As a bonus; every two years or so, Sam would call and say, "I'm in New York. Do you want to go to the Giants game tomorrow?"

Going to a pro football game with Sam was an experience. You were chauffeured to and from the stadium. Your seats were on the fifty-yard line. And best of all, you got to spend an entire afternoon with Sam.

In early 2013, Sam telephoned to chat. I asked how he was, and he answered, "I'm fine, except I'm dying."

I thought he was joking. Sam had a strange sense of humor. It was part of his genius.

"I have cancer. And it's not good."

The previous autumn, Sam hadn't been feeling well. He went to his doctor, hoping it was just a virus. After a battery of tests, he was told he had colon cancer that had metastasized to his liver, kidneys, and lymph nodes.

"The question now is how long the doctors can keep me alive. Some people say, 'Oh, woe is me,' and roll over and die. That's not me. All my life, I've been accused of having a bad attitude, of being combative and thinking that rules don't apply to me. When the best doctors in the world tell you that you have three to six months to live, that's a good attitude to have."

The cancer was a particularly cruel twist of fate given the fact that Sam had followed standard medical practice by undergoing a colonoscopy every five years.

"With your family's medical history, you should have had colonoscopies more often," one of his doctors told him.

"Now you tell me," Sam responded.

I never saw Sam again. But we continued our telephone conversations. Sam was one of the people I exchanged ideas with when I wrote essays during the past two years about the Beatles and Frank Sinatra. Sam recounted watching the "Fab Four" on the Ed Sullivan Show on that magical night in February 1964 when he was eight years old. The next day, almost every boy in school who had hair that was long enough, including Sam, showed up with his hair combed down over his forehead.

With Sam's knowledge, I took notes on our conversations. We talked about boxing and also his illness. His moods encompassed a range of emotions. Some of his thoughts follow:

★ "I've had a particularly rough time with the chemo. I know chemo is hard on everyone. But for whatever reason, it's been particularly hard on me. But there are days now when I feel pretty good. Hopefully, something good is happening."

★ "I had a gloomy conversation with my doctor today. I'll be on chemo for the rest of my life, however long that is. The side effects are pretty unpleasant and will become permanent. I'm on a trial drug now, but it doesn't seem to be working."

★ "I'm pretty good, considering that I'm in hospice care. I had a scare with liver failure last month but bounced back. They found a chemo drug that I'm doing pretty well on. The problem is, they expect it will stop working soon and they'll have to experiment with something else."

★ "I'm working one day a week now on this Charlie Sheen show. There's something wrong with that. I spend my career working on some of the greatest shows in the history of television and wind up working on Charlie Sheen."

Near the end, Sam shared some thoughts with Maria Shriver during an interview on NBC. They bear repeating now as part of his legacy:

"Cancer is a horrible disease. It's everything that everybody always tells you. But somehow I ended up surrounded by people who love me and take care of me and will do anything for me. That is called happiness. I think I may have had a problem letting it in before. Cancer has been a fight, a journey, an adventure, and the most amazing experience of my life."

This article was first published by SB Nation and is among the most important pieces I've written.

Can Boxing Trust USADA?

Shortly after 3 p.m. on Friday, May 1, Floyd Mayweather and Manny Pacquiao weighed in for their historic encounter that would be contested the following night at the MGM Grand Garden Arena in Las Vegas. Later on Friday afternoon, collection agents for the United States Anti-Doping Agency (USADA), which had contracted to oversee drug testing for the Mayweather-Pacquiao fight, went to Mayweather's Las Vegas home to conduct a random unannounced drug test.

The collection agents found evidence of an IV being administered to Mayweather. Bob Bennett, the executive director of the Nevada State Athletic Commission, which had jurisdiction over the fight, says that USADA did not tell the commission whether the IV was actually being administered when the agents arrived. USADA did later advise the NSAC that Mayweather's medical team told its agents that the IV was administered to address concerns related to dehydration.

Mayweather's medical team also told the collection agents that the IV consisted of two separate mixes. The first was a mixture of 250 milliliters of saline and multi-vitamins. The second was a 500-milliliter mixture of saline and Vitamin C. 750 milliliters equals 25.361 ounces, an amount equal to roughly 16 percent of the blood normally present in an average adult male.

The mixes themselves are not prohibited by the World Anti-Doping Agency (WADA), which sets the standards that USADA purports to follow. However, their intravenous administration is prohibited by WADA.

More specifically, the 2015 WADA "Prohibited Substances and Methods List" states, "Intravenous infusions and/or injections of more than 50 ml per 6 hour period are prohibited except for those legitimately received in the course of hospital admissions, surgical procedures, or clinical investigations."

This prohibition is in effect at all times that the athlete is subject to testing. It exists because, in addition to being administered for the purpose of adding specific substances to a person's body, an IV infusion can dilute or mask the presence of another substance that is already in the recipient's system or might be added to it in the near future.

What happened next with regard to Mayweather is extremely troubling.

The first fighter of note to test positive for steroids after a professional championship fight was Frans Botha, who decisioned Axel Schulz in Germany to win the vacant International Boxing Federation heavyweight crown in 1995 but was stripped of the title by the IBF after a urine test indicated the use of anabolic steroids.

It's a matter of record that, since then, Fernando Vargas (stanozolol), Lamont Peterson (an unspecified anabolic steroid), Andre Berto (norandrosterone), Antonio Tarver (drostanolone), Roy Jones (an unspecified anabolic steroid), James Toney (nandrolone, boldenone metabolite, and stanozolol metabolite), Brandon Rios (methylhexaneamine), Erik Morales (clenbuterol), Richard Hall (an unspecified anabolic steroid), Cruz Carbajal (nandrolone and hydrochlorothiazide), Orlando Salido (nandrolone), and Tony Thompson (hydrochlorothiazide) are among the fighters who have tested positive for the presence of a prohibited performance-enhancing drug or masking agent in their system.

Almost always, fighters who test positive express disbelief and maintain that the prohibited substance was ingested without their knowledge. In most instances, punishment has been minimal or there has been no punishment at all.

Other fighters like former heavyweight champion Evander Holyfield, Shane Mosley (who won belts in three different weight classes), and heavyweight contender Jameel McCline, did not test positive but were named in conjunction with PED investigations conducted by federal law-enforcement authorities.

By way of example, on August 29, 2006, federal Drug Enforcement Agency officials in Alabama raided a compounding pharmacy (a pharmacy that makes its own drugs generically) called Applied Pharmacy Services. The documents seized included records revealing that a patient named "Evan Fields" picked up three vials of testosterone and related injection supplies from a doctor in Columbus, Georgia, in June 2004. That same month, Fields received five vials of a human growth hormone called Saizen. The documents further revealed that, in September 2004, Fields underwent treatment for hypogonadism (a condition in which the body does not produce enough natural testosterone, often a consequence of the use of performance-enhancing drugs). The home address, telephone number, and date of birth listed for Evan Fields in Applied Pharmacy's records were identical to those of Evander Holyfield.

Similarly, Shane Mosley never tested positive for illegal performance-enhancing drugs. But his testimony before a grand jury investigating the Bay Area Laboratory Co-Operative (BALCO) made it clear that he used prohibited PEDs prior to his 2003 victory over Oscar De La Hoya.

Many types of PED use are prohibited in boxing and other sports because of health concerns and the fact that they give athletes an unfair competitive advantage. Their use also often violates federal laws regarding controlled substances. But PED use is more prevalent in boxing today than ever before, particularly at the elite level. Some conditioning coaches have well-known reputations for shady tactics. In many gyms, there is a person on site who serves as a pipeline to PED suppliers.

Indeed, for many fighters, the prevailing ethic seems to be, "If you're not cheating, you're not trying." In a clean world, fighters don't get older, heavier, and faster at the same time. But that's what's happening in boxing. Fighters are reconfiguring their bodies and, in some instances, look like totally different physical beings. Improved performances at an advanced age are becoming common. Fighters at age thirty-five are outperforming what they could do when they were thirty. In some instances, fighters are starting to perform at an elite level at an age when they would normally be expected to be on a downward slide.

Victor Conte was the founder and president of BALCO and at the vortex of several well-publicized PED scandals. He spent four months in prison after pleading guilty to illegal steroid distribution and tax fraud in 2005. Since then, Conte has undergone a remarkable transformation and is now a forceful advocate for clean sport. What makes him a particularly valuable asset is his knowledge of how the performance-enhancing drugs game was—and is—played. Indeed, former federal prosecutor

Jeff Novitzky, who was instrumental in putting Conte behind bars, acknowledged in a recent interview on *The Joe Rogan Experience* that Conte now has "an anti-doping platform" and has come "over to the good side."

"The use of performance-enhancing drugs is rampant in boxing, particularly at the elite level," Conte recently told this writer. "If there was serious testing and the fighters believed that the testing was effective, they'd be less inclined to use prohibited drugs. But almost across the board, state athletic commissions have minimal expertise, limited funding, and little or no will to address the problem. So knowing that the testing programs are inept, many fighters feel that they're forced to use these drugs to compete on a level playing field."

In recent years, the United States Anti-Doping Agency has stepped into the enforcement void.

USADA was created in 1999 pursuant to the recommendation of a United States Olympic Committee task force that recognized the need for credible PED testing of all Olympic and Paralympic athletes representing the United States.

Despite its name, USADA is neither a government agency nor part of the United States Olympic Committee. It is an independent "not-for-profit" corporation headquartered in Colorado Springs that offers drug-testing services for a fee. Most notably, the United States Olympic and Paralympic movements utilize its services. Because of this role, USADA receives approximately $10 million annually in Congressional funding, more in Olympic years.

USADA's website states, "The organization continues to aspire to be a leader in the global anti-doping community in order to protect the rights of clean athletes and the integrity of competition around the world. We hold ourselves to the same high standards exhibited by athletes who fully embrace true sport. We commit to the following core values to guide our decisions and behaviors." The core values listed are integrity, respect, teamwork, responsibility, and courage.

Travis Tygart, the chief executive officer of USADA, has spearheaded the organization's expansion into professional boxing. That opportunity initially arose in late 2009, when drug testing became an issue in the first round of negotiations for a proposed fight between Floyd Mayweather and Manny Pacquiao. When those negotiations fell through, Mayweather opted instead for a May 1, 2010, bout against Shane Mosley.

During a March 18, 2010, conference call to promote Mayweather-Mosley, Tygart advised the media, "Both athletes have agreed to USADA's testing protocols, including blood and urine testing, which is unannounced, which is anywhere and anytime. There is no limit to the number of tests that we can complete on these boxers."

Thereafter, Tygart moved aggressively to expand USADA's footprint in boxing and forged a working relationship with Richard Schaefer, who until 2014 served as CEO of Golden Boy Promotions, one of boxing's most influential promoters. USADA also became the drug-testing agency of choice for fighters advised by Al Haymon, who is now the most powerful person in boxing. In addition to representing Mayweather, Haymon is the driving force behind *Premier Boxing Champions*. He has bought time on CBS, NBC, ESPN, Spike, and several other networks to showcase his product. Most boxing matches televised by Showtime also feature Haymon fighters.

Drug testing, if it is to inspire confidence, should be largely transparent. Much of USADA's operation insofar as boxing is concerned is shrouded in secrecy. Sometimes there's an announcement when USADA oversees drug testing for a fight. Other times, there is not. The organization has resisted filing its boxer drug-testing contracts with governing state athletic commissions. On several occasions, New York and Nevada have forced the issue. Compliance has often been slow in coming.

When asked to identify the boxing matches for which a USADA drug-testing contract was filed with either the New York or Nevada State Athletic Commissions, Travis Tygart declined through a spokesperson (USADA senior communications manager Annie Skinner) to answer the question.

USADA's fee structure (which USADA has endeavored to shield from public view) has also raised eyebrows.

The primary alternative to USADA insofar as PED testing for boxers is concerned is the Voluntary Anti-Doping Association (VADA). Like USADA, VADA's testing laboratories are accredited by the World Anti-Doping Agency, and it uses internationally recognized collection agencies. Unlike USADA, VADA utilizes carbon isotope ratio (CIR) testing on every urine sample it collects from a boxer. USADA often declines to administer CIR testing on grounds that it's unnecessary and too expensive. Of course, the less expensive that tests are to administer, the better it is for USADA's bottom line.

VADA charged a total of $16,000 to administer drug testing for the April 18, 2015, junior-welterweight fight between Ruslan Provodnikov and Lucas Matthysse. By contrast, USADA charged $36,000 to administer drug testing for the April 11, 2015, middleweight encounter between Andy Lee and Peter Quillin.

The Lee-Quillin bout was part of Al Haymon's *Premier Boxing Champions* series. USADA is often paid quite generously for services rendered in conjunction with fights in which Haymon plays a role.

A notable example is the fee paid to USADA for administering drug testing in conjunction with the May 2, 2015, Mayweather-Pacquiao fight. Haymon advises Mayweather, and Team Mayweather controlled the promotion. USADA's contract called for it to receive an up-front payment of $150,000 to test Mayweather and Pacquiao.

More troubling than USADA's fee structure are the accommodations that it seems to have made for clients who either pay more for its services or use USADA on a regular basis. The case of Erik Morales, who has held world titles in three weight divisions, is an example.

Under standard sports drug-testing protocols, when blood or urine is taken from an athlete, it is divided into an "A" and "B" sample. The "A" sample is tested first. If it tests negative, end of story; the athlete has tested "clean." If, however, the "A" sample tests positive, the athlete has the right to demand that the "B" sample be tested. If the "B" sample tests negative, the athlete is presumed to be clean. But if the "B" sample also tests positive, the first positive finding is confirmed and the athlete has a problem.

In 2012, Erik Morales was promoted by Golden Boy, which, as earlier noted, was under the leadership of Richard Schaefer. Golden Boy was the lead promoter for an October 20 fight card at Barclays Center in Brooklyn that was to be headlined by Morales vs. Danny Garcia.

On Thursday, October 18, 2012, the website Halestorm Sports reported that Morales had tested positive for a banned substance. Thereafter, Golden Boy and USADA engaged in damage control.

Dan Rafael of ESPN.com spoke with two sources and wrote, "The reason the fight has not been called off, according to one of the sources, is because Morales' 'A' sample tested positive but the results of the 'B' sample test likely won't be available until after the fight. '[USADA] said it could be a false positive,' one of the sources with knowledge of the disclosure said."

Richard Schaefer told Chris Mannix of SI.com, "USADA has now started the process. The process will play out. There is not going to be a rush to judgment. Morales is a legendary fighter. And really, nobody deserves a rush to judgment. You are innocent until proven guilty."

Then, on Friday, one day before the scheduled fight, Keith Idec revealed on BoxingScene.com that samples had been taken from Morales on at least three occasions. Final test results from the samples taken on October 17 were not in yet. But both the "A" and "B" samples taken from Morales on October 3 and October 10 had tested positive for clenbuterol. In other words, Morales had tested positive for clenbuterol four times.

Clenbuterol, a therapeutic drug first developed for people with breathing disorders such as asthma, is widely used by bodybuilders and athletes. It helps the body increase its metabolism and process the conversion of carbohydrates, proteins, and fats into useful energy. It also boosts muscle growth and eliminates excess fats caused by the use of certain steroids. Its therapeutic use is banned in the United States, as is its use in animals raised for human consumption. It is also banned by WADA.

Under the WADA prohibited list, no amount of clenbuterol is allowed in a competitor's body. The measure is qualitative, not quantitative. Either clenbuterol is there or it is not.

According to a report in the *New York Daily News*, after Morales was confronted with the positive test results, he claimed a USADA official suggested that he might have inadvertently ingested clenbuterol by eating contaminated meat. Meanwhile, the New York State Athletic Commission issued a statement referencing a representation by Morales that he "unintentionally ingested contaminated food."

However, no evidence was offered in support of the contention that Morales had ingested contaminated meat.

The moment that the "B" sample from Morales' first test came back positive, standard testing protocol dictated that this information be forwarded to the New York State Athletic Commission. But neither USADA nor Richard Schaefer did so in a timely manner. Rather, it appears as though the commission and the public may have been deliberately misled in regard to the testing and how many tests Morales had failed.

New York State Athletic Commission sources say that the first notice the NYSAC received regarding Morales's test results came in a three-way telephone conversation with representatives of Golden Boy and USADA after the story broke on Halestorm Sports. In that conversation, the commission was told that there were "some questionable test results" for Morales but that testing of Morales' "B" sample would not be available until after the fight.

Travis Tygart has since said, "The licensing body was aware of the positive test prior to the fight. What they did with it was their call."

That's terribly misleading.

This writer submitted a request for information to the New York State Athletic Commission asking whether it was advised that Erik Morales had tested positive for clenbuterol prior to the October 18, 2012, revelation on Halestorm Sports.

On August 10, 2015, Laz Benitez (a spokesperson for the New York State Department of State, which oversees the NYSAC) advised in writing, "There is no indication in the Commission's files that it was notified of this matter prior to October 18, 2012."

The Garcia-Morales fight was allowed to proceed on October 20, in part because the NYSAC did not know of Morales's test history until it was too late for the commission to fully consider the evidence and make a decision to stop the fight. Since then, people in the PED-testing community have begun to openly question the role played in boxing by USADA. What good are tests if the results are not properly reported?

Don Catlin founded the UCLA Olympic Analytical Laboratory in 1982 and is one of the founders of modern drug testing in sports. Three years ago, Catlin told this writer, "USADA should not enter into a contract that doesn't call for it to report positive test results to the appropriate governing body. If it's true that USADA reported the results [in the Morales case] to Golden Boy and not to the governing state athletic commission, that's a recipe for deception."

When asked about the possibility of withholding notification because of inadvertent use (such as eating contaminated meat), Catlin declared, "No! The International Olympic Committee allowed for those waivers 25 years ago, and it didn't work. An athlete takes a steroid, tests positive, and then claims it was inadvertent. No one says, 'I was cheating. You caught me.'"

Victor Conte is in accord and says, "The Erik Morales case was a travesty. If you're doing honest testing, you don't have a positive "A" and "B" sample and then another positive "A" and "B" sample and keep going until you get a negative result."

In the absence of a credible explanation for what happened or an acknowledgment by USADA that there was wrongdoing that will not be repeated, the Erik Morales matter casts a pall over USADA.

The way things stand now, how can any of USADA's testing in any sport be trusted by the sports establishment or the public? Would USADA handle the testing of an Olympic athlete the way it handled the testing of Erik Morales?

That brings us to Floyd Mayweather and USADA.

Mayweather has gone to great lengths to propagate the notion that he is in the forefront of PED testing to "clean up" boxing. Beginning with his 2010 fight against Shane Mosley, he has mandated that he and his opponent be subjected to what he calls "Olympic-style testing" by USADA.

At a media "roundtable" in New York before the June 24, 2013, kick-off press conference for Mayweather vs. Canelo Alvarez, Mayweather Promotions CEO Leonard Ellerbe declared, "We've put in place a mechanism where all Mayweather Promotions fighters will do mandatory blood and urine testing 365-24-7 by USADA."

But neither Mayweather nor the fighters that Mayweather Promotions has under contract have undergone 365-24-7 testing—tests that can be administered any place at any time and would make it more risky for an athlete to use prohibited PEDs.

Drug testing for a Mayweather fight generally begins shortly after the fight is announced. Mayweather and his opponent agree to keep USADA advised as to their whereabouts at all times and submit to an unlimited number of unannounced blood and urine tests. That sounds good. But in effect, USADA allows Mayweather to determine when the testing begins. That leaves a long period of time during which there are no checks on what substances he might put into his body.

For example, Mayweather didn't announce Andre Berto as the opponent for his upcoming September 12 fight until August 4, only thirty-nine days before the fight. That didn't leave much time for serious drug testing. From the conclusion of the May 2 Pacquiao fight until the Berto announcement, Mayweather was not subject to USADA testing.

Here, the thoughts of Victor Conte are instructive.

"Mayweather is not doing 'Olympic-style testing,'" Conte states. "Olympic testing means that you can be tested twenty-four hours a day, 365 days a year. If USADA was serious about boxing becoming a clean sport, it would say, 'We don't do one-offs. If you sign up for USADA testing, we reserve the right to test you at any time 365-24-7.' But that's not what USADA does with Mayweather or any other fighter that I know of."

"The benefits that an athlete retains from using anabolic steroids and certain other PEDs carry over for months," Conte continues. "Anybody who knows anything about the way these drugs work knows that you don't perform at your best when you're actually on the drugs. *You get maximum benefit after the use stops.* I can't tell you what Floyd Mayweather is and isn't doing. What he could be doing is this. The fight is over. First, he uses these drugs for tissue repair. Then he can stay on them until he announces his next fight, at which time he's the one who decides when the next round of testing starts. And by the time testing starts, the drugs have cleared his system.

"Do I know that's what's happening? No, I don't. I do know that the testing period for Mayweather's fights is getting shorter and shorter. What is it for this one? Five weeks? The whole concept of one man dictating the testing schedule is wrong. But USADA lets Mayweather do it. USADA is not doing effective comprehensive testing on Floyd Mayweather. Testing for four or five weeks before a fight is nonsense."

As noted earlier, USADA CEO Travis Tygart declined to be interviewed for this article. Instead, senior communications manager Annie Skinner emailed a statement to this writer that outlines USADA's mission and reads in part, "Just like for our Olympic athletes, any pro-boxing program follows WADA's international standards, including: the Prohibited List, the International Standard for Testing & Investigations

(ISTI), the International Standard for Therapeutic Use Exemptions (ISTUEs) and the International Standards for Protection of Privacy and Personal Information (ISPPPI)."

Skinner's statement is incorrect. This writer has obtained a copy of the contract entered into between USADA, Floyd Mayweather, and Manny Pacquiao for drug testing in conjunction with Mayweather-Pacquiao.

Paragraph 30 of the contract states, "If any rule or regulation whatsoever incorporated or referenced herein conflicts in any respect with the terms of this Agreement, this Agreement shall in all such respects control. Such rules and regulations include, but are not limited to: the Code [the World Anti-Doping Code]; the USADA Protocol; the WADA Prohibited List; the ISTUE [WADA International Standard for Therapeutic Use Exemptions]; and the ISTI [WADA International Standard for Testing and Investigations]."

In other words, USADA was not bound by the drug testing protocols that one might have expected it to follow in conjunction with Mayweather-Pacquiao. And this divergence was significant vis-a-vis its rulings with regard to the IV that was administered to Mayweather on May 1. 2015.

In evaluating USADA's conduct with regard to Mayweather's IV, the evolution of the USADA-Mayweather-Pacquiao contract is important.

It was announced publicly that the bout contract Mayweather and Pacquiao signed in February 2015 to fight each other provided that drug testing would be conducted by USADA. But the actual contract with USADA remained to be negotiated. In early March, USADA presented the Pacquiao camp with a contract that allowed the testing agency to grant a retroactive therapeutic use exemption (TUE) to either fighter in the event that the fighter tested positive for a prohibited drug. That retroactive exemption could have been granted without notifying the Nevada State Athletic Commission or the opposing fighter's camp.

Team Pacquiao thought that was outrageous and an opportunity for Mayweather to game the system. Pacquiao refused to sign the contract.

Thereafter, Mayweather and USADA agreed to mutual notification and the limitation of retroactive therapeutic use exemptions to narrowly delineated circumstances. With regard to notice, a copy of the final USADA-Mayweather-Pacquiao contract provides: "Mayweather and Pacquiao agree that USADA shall notify both athletes within 24 hours of any of the following occurrences: (1) the approval by USADA of a TUE application submitted by either athlete; and/or (2) the existence of and/or any modification to an existing approved TUE. Notification pursuant to this paragraph shall consist of and be limited to: (a) the date of the application; (b) the prohibited substance(s) or method(s) for which the TUE is sought; and (c) the manner of use for the prohibited substance(s) or method(s) for which the TUE is sought."

How was Mayweather's IV handled by USADA?

As previously noted, the weigh-in and IV administration occurred on May 1. The fight was on May 2. For twenty days after the IV was administered, USADA chose not to notify the Nevada State Athletic Commission about the procedure.

Finally, on May 21, USADA sent a letter to Francisco Aguilar and Bob Bennett (respectively, the chairman and executive director of the NSAC) with a copy to Top Rank (Pacquiao's promoter) informing them that a retroactive therapeutic use exemption had been granted to Mayweather. The letter did not say when the request for the retroactive TUE was made by Mayweather or when it was granted by USADA.

Subsequent correspondence in response to requests by the NSAC and Top Rank for further information revealed that the TUE was not applied for until May 19 and was granted on May 20.

In other words, eighteen days after the fight, USADA gave Mayweather a retroactive therapeutic use exemption for a procedure that is on the WADA "Prohibited Substances and Methods List." And because of a loophole in its drug-testing contract, USADA wasn't obligated to notify the Nevada State Athletic Commission or Pacquiao camp regarding Mayweather's IV until after the retroactive TUE was granted.

Meanwhile, on May 2 (fight night), Pacquiao's request to be injected with Toradol (a legal substance) to ease the pain caused by a torn rotator cuff was denied by the Nevada State Athletic Commission because the request was not made in a timely manner.

A conclusion that one might draw from these events is that it helps to have friends at USADA.

"It's bizarre," Don Catlin says with regard to the retroactive therapeutic use exemption that USADA granted to Mayweather. "It's very troubling to me. USADA has yet to explain to my satisfaction why

Mayweather needed an IV infusion. There might be a valid explanation, but I don't know what it is."

Victor Conte is equally perturbed.

"I don't get it," Conte says. "There are strict criteria for the granting of a TUE. You don't hand them out like Halloween candy. And this sort of IV use is clearly against the rules. Also, from a medical point of view, if they're administering what they said they did, it doesn't make sense to me. There are more effective ways to rehydrate. If you drank ice-cold Celtic seawater, you'd have far greater benefits. It's very suspicious to me. I can tell you that IV drugs clear an athlete's system more quickly than drugs that are administered by subcutaneous injection. So why did USADA make this decision? Why did they grant something that's prohibited? In my view, that's something federal law enforcement officials should be asking Travis Tygart."

Bob Bennett (who worked for the FBI before assuming his present position as executive director of the Nevada State Athletic Commission) has this to say: "The TUE for Mayweather's IV—and the IV was administered at Floyd's house, not in a medical facility, and wasn't brought to our attention at the time—was totally unacceptable. I've made it clear to Travis Tygart that this should not happen again. We have the sole authority to grant any and all TUEs in the state of Nevada. USADA is a drug-testing agency. USADA should not be granting waivers and exemptions. Not in this state. We are less than pleased that USADA acted the way it did."

If Bennett looks at what transpired before he became executive director of the NSAC, he might have further reason to question USADA's performance.

The use of carbon isotope ratio (CIR) testing as a means of identifying the presence of exogenous (synthetic) testosterone in an athlete's body was developed in part under the direction of Don Catlin. It has been used in conjunction with Olympic testing since the 1998 Winter Games in Nagano.

As noted earlier, USADA often declines to administer CIR testing to boxers on grounds that it is unnecessary and too expensive. The cost is roughly $400 per test, although VADA CEO Dr. Margaret Goodman notes, "If you do a lot of them, you can negotiate price."

If VADA (which charges far less than USADA for drug testing) can afford CIR testing on every urine sample that it collects from a boxer, then USADA can afford it too.

"If you're serious about drug testing," says Victor Conte, "you do CIR testing."

But CIR testing has been not been fully utilized for Floyd Mayweather's fights. Instead, USADA has chosen to rely primarily on a testosterone-to-epitestosterone ratio test to determine if exogenous testosterone is in an athlete's system.

Testosterone and epitestosterone are naturally occurring hormones. Testosterone is performance-enhancing. Epitestosterone is not.

A normal testosterone-to-epitestosterone ratio is slightly more than 1-to-1. Conte says that one recent study of the general population "placed the average T-E ratio for whites at 1.2-to-1 and for blacks at 1.3-to-1."

Under WADA standards, a testosterone-to-epitestosterone ratio of up to 4-to-1 is acceptable. That allows for any reasonable variation in an athlete's natural testosterone level (which, for an elite athlete, might be particularly high). If the ratio is above 4-to-1, an athlete is presumed to be doping.

Some athletes who use exogenous testosterone game the system by administering exogenous epitestosterone to drive their testosterone-to-epitestosterone ratio down beneath the permitted ceiling. This can be done by injection or by the application of epitestosterone as a cream. In the absence of a CIR test, this masks the use of synthetic testosterone.

But there's a catch. If an athlete tries to manipulate his or her testosterone-to-epitestosterone ratio, it is difficult to balance the outcome. If an athlete uses too much epitestosterone—and the precise amount is difficult to calibrate—the result can be an abnormally low T-E ratio.

"In and of itself," Conte explains, "an abnormally low T-E ratio is not proof of doping. The ratio can vary for the same athlete from test to test. But an abnormally low T-E ratio is a red flag. And if you're serious about the testing, the next thing you do [after a low T-E ratio test result] is administer a CIR test on the same sample."

Earlier this year, in response to a request for documents, the Nevada State Athletic Commission produced two lab reports listing the testosterone-to-epitestosterone ratio on tests that it (not USADA) had overseen on

Floyd Mayweather. In one instance, blood and urine samples were taken from Mayweather on August 18, 2011 (prior to his September 17 fight against Victor Ortiz). In the other instance, blood and urine samples were taken from Mayweather on April 3, 2013 (prior to his May 4 fight against Robert Guerrero).

Mayweather's testosterone-to-epitestosterone ratio for the April 3, 2013, sample was .80. His testosterone-to-epitestosterone ratio for the August 18, 2011, sample was .69.

"That's a warning flag," says Don Catlin. "If you're serious about the testing, it tells you to do the CIR test."

The Nevada State Athletic Commission wasn't as knowledgeable with regard to PED testing several years ago as it is now. Commission personnel might not have understood the possible implications of the .69 and .80 numbers. But USADA officials were knowledgeable.

Did USADA perform CIR testing on Mayweather's urine samples during that time period? What were the results? And if there was no CIR testing, what testosterone-to-epitestosterone ratio did USADA's tests show? At present, the answers to these questions are not publicly known.

Note to investigators: CIR tests can be performed retroactively on frozen samples.

All of this leads to another issue. As acknowledged by NSAC executive director Bob Bennett, "As of now, USADA does not give us the full test results. They give us the contracts for drug testing and summaries that tell us whether a fighter has tested positive or negative. It is incumbent on them to notify us if a fighter tests positive. But no, they don't give us the full test results."

Laz Benitez reports a similar lack of transparency in New York. On August 10, Benitez advised this writer that the New York State Athletic Commission had received information from USADA regarding test results for four fights where the drug testing was conducted by USADA. But Benitez added, "The results received were summaries."

Why is that significant? Because full test results can raise a red flag that's not apparent on the face of a summary. Once again, a look at the relationship between USADA and Floyd Mayweather is instructive.

On December 30, 2009, Manny Pacquiao sued Mayweather for defamation. Pacquiao's complaint, filed in the United States District

Court for Nevada, alleged that Mayweather and several other defendants had falsely accused him of using, and continuing to use, illegal performance-enhancing drugs. The court case moved slowly, as litigation often does. Then things changed dramatically.

As reported by this writer on MaxBoxing in December 2012, information filtered through the drug-testing community on May 20, 2012, to the effect that Mayweather had tested positive on three occasions for an illegal performance-enhancing drug. More specifically, it was rumored that Mayweather's "A" sample had tested positive three times and, after each positive test, USADA had given Floyd an inadvertent use waiver. These waivers, if they were in fact given, would have negated the need to test Floyd's "B" samples. And because the "B" samples were never tested, a loophole in Mayweather's USADA contract would have allowed testing to continue without the positive "A" sample results being reported to Mayweather's opponent or the Nevada State Athletic Commission.

Pacquiao's attorneys became aware of the rumor in late May. On June 4, 2012, they served document demands and subpoenas on Mayweather, Mayweather Promotions, Golden Boy (Mayweather's co-promoter), and USADA demanding the production of all documents relating to PED testing of Mayweather in conjunction with his fights against Shane Mosley, Victor Ortiz, and Miguel Cotto. These were the three fights that Mayweather had been tested for by USADA up until that time.

The documents were not produced. After pleading guilty to charges of domestic violence and harassment, Mayweather spent nine weeks in the Clark County Detention Center. He was released from jail on August 2. Then settlement talks heated up.

A stipulation of settlement ending the defamation case was filed with the court on September 25, 2012. The parties agreed to a confidentiality clause that kept the terms of settlement secret. However, prior to the agreement being signed, two sources with detailed knowledge of the proceedings told this writer that Mayweather's initial monetary settlement offer was "substantially more" than Pacquiao's attorneys had expected it would be. An agreement in principle was reached soon afterward. The settlement meant that the demand for documents relating to USADA's testing of Mayweather became moot.

If Mayweather's "A" sample tested positive for a performance-enhancing drug on one or more occasions and he was given a waiver by USADA that concealed this fact from the Nevada State Athletic Commission, his opponent, and the public, it could contribute to a scandal that undermines the already-shaky public confidence in boxing. At present, the relevant information is not a matter of public record.

USADA CEO Travis Tygart (through senior communications manager Annie Skinner) declined to state how many times the "A" sample of a professional boxer tested by USADA has come back positive for a prohibited substance.

What is clear though, is that USADA is not catching the PED users in boxing. Tygart says that's because his organization's educational programs and the knowledge that USADA will catch cheaters deters wrongdoing. But the changing physiques and performance levels of some of the elite fighters tested by USADA suggest otherwise.

A simple comparison will suffice. As of August 1, 2015, VADA had conducted drug testing for eighteen professional fights. Three of the fighters tested by VADA (Andre Berto, Lamont Peterson, and Brandon Rios) tested positive for a banned substance.

Contrast that with USADA. Annie Skinner says that Mayweather-Berto will be the forty-sixth fight for which USADA has conducted drug testing. In an August 14, e-mail she acknowledges, "At this time, the only professional boxer under USADA's program who has been found to have committed an anti-doping rule violation is Erik Morales."

One can speculate that, had Halestorm Sports not broken the Morales story, USADA might not have "found" that Morales committed an anti-doping violation either.

"USADA's boxing testing program is propaganda; that's all," says Victor Conte. "It has one set of rules for some fighters and a different set of rules for others. That's not the way real drug testing works. Travis Tygart wants people to think that anyone who questions USADA is against clean sport. But that's nonsense."

After Lance Armstrong's defoliation for illegal PED use, Tygart was interviewed by Scott Pelley on *60 Minutes*. Armstrong, Tygart declared, was "cowardly" and had "defrauded millions of people."

Pelley then asked, "If Lance Armstrong had prevailed in this case and you had failed, what would the effect on sport have been?"

"It would have been huge," Tygart answered, "because athletes would have known that some are too big to fail."

"And the message that sends is what?" Pelley pressed.

"Cheat your way to the top. And if you get too big and too popular and too powerful, if you do it that well, you'll never be held accountable."

USADA is the dominant force in American sports insofar as drug testing is concerned. But it is not too big and powerful to be held accountable.

The essence of boxing is such that all participants are at risk. The increasing use of performance-enhancing drugs makes these risks unacceptable.

Fighters are entitled to an initial presumption of innocence when questions arise regarding the use of performance-enhancing drugs. Based on their performance, Muhammad Ali (blessed with preternatural speed and stamina) and Rocky Marciano (who absorbed incredible punishment and seemed to grow stronger as a fight wore on) might have been suspected of illegal drug use had PEDs been available to them.

But fighters who are clean are also entitled to know that they're not facing an opponent who has augmented his firepower through the use of performance-enhancing drugs. And any state athletic commission that fails to limit the use of PEDs within its jurisdiction is unfit to regulate boxing.

Richard Pound was one of the founders and the first president of the World Anti-Doping Agency. On May 13, 2013, a committee that Pound chaired submitted a report entitled "Lack of Effectiveness of Testing Programs" to WADA.

In part, that report states, "The primary reason for the apparent lack of success of the testing programs does not lie with the science involved. While there may well be some drugs or combinations of drugs and methods of which the anti-doping community is unaware, the science now available is both robust and reliable. The real problems are the human and political factors. There is no general appetite to undertake the effort and expense of a successful effort to deliver doping-free sport. This applies with varying degrees at the level of athletes, international sport organizations, national Olympic committees, national anti-doping organizations, and governments. It is reflected in low standards of compliance measurement, unwillingness to undertake critical analysis of the necessary requirements, unwillingness to follow-up on suspicions and information, unwillingness to share available information, and unwillingness to commit the necessary informed intelligence, effective actions, and other resources to the fight against doping in sport."

A website and those who write for it are not the final arbiters of whether USADA has acted properly insofar as drug testing in boxing is concerned. Nor can they fully investigate USADA. But Congress and various law enforcement agencies can.

There's an open issue as to whether USADA has become an instrument of accommodation. For an agency that tests United States Olympic athletes and receives $10 million a year from the federal government, that's a significant issue.

Meanwhile, the presence of performance-enhancing drugs in boxing cries out for action. To ensure a level playing field, a national solution with uniform national testing standards is essential. A year-round testing program is necessary. It should be a condition of being granted a boxing license in this country that any fighter is subject to blood and urine testing at any time. While logistics and cost would make mandatory testing on a broad scale impractical, unannounced spot testing could be implemented, particularly on elite fighters.

All contracts for drug testing should be filed upon execution with the Association of Boxing Commissions and the governing state athletic commission. Full tests results, not just summaries, should be disclosed immediately to the governing commission. A commission doctor should review all test results as they come in.

As the Pound Report states, "The objective is to improve the efficacy of testing procedures and other anti-doping activities, not merely to rely on having performed a certain number of tests." Also, as recommended by the Pound Report, "CIR testing for artificial testosterone should be increased forthwith."

Ten years ago, John Ruiz lost a twelve-round decision to James Toney in a heavyweight championship fight at Madison Square Garden. Then Toney tested positive for nandrolone. The outcome of the fight was changed to no decision. Toney was suspended for ninety days, and Ruiz was reinstated as champion.

"The only sport in which steroids can kill someone other than the person using them is boxing," Ruiz said afterward. "You're stronger when you use steroids. You're quicker and faster. If a baseball player uses steroids, he hits more home runs. So what? I'm not saying that it's right, but you're not putting anyone else at risk. When a fighter is juiced, it's dangerous. People go crazy about the effect that steroids have when a bat hits a ball. What about when a fist hits a head?"

Events after "Can Boxing Trust USADA?" was published warranted a follow-up article.

Was Floyd Mayweather Really Dehydrated?

On September 9, 2015, an article I wrote entitled "Can Boxing Trust USADA?" was posted online.

Among other things, the article reported that, eighteen days after the May 2, 2015, fight between Floyd Mayweather and Manny Pacquiao, the United States Anti-Doping Agency (which had contracted to oversee drug testing for the bout) granted Mayweather a retroactive therapeutic use exemption for a procedure that's on the World Anti-Doping Agency (WADA) "Prohibited Substances and Methods List."

More specifically, on May 19, Mayweather applied for (and, on May 20, was granted) a therapeutic use exemption for what he says was an IV infusion of saline and vitamins that was administered on May 1.

The IV administration of legal substances of up to 50 milliliters per six-hour period is permitted under WADA and USADA regulations. The adminstration of more than 50 milliliters per six-hour period is prohibited because an IV infusion can dilute or mask the presence of another substance that is already in the recipient's system or might be added to it in the near future.

Mayweather acknowledges having received an IV infusion of 750 milliliters (25.361 ounces), an amount equal to roughly 16 percent of the blood normally present in an average adult male.

A September 10, 2015, statement from USADA in response to "Can Boxing Trust USADA?" reads in part, "Because Mr. Mayweather was voluntarily taking part in a USADA program, and therefore subject to the rules of the WADA Code, he took the additional step of applying for a TUE after the IV infusion was administered in order remain in compliance with the USADA program."

In other words, USADA concedes that, without the retroactive therapeutic use exemption, Mayweather would have been in violation of the WADA code.

"Can Boxing Trust USADA?" raised other issues as well. Most notable among these were questions regarding the results of two testosterone-to-epitestosterone ratio tests administered to Mayweather and USADA's handling of tests that found Clenbuterol (a prohibited drug) in Erik Morales's system. However, public reaction to the article focused on the IV that was administered to Mayweather.

In the first twenty-four hours after "Can Boxing Trust USADA?" was posted online, links to the article were tweeted more than two thousand times. At one point on September 10, the issue of Mayweather and USADA was the number one trending story on Facebook.

That same day, an interviewer for ESPN SportsCenter was bypassed during a series of satellite interviews designed to promote the September 12 pay-per-view fight between Mayweather and Andre Berto because ESPN refused to commit to not asking about the issue of Mayweather's IV.

The widely reported justification for Mayweather's IV is that it was administered to remedy dehydration. On September 11, Mayweather told an interviewer for FightHype.com that he'd been "just rehydrating." That's also what USADA suggested to the Nevada State Athletic Commission when it advised the NSAC on May 21 (nineteen days after Mayweather-Pacquiao) that "the infusion was administered to address concerns related to dehydration."

But that statement was made by USADA at a time when it was likely that Mayweather's IV would pass without public notice. Since then, USADA has declined to state what the medical justification for the otherwise-prohibited IV procedure was.

On September 17, USADA released what it called a "Detailed Correction" of "Can Boxing Trust USADA?" The "correction" (which will be discussed at length later in this article) is 9,992 words long. It references Victor Conte (who was imprisoned for conduct related to the BALCO scandal) by name twenty-one times. It describes this writer with words like "reckless" and "totally irresponsible."

One word that USADA's "Detailed Correction" does not mention is "dehydrated." Nor does it use "dehydration" or any derivative thereof.

Most likely, that's because the available evidence strongly suggests that Floyd Mayweather was not dehydrated.

Too often, people enter into a discussion with their minds already made up. I urge everyone on both sides of the Mayweather-USADA issue to read this article and the article that preceded it in their entirety. Carefully. The issues that the articles raise are important to everyone who cares about boxing and clean sport.

Then let's have an intelligent dialogue.

USADA's explanation of the events surrounding the IV that was administered to Floyd Mayweather raises more questions than it answers. This is the timeline that USADA offered in its September 17 statement.

A doping control officer arrived at Mayweather's home at approximately 1:45 p.m. on the day of the weigh-in for Mayweather-Pacquiao to collect a urine sample. As previously noted, USADA's "Detailed Correction" does not say that Mayweather was dehydrated. It references an unspecified "physical condition" and says that he "provided partial urine samples to USADA both prior to and following the infusion [which was after the weigh-in]." USADA did not state with greater specificity when the first partial urine sample was provided.

Mayweather went to the MGM Grand Garden Arena for the weigh-in, conducted interviews after the weigh-in, and returned to his home at an unspecified hour. Presumably, if he was dehydrated, he had the opportunity to drink water, Gatorade, or another beverage of his choosing after the weigh-in.

Be that as it may; at an unspecified time, the USADA collection officer "observed Mr. Mayweather's condition that precipitated the need for an IV."

We are not told specifically what this condition was, but might speculate that Mayweather told the collection officer that he couldn't urinate since there was only a "partial" urine collection before the IV. USADA also tells us that "Mr. Mayweather declared the infusion in advance to the USADA DCO, who was made aware of the need for the IV due to Mr. Mayweather's physical condition."

What exactly was Mayweather's "physical condition"? What was the medical justification that led to the decision that an onsite IV was the appropriate treatment? Who made the determination that the IV was medically necessary? A doping control officer can't make that determination.

USADA further tells us, "The DCO was also in the home when the paramedic was called and remained in the home while the paramedic provided the IV."

Who called the paramedic? Which medical service did the paramedic come from? Where is the full paramedic report of the incident?

In addition, USADA states, "The USADA DCO continued to monitor Mr. Mayweather throughout the administration of the IV by the paramedic and thereafter until a full sample was collected from Mr. Mayweather."

In other words, according to USADA, its on-site doping control officer was informed in advance that Mayweather intended to undergo a procedure that was in violation of WADA protocols and then watched while the procedure was in progress. Thereafter, USADA withheld notification from the Nevada State Athletic Commission for twenty days.

And USADA knew the procedure was in violation of WADA protocols because it had to grant Mayweather a therapeutic use exemption in order to justify it. In fact, USADA's "Detailed Correction" acknowledges, "The use of IVs in this manner is prohibited without a TUE."

This, in turn, leads to more questions.

Did USADA independently analyze the solution that was administered to Mayweather by IV? Or did it take the word of Mayweather's camp that it was saline and vitamins?

Who "approved" the IV procedure on site?

What was the medical justification and supporting data that led to USADA granting a retroactive therapeutic use exemption for an otherwise prohibited IV procedure?

Who at USADA made the decision to grant Mayweather a retroactive therapeutic use exemption eighteen days after the fight?

If the procedure was "approved on site," why did Mayweather need to apply for and receive a therapeutic use exemption almost three weeks later?

USADA reported to the Nevada State Athletic Commission that the last blood sample it took from Mayweather prior to the fight was on April 21. *Shouldn't USADA have taken samples on May 1, immediately prior to and after administration of the IV?*

On how many previous occasions has Mayweather received an IV infusion after the weigh-in for one of his fights? If such infusions did in fact occur, was he given a therapeutic use exemption in each instance?

And at the risk of sounding simplistic: If Mayweather was dehydrated, why didn't he simply drink several glasses of water after the weigh-in to remedy the problem?

The answer to the last question is that, as earlier noted, the available evidence strongly suggests that Mayweather was not dehydrated. And certainly not dehydrated enough to need an IV infusion equal to roughly 16 percent of his total blood volume.

Let's review what we know at the present time.

The contract weight for Mayweather-Pacquiao was 147 pounds.

Thirty days before the fight, Mayweather weighed in for the World Boxing Council and tipped the scales at 150-1/2 pounds.

Much has been made of the pre-fight medical questionnaire that Manny Pacquiao filled out on May 1, 2015 (the day of the Mayweather-Pacquiao weigh-in). The questionnaire specifically asked, "Have you had any injury to your shoulders, elbows, or hands that needed evaluation or examination?" Hiding the fact of his partial rotator-cuff tear, Pacquiao (or his representative) falsely answered "no."

But Mayweather's pre-fight medical questionnaire is also instructive. In response to the question, "What was your weight 2 weeks ago," Mayweather answered "149 pounds." In response to the question, "What was your weight 1 week ago," Mayweather answered "148-½ pounds."

And Mayweather weighed in for the Mayweather-Pacquiao fight at 146 pounds (one pound under the contract weight), which is a further indication that he didn't need to dangerously dehydrate to make weight.

Also, Mayweather was given a pre-fight physical examination by the Nevada State Athletic Commission on the day of the weigh-in. Did he disclose to commission doctors at that time that he was so badly dehydrated that he needed an IV infusion? No, he did not. Nor, according to NSAC records, did the examining physician find evidence of dehydration.

If a fighter is dehydrated, his blood pressure is likely to be low and his pulse rate high. That wasn't the case with Mayweather as evidenced by the Nevada State Athletic Commission medical data sheet.

Mayweather's blood pressure was 118/84. In other words, his sys-tolic blood pressure (pressure when the heart is contracting and pumping blood out) was 118. And his diastolic blood pressure (pressure when the heart is resting between beats) was 84. That's normal for a professional athlete.

Mayweather's pulse rate—60 sitting and 66 standing—was also normal.

When a ring doctor tells a fighter to open his mouth wide at a pre-fight physical examination, the doctor isn't looking for cavities. He's checking for loose teeth and cuts inside the mouth. The doctor is also checking the mucous membrane lining inside the fighter's mouth for signs of dehydration. Furthermore, if a fighter is dehydrated, there are additional signs of that condition in his skin turgor (the time it takes for skin to return to its original position after being pinched). Neither of these conditions was noted by the examining doctor.

To repeat: Mayweather showed no significant signs of dehydration at his pre-fight physical examination.

Moreover, if USADA did determine that Mayweather was so badly dehydrated as to warrant the emergency treatment of adding 25.361 ounces of fluid to his blood, it's unconscionable that USADA didn't transmit this information to the Nevada State Athletic Commission and the ring doctors who would be overseeing the fight the following night.

So . . . If the purpose of the IV that was administered to Mayweather wasn't to combat dehydration, what was it for?

Let's start with some thoughts from Jeff Novitzky, the former federal agent who played a key role in the investigation of Lance Armstrong, Barry Bonds, and Victor Conte.

In August of this year, Novitzky appeared on *The Joe Rogan Experience* #685, and the following exchange occurred:

Joe Rogan: What's the reason why they can't use an IV? Is it to mask possible performance enhancing drugs?

Jeff Novitzky: That's the primary reason. I saw it up front and center in cycling. They were using IVs of saline solution to manipulate their blood level readings, which were being used to determine if they were blood doping. It could also be used to flush a system. It dilutes blood and urine so that natural steroid profiles are very hard to read after you've taken an IV bag. That's the primary reason. WADA also prohibits them for some health reasons. When an IV is administered, especially close to a competition, there's a possibility of blowing out a vein or having clotting after the IV is taken out. There could be some issues with edema and swelling. If the idea is to rehydrate, it's much safer to do it orally. Studies show that orally rehydrating is better for you if you're mildly dehydrated. There's two things that they show consistently. Number one, it's obviously safer to put something through your mouth than put it in a needle in your vein. Number two, your perceived rate of exertion, how hard you feel you're working after rehydrating orally, is less than if you rehydrate via IV. If you rehydrate orally properly, the next day you're going to feel a whole lot better when you're exerting yourself.

"Now that's mild dehydration," Novitzky added. Where extreme dehydration is concerned, Novitzky suggested, "You probably should go to a hospital. [And] I think you need to notify the commission where you're fighting."

Sports fans now know that an IV infusion can dilute or mask the presence of another substance that is already in an athlete's system or might be added to the athlete's system in the near future. Let's put some meat on that statement, taking erythropoietin (EPO) as an example.

A person's red and white blood cells are suspended in plasma (a fluid that, by itself, is yellow in color).

Red blood cells deliver oxygen to muscle tissue.

Erythropoietin is a hormone that stimulates the production of red blood cells. Synthetic EPO can be administered by injection and, by creating more red blood cells, increases the flow of oxygen to an athlete's muscle tissue. It also hastens the removal of metabolic waste. As such, EPO increases an athlete's aerobic capacity and endurance.

Once the desired level of EPO is reached in an athlete's system, the level of red blood cells can be maintained by a weekly injection.

There are two ways to determine the presence of synthetic EPO in an athlete's system. The first is a urine test that directly determines its presence. When EPO is administered by subcutaneous injection, it clears an athlete's system in roughly 43 hours. If EPO is administered by IV, it clears an athlete's system on average in 19 hours.

The second way to test for synthetic EPO is a hematocrit blood test. This test doesn't directly measure the presence of EPO. Rather, it tests for the result of EPO administration.

A person's hematocrit level is the percentage of red blood cells to that person's total whole blood volume. The hematocrit level for an average adult male is roughly 45 percent. Anything below 37 percent or above 51 percent indicates an irregularity.

If an athlete is using synthetic EPO, his or her hematocrit level rises. Adding saline solution to the athlete's blood intravenously increases the plasma component of the blood, thus bringing down the ratio of red blood cells to total whole blood volume. As such, the saline solution reduces the athlete's hematocrit level to an acceptable level.

Let's say, hypothetically, that a hematocrit blood test would show that the percentage of red blood cells to an athlete's total whole blood volume is 55 percent. If the athlete adds 750 milliliters (25.361 ounces) of saline solution and vitamins via IV, it won't diminished the number of red blood cells in that athlete. His red blood cells will still be at an elevated level. But the percentage of red blood cells to that athlete's total whole blood volume will drop to 47 percent because he will be increasing his total whole blood volume.

That's an example of what is meant by "diluting and masking" through the use of an intravenous infusion.

I don't know whether or not Floyd Mayweather used prohibited performance-enhancing drugs.

To repeat: I don't know whether or not Floyd Mayweather used prohibited performance-enhancing drugs.

I do know that the facts surrounding Mayweather's May 1 IV have not been fully explored. And I have a problem with the concept of a doping control officer going to Mayweather's home, and Mayweather telling the DCO that he'll provide a full urine sample AFTER he takes an IV infusion of 25.361 ounces of fluid.

To date, the Nevada State Athletic Commission has been supportive of Mayweather. At the start of Showtime's pay-per-view telecast of the September 12 fight between Mayweather and Andre Berto, NSAC executive director Bob Bennett told Jim Gray, "Mr. Mayweather has done nothing wrong. The Nevada State Athletic Commission has no interest in any type of investigation regarding his IV."

But the issues regarding Mayweather and USADA go far beyond the May 1 IV.

In response to a request for documents, the Nevada State Athletic Commission produced two lab reports earlier this year that listed the testosterone-to-epitestosterone ratio on tests that it (not USADA) had overseen on Mayweather. In one instance, blood and urine samples were taken from Mayweather on August 18, 2011 (prior to his September 17 fight against Victor Ortiz). In the other instance, blood and urine samples were taken from Mayweather on April 3, 2013 (prior to his May 4 fight against Robert Guerrero). In each instance, Mayweather's testosterone-to-epitestosterone ratio was unusually low, which is sometimes a sign that synthetic epitestosterone has been administered to cover up the use of synthetic testosterone.

Also, USADA previously posted on its website the dates on which it took blood and urine samples from Mayweather dating back to his 2010 fight against Shane Mosley. These posts have now been removed.

Other sources have provided the testing dates for Mayweather's fights against Mosley, Miguel Cotto, and Manny Pacquiao. In the case of Mayweather-Mosley, the final pre-fight blood sample was taken from Mayweather eighteen days before the fight. In the case of Mayweather-Cotto, the final pre-fight blood sample was taken from Mayweather sixteen days before the fight. For Mayweather-Pacquiao, there was an eleven-day gap.

That's a lot of time.

Meanwhile, the Nevada State Athletic Commission is unhappy with USADA.

After "Can Boxing Trust USADA?" was posted, NSAC chairman Francisco Aguilar told the Las Vegas Review Journal, "USADA does not have the jurisdiction to approve and administer a TUE. That and the fact we were not notified until well after the fact of Mr. Mayweather's being administered the TUE are very troubling and concerning to us. USADA is supposed to be a drug-testing agency and not a TUE administrating organization. We were not made aware of this until several weeks after the fight, which is not acceptable procedure for the commission."

Similarly, Bob Bennett told the Los Angeles Times, "USADA has historically been recognized as the world's leading anti-doping authority. However, my experiences to date with them have been less than acceptable and less than professional. He [Mayweather] cannot have it done at his house and USADA can't authorize it. I have specifically articulated and memorialized to USADA that [the NSAC] is the sole authority that can authorize a therapeutic use exemption for a fighter in the state of Nevada. USADA never told us prior to the IV that they had their own TUE, and they never kept us informed about it being administered. If they think they can do what they want, where and whenever they want in the State of Nevada, they are grossly mistaken."

Also, let's keep in mind that the original draft of the USADA-Mayweather-Pacquiao drug-testing contract would have allowed USADA to grant a retroactive therapeutic use exemption to either fighter *without notifying the Nevada State Athletic Commission or the opposing fighter's camp.* Indeed, even USADA's "Detailed Correction" concedes, "USADA agreed to the request from Mr. Pacquiao's representatives that USADA provide mutual notification to both fighters upon the approval of a TUE."

In other words, if Pacquiao's representatives hadn't insisted upon notification, Mayweather's retroactive therapeutic use exemption would most likely have remained a secret between Mayweather and USADA.

That brings us back to USADA's twenty-five-page "Detailed Correction."

"Can Boxing Trust USADA?" was posted on September 9. Eight days later, USADA issued its response. Its "Detailed Correction" purports to give readers "accurate facts"—a redundancy that underscores USADA's lack of understanding of what constitutes truth.

The dictionary defines "fact" as "something that actually exists, reality, truth." A fact is a fact. If it isn't accurate, it's not a fact.

USADA's "Detailed Correction" reads like talking points that have been prepared for a political candidate who wants to distort the facts.

There's one significant correction in it that I accept. Prior to USADA's September 17 statement, it was widely believed that its doping control officer went to Mayweather's Las Vegas home to conduct an unannounced drug test and found evidence of an IV being administered to Mayweather. USADA maintains—and I will accept—that "Mr. Mayweather declared the infusion in advance to the USADA DCO." However, that leads to the questions about the IV posed earlier in this article.

Beyond that, USADA's "Detailed Correction" consists for the most part of misstatements, distortions, and platitudes about "clean sport."

It purports to present "a side by side comparison of the claims of Mr. Hauser's article to the truth." But USADA's "truth" is often misleading or a reaffirmation of what I wrote.

For example, the USADA "Detailed Correction" states, "Mr. Hauser fails to specifically identify any provisions in the Testing Agreement that conflict with USADA's statement that our professional boxing testing programs are in accordance with the WADA International Standards."

That's simply wrong.

A copy of the drug-testing agreement entered into between USADA, Floyd Mayweather, and Manny Pacquiao was attached as an exhibit to "Can Boxing Trust USADA?" Paragraph 30 of the contract states, "If any rule or regulation whatsoever incorporated or referenced herein conflicts in any respect with the terms of this Agreement, this Agreement shall in all such respects control. Such rules and regulations include, but are not limited to: the Code [the World Anti-Doping Code]; the USADA Protocol; the WADA Prohibited List; the ISTUE [WADA International Standard for Therapeutic Use Exemptions]; and the ISTI [WADA International Standard for Testing and Investigations]."

USADA also objects to a quote from Victor Conte in "Can Boxing Trust USADA?" in which Conte states, "USADA's boxing testing program . . . has one set of rules for some fighters and a different set of rules for others. That's not the way real drug testing works."

In response, USADA's "Detailed Correction" claims, "USADA applies the same set of rules to all fighters who voluntarily agree to participate in a USADA professional boxing testing program."

But in the same "Detailed Correction," USADA acknowledges that paragraph thirty of the USADA-Mayweather-Pacquiao drug testing agreement (referenced above) varied from its standard professional boxing testing agreement.

There's more.

"Can Boxing Trust USADA?" notes that, after hearing reports that three Floyd Mayweather "A" samples had tested positive, Manny Pacquiao's attorneys served document demands and subpoenas on various entities including USADA, demanding the production of all documents relating to PED testing of Mayweather in conjunction with three fights.

"The documents," I wrote, "were not produced."

In response, the "Detailed Correction" states, "This is inaccurate. USADA produced a total of 2,695 pages of documents in response to the subpoena from Mr. Pacquiao's legal counsel."

Now let's look at the truth.

USADA produced a mountain of paper in response to the subpoena, including rules and regulations that were already a matter of public record and some test results. But it withheld other documents and, on June 22, 2012, filed a motion to quash the subpoena, arguing, "First, the requested documents include medical records and documentation relating to Mr. Mayweather Jr which may constitute confidential medical records requiring his consent and release. Second, the requested documents include documents protected by the attorney-client privilege, work product doctrine and/or the investigative privilege. Third, the subpoena purports to require production in Los Angeles, California, more than 100 miles from USADA's offices and the location of the requested documents."

USADA's motion to quash was never ruled upon by the court because the case was settled by the payment of an undisclosed sum of money by Mayweather to Pacquiao. It would be interesting to review the documents that USADA did not produce.

The list of distortions in USADA's "Detailed Correction" goes on.

In "Can Boxing Trust USADA?," I wrote, "Drug testing, if it is to inspire confidence, should be largely transparent. Much of USADA's operation insofar as boxing is concerned is shrouded in secrecy . . . The organization has resisted filing its boxer drug-testing contracts with governing state athletic commissions. On several occasions, New York and Nevada have forced the issue. Compliance has often been slow in coming. When asked to identify the boxing matches for which a USADA drug-testing contract was filed with either the New York or Nevada State Athletic Commissions, [USADA CEO] Travis Tygart declined through a spokesperson (USADA senior communications manager Annie Skinner) to answer the question."

In response, USADA's "Detailed Correction" claims, "This is inaccurate. Mr. Hauser fails to attribute this information to a source or specifically indicate the 'several occasions' on which the referenced commissions allegedly forced USADA to disclose its testing agreements. USADA has never been forced to disclose a testing agreement. When requested, *for valid reasons given*, we have provided copies of those contracts to the appropriate commission. That includes both the Nevada and New York commissions [italics added]."

All right. To cite an example, USADA declined to give its drug-testing contract for the April 11, 2015, fight between Andy Lee and Peter Quillin to the New York State Athletic Commission. Ultimately, the commission obtained a copy from DiBella Entertainment (Lee's promoter). And that copy wasn't even signed by Quillin.

More to the point; what right does USADA have to decide whether a request by a state athletic commission for a drug-testing contract is "valid"? The state athletic commission is the government entity with jurisdiction over the fight. USADA shouldn't be deciding what the commission is and isn't entitled to.

Similarly, "Can Boxing Trust USADA?" notes that USADA does not give full test results to the state athletic commission that governs a fight. It gives the commission summaries that state whether a fighter has tested positive or negative.

USADA responded in its "Detailed Correction," "USADA has no objection in principle to providing State Athletic Commissions access to test results if used appropriately under the WADA ISPPPI and only for legitimate anti-doping purposes."

Again; what right does USADA have to determine what is legitimate and appropriate?

There are times when USADA's "Detailed Correction" reads like a bad joke.

"Can Boxing Trust USADA?" states, "Thereafter, [Travis] Tygart moved aggressively to expand USADA's footprint in boxing and forged a working relationship with Richard Schaefer, who until 2014 served as CEO of Golden Boy Promotions, one of boxing's most influential promoters."

The "Detailed Correction" indignantly responds, "This is misleading. It's unclear what Mr. Hauser is trying to insinuate. There is no personal relationship between Mr. Tygart and Mr. Schaefer and the two have never met in person."

I didn't write that there was a "personal" relationship between Travis Tygart and Richard Schaefer. I wrote that they "forged a working relationship." Yet this passage is specifically cited as an example of how "USADA has been viciously and unjustifiably maligned by Mr. Hauser." Strange reaction on the part of USADA. I didn't comment on or ask about Travis Tygart's personal relationships.

Moreover, USADA's "Detailed Correction" fails to satisfactorily explain the agency's behavior with regard to the Erik Morales fiasco.

USADA now claims that it notified the New York State Athletic Commission by telephone on October 17, 2012, that Morales had tested positive for Clenbuterol. But as noted in "Can Boxing Trust USADA?," on August 10, 2015, Laz Benitez (a spokesperson for the New York State Department of State, which oversees the NYSAC) advised in writing, "There is no indication in the Commission's files that it was notified of this matter prior to October 18, 2012."

Since then, a September 18, 2015, response by Helen Wilbard (an assistant records access officer for the New York State Department of State) to a Freedom of Information Law request has confirmed that the NYSAC has no record of any communication from USADA regarding Erik Morales testing positive for Clenbuterol prior to that information becoming public knowledge on October 18.

Would USADA really notify a state athletic commission about a serious drug violation by telephone only? Where is the back-up documentation?

There isn't any. USADA concedes in its "Detailed Correction" that it "did not send any written follow-up" to the NYSAC regarding the supposed October 17 telephone conversation.

Then there's the crowning jewel in USADA's "Detailed Correction" regarding Erik Morales. USADA proclaims that, eventually, it "commenced an anti-doping rule violation proceeding against Mr. Morales that resulted in the athlete being sanctioned with a two-year period of ineligibility."

The problem with that is, USADA had no authority to suspend Morales. Indeed, USADA's own "Detailed Correction" later acknowledges, "USADA does not have the authority to prevent a fight from occurring."

I could go on. But the facts (or, as USADA would say, the "accurate facts") speak for themselves.

It's hard to imagine how many corporate executives, lawyers, and public relations experts worked on USADA's "Detailed Correction" statement. If this is the best that they could come up with after eight days of trying, then USADA has a problem.

USADA can recite "The Lord's Prayer" backwards in its PR handouts, but that won't change what it has done.

And let's not forget; USADA is hired by and contracts with the fighters it's supposed to be testing. Indeed, there are times when it seems as though USADA collects drug-testing payments the way boxing's world sanctioning organizations collect sanctioning fees.

The cost of USADA's testing that we know of has ranged from $36,000 for Andy Lee vs. Peter Quillin to $150,000 for Floyd Mayweather vs. Manny Pacquiao.

Does anyone see a problem here? A Major League Baseball player can't choose the drug-testing agency that tests him and negotiate a fee with that agency. It would be laughable to suggest that New York Yankees star Alex Rodriguez (who was suspended for the entire 2014 season after being found in violation of Major League Baseball's drug policy) could designate which agency tests him and then pay that agency out of his own pocket.

A National Football League player can't say, "I don't want this testing agency. They caught me using a banned substance last year." But that's precisely what happens in boxing. VADA (the Voluntary Anti-Doping Agency) tested Andre Berto and Lamont Peterson, both of whom tested positive for the presence of prohibited performance-enhancing drugs in their system. What happened next? Both fighters refused to test again with VADA and opted for USADA.

USADA allows Floyd Mayweather and some of the other boxers it tests to dictate when drug testing begins. If Olympic athletes could dictate the date on which drug testing began, world records for races from 100 meters to the marathon would be considerably lower than they are today.

How many US Olympic athletes in the condition that Floyd Mayweather was in on May 1 have received IVs of 750 milliliters or more while a USADA doping control officer was present? How many US Olympic athletes have been given a retroactive therapeutic use exemption for a similar IV eighteen days after competing in their Olympic event?

And one more question. In responding to "Can Boxing Trust USADA?," the United States Anti-Doping Agency issued a September

10 statement that read, "There are certainly those in the sport of professional boxing who appear committed to preventing an independent and
comprehensive anti-doping program from being implemented in the
sport, and who wish to advance an agenda that fails to put the interests
of clean athletes before their own."

I can think of several physical conditioners and fighters who might
be against an independent and comprehensive anti-doping program.
Who did USADA have in mind when it made that statement? If USADA
is suggesting by innuendo that I'm on that list, I categorically reject that
notion.

By and large, the people who are asking questions about the imple-
mentation of USADA's drug testing program for boxing are the people
who care about boxing the most.

Hours before Manny Pacquiao entered the ring to fight Floyd
Mayweather, his request to be injected with Toradol (a legal substance)
to ease the pain caused by a torn rotator cuff was denied by the Nevada
State Athletic Commission because the request was not made in a timely
manner. In explaining the NSAC's decision, commission chairman
Francisco Aguilar told the media, "There is a process. And when you try
to screw with the process, it's not going to work for you."

USADA and Mayweather appear to have screwed with the process.
Let's see if it works for them in the end.

As Winston Churchill once proclaimed, "The truth is incontrovert-
ible. Malice may attack it. Ignorance may deride it. But in the end, there
it is."